the Hungarian girl trap

the hungarian girl trap

ray
dexter

First published in 2006

Copyright© 2006 Ray Dexter

The moral right of the author has been asserted

All rights reserved.
No part of this publication may be reproduced, stored in a retrieval system, or transmitted, in any form or by any means, without the prior permission in writing of the publisher, nor be otherwise circulated in any form of binding or cover than that in which it is published and without a similar condition being imposed on the subsequent purchaser.

Cover by RGD, with thanks to Richard and Steve for some of the pics

For Áron, for whom this is the prologue.

Based on true events.

Boy meets girl.
Boy is English, girl Hungarian
Boy has a good job at a very well-known boarding school in England; girl is an *au pair* who wants to get back to Hungary as soon as possible.
Boy discovers he knows a man who is running an International school in Hungary and he is desperate for boy to work for him.
Boy decides you can't fight that sort of coincidence, chucks in the good job at the well-known boarding school and follows the girl to Budapest…

This is what happened…

August

Wednesday, 27th August

Budapest

The Churchill International School of Hungary was not as important as its name implied. It was in Óbuda[1], at the end of a quiet, leafy suburban street, so its surroundings were pleasant enough. Even the rusty, graffiti strewn bridge carrying the railway line to Austria was not too intrusive. The problem was that the building itself and all the neighbouring dwellings, although once impressive, were now decaying and dusty and suffering from a lack of love. It was rather like seeing a once beautiful actress in old age. I had arrived in Hungary yesterday and was greeted at the airport by Andrea of course and her father, a great bear of a man, whose expressive and lived-in features immediately gave away what part of the world he was from. He was tall, with a physique that could only be described as generous, with a huge beard. He was an architect and pretty much had the word 'Bohemian' tattooed on his ample chest. I had heard stories about his refusal to tolerate mobile phones, and preferring to talk to buskers on the streets than important business men in their offices. His first sight of me was worrying. He looked me up and down sternly and said in his broken English, "my daughter is not for sale". As I fumbled for an answer he burst out laughing, bear hugged me and pressed a small bottle of *Unicum*[2] into my hand.

We drove from the airport into Budapest. I experienced great culture shock: cobbled roads filled with Wartburgs, Trabants, Ladas and Dacias (whatever they were); the buildings were a different shape; billboards offered familiar products in incomprehensible language and cigarette smoke filled the air. The sound-track to my thoughts was Andrea's father pointing out the most beautiful and innovative buildings in the city and who designed them. The city all seemed to live in apartments above parades of shops and businesses. I spent the rest of the day desperately trying to deny to my system how much alcohol Andrea's father tried to ply me with. In England we would have a cup of tea upon arrival at someone's house. Here it's whisky.

Today was my first full day in the city and I needed to see the school. I walked through the glass fronted entrance of the school into a typically East European lobby. It was full of austere grey marble and large, tubular ashtrays. In the

---

[1] Budapest is made up of three cities, Buda, Pest, and Óbuda. Tourist guides will tell you that Buda is the hilly, pretty side of the Danube, Pest is the flat, business side of the Danube and Óbuda is basically forgotten about. It is on the Buda side, north of Buda.

[2] Popular Hungarian liqueur, with the colour and consistency of crude oil and similar to *Jägermeister* in flavour. Said to have medicinal properties.

corner stood a forlorn looking snack kiosk. I looked for directions, or any sign that this building housed an International School, but there was nothing in English and the hundreds of notices in Hungarian seemed to consist of only the letters k, z and vowels with umlauts. Suddenly a small, old, unshaven man leapt out of a cupboard brandishing a broom and barked a few words of Hungarian at me. A black and white television flickered inside the cupboard. I had no idea what he said and I had no idea a language could be so impenetrable.

"Churchill International School?" I said hopefully.

The man swayed a little on his feet. I could smell strong liquor. He jabbered away again, gesticulating towards the exit.

"Dr Arpád Szentesi? Here?" I said.

The man looked at me again, cocking his head, bird-like, but didn't seem to understand. I feared he was going to push me out of the building with his broom. We would have stood there for hours not understanding each other but for the fortunate intervention of a shout from along the corridor. It was Gerry Ashcroft's voice, and the sight of his portly frame hurrying towards me was welcome indeed.

"Don't worry about Láci Bácsi[3]," said Gerry, grinning, as we shook hands, "he's always pissed."

"Does he work here?" I asked as we shook hands like old friends.

"Theoretically… he's the caretaker," explained Gerry. "Láci Bacsi meet Ray Dexter."

The man smiled a toothless smile and said something to me, extending a grubby hand.

"He says, it's a pleasure to meet you," said Gerry.

Gerry then turned to Láci Bácsi and said very slowly, "Too many cooks spoil the broth."

Láci grinned and said something back.

"He says I hope you settle in well at our humble school," said Gerry.

"Tell him thanks," I said.

"Now – is – the – winter - of - our - discontent - and – alas - poor - Yor - ick," said Gerry. He pronounced each word loudly his lips mouthing the syllables with theatrical aplomb. Then he turned to me, smiling; "You can say anything you like to him he doesn't understand a bloody word. We're not even too sure about his Hungarian. The alcohol has had a pickling effect on his brain cells."

Láci Bácsi staggered off towards the door, missed it and fell over what sounded like a bucket.

"You can't get the staff you see," said Gerry. He was in a good mood.

"So you speak Hungarian?" I said impressed.

"Not a word," he said.

"But you translated what he said."

---

[3] Laci is short for László, the Bácsi is a pet name meaning uncle, often attached to older men

"Nope, made it up completely. Hungarian is the hardest language to learn in Western Europe. You haven't got a prayer. Now you must come and meet the Headmaster."

Gerry Ashcroft was the reason I was here. He was the Trustee of the Churchill International School, the only Briton on the board and the only one with any experience of a British secondary school. I was here to help him out, a last mad trip before the sensible life.

Gerry took me to the Headmaster's office. Éva, the secretary sat in the first office. She had shiny black hair, but the roots were grey. She eyed me suspiciously as Gerry introduced me.

"Coffee?" she asked.

"Please," I said nervously. Éva frowned, but showed us into the Headmaster's room. He was on the telephone. This was the first time I had met him. Up until then all my interviews had been conducted in England with Gerry. As I shook hands with Doctor Árpád Szentesi I realised why Gerry had done the recruiting. Szentesi was a man who could never inspire one with confidence. He didn't look Headmasterly. He had a bookish air and if chaos were tangible you would see it flying round his head in great waves. He had slightly weak features with a large nose and silver framed glasses. His hair was dark and greasy and was combed as an afterthought rather than out of pride in his appearance. He wore jackets that didn't really go with his trousers and I would only once see him in a tie. He looked dusty, as if he had been sitting in one place for too long. If you met him for the first time and were told he was a Headmaster you would laugh. I wondered why parents sent their children here. He seemed more suited to an office job with large ledgers and very little light or human contact.

"I presume my work permit is on its way," I said.

"Well," he said evasively, his voice a little reedy. "There is a lot of paperwork involved. I think you should work for a while, pretend you are on vacation and once you are established here I will organise one. What I really want to talk about," he continued, changing the subject smoothly, "is if you could be in charge of examinations at the school." Later, after agreeing readily, I realised this appointment was not because of my vast experience with the administration of examinations, but because I knew what the letters GCSE stood for.

Éva entered with the coffee. There were two small cups on a silver tray. Each cup had less than a mouthful of thick, black liquid. Sugar lumps were provided but they were so large that there wasn't enough coffee to dissolve them. I took a sip of the sugary goo and pulled a face. The coldness of the liquid hit me first, followed by the bizarre mixture of harsh coffee and too much sugar. I decided to stick to tea in the future.

I got back to business. Earlier in the year the Headmaster, via Gerry, had asked me to provide him with a list of vital scientific equipment needed to teach science properly. I posted the list to him in June. It mentioned such things as Bunsen burners, test tubes, batteries, wires, masses, microscopes, beakers, thermometers, rulers, measuring cylinders, safety glasses, litmus paper.

"Have you ordered the things I suggested on the list?" I asked.

The Headmaster rummaged through a mass of paperwork on his desk. After about five minutes he located the document. From his expression I was certain that this was the first time he had actually looked at the list. He scanned the figures with a concerned look on his face. He turned the pages and seemed even more dismayed at the length.

"All this?" he said eventually, with a sad look and the shake of a head. "Is all this really necessary?"

"This is just the bare bones," I said. "You do want to teach science the English way don't you?"

"Of course," said the Headmaster. "But in Hungary we don't do so many practicals. We don't think it is important. Let me look at this list. It all looks very expensive."

He read the list. I had given serial numbers and suppliers in England. "We can get these things a lot cheaper in Hungary I'm sure."

"Yes but have you ordered anything yet?"

"No because I have to check with suppliers…"

"I gave you that list two months ago. We will be open on Monday and there will be no experiments."

"I will check with suppliers," repeated the Headmaster.

Gerry and I went outside. Gerry turned to me with a grin. "He's quite a card isn't he! The best thing about Árpád is that when it comes to money he will say 'no' nine times. When he gets to the ninth 'no' then he believes that is the basis for a negotiation to start!"

"I see," I said, not seeing at all.

The Headmaster and Gerry forgot about me soon afterwards as an Egyptian family walked in unannounced to see the school. Left to my own devices I walked into the staff room, looked around and smiled at the young woman in there. She smiled back with about a million teeth and said something in Hungarian. I must have looked particularly confused because she switched to English.

"Oh sorry, are you American?"

"No English, I'm Ray, I'm the new science teacher. I'm sorry I don't speak Hungarian yet," I said.

"Great," said the girl, beaming even harder. "I can't either really, just a few words. I'm American. My name's Jessica and wow, you're a science teacher," she said, seemingly the first person to ever be impressed by such a profession. "Say, is Árpád free yet? I've been trying to get to see him all morning but Éva, the evil secretary won't let me past."

"Is she always that scary?" I asked.

"Yeah, it's kind of the way secretaries are here," said Jessica. "So is he free?"

"Well I got to see him for a while but then some prospective parents showed up so he's busy again."

"Ah shimmy," said Jessica. She had a nose stud, cascading curly, auburn hair and a permanent smile. She had been in Budapest one year and would teach the school's elementary class, which was fine with me until she revealed she had never done such a thing before.

"I don't have a work permit yet and I need one," she said.

"Don't worry," I said, "I haven't got one either. Árpád seems unconcerned about it."

"How come you got shown in to see him straight away?" she moaned.

"I bribed him," I said

"Does anyone have a work permit?" she said. "What *is* this place?"

She also showed me her room. It had no resources in, not even chairs. "Can you believe it?" she said, a slight hysterical edge appearing in her voice. "And people are paying a lot of money for this."

"From what I've seen so far it doesn't really surprise me," I said and told her about my problems with the lack of equipment.

"I'm just really worried about not having a work permit," she said wringing her hands. "I don't want to get deported. I have my cat with me and she's a house cat and if I had to leave she wouldn't be able to fend for herself."

I pointed out that she should let Árpád worry about that because he needed us more than we needed him and he would be the one in trouble if we were deported. "And I am sure you could find someone to look after the cat."

"How long have you been here?" she asked.

I told her I had arrived last night.

"Have you been shopping yet?"

"I was going this afternoon."

"Always get a basket no matter what shop you go into," she said. "Even if it's a bookstore. In America you don't have to but here they think you are a thief if you don't take a basket. Oh sorry," she said and put her hand over her mouth.

"What?" I said.

"They don't do that in England do they?"

"What?" I said again.

"You know, insist you have a basket when you go into a shop."

"Don't worry," I said. "We English think we're the fifty first state of the union."

"Really, that's neat. Do we get the Queen then?"

"I was joking," I said.

"Oh sorry," said Jessica giggling. "You see I didn't want to embarrass you with my basket problems if you were like used to it or something. So GOOD you don't do the basket thing in England."

"And we use miles and yards too."

"I know they are so much easier aren't they," said Jessica happily.

"Yeah these world-wide accepted units of tens and hundreds get darned confusing compared with entirely random divisions of matter and liquid."

"No it's just that I know feet and inches…you're joking again aren't you."

"Yes I am," I said.

"I have got to get used to that I'm sorry."

"We do use stones though," I said.

"A what?" said Jessica.

"Fourteen pounds is one stone in England."

"Now that is really confusing," said Jessica. "What was I talking about? Oh shimmy where was I?"

"Shimmy?" I said.

"Don't you use shimmy? It kinda sounds like a bad word but it isn't. I use it when I feel the need to swear. I REMEMBER, WE WERE TALKING ABOUT SHOPPING! In my first days I was shouted at for not having a basket but I didn't know why they were shouting because I didn't understand Hungarian so I would leave the shop saying to myself, I'm not hungry really I don't wanna eat."

"I will be very careful," I said.

I liked her; I just wondered how she had managed to live as long as she had.

Thursday 28th August

Andrea had a flat in the highly salubrious Örs Vezér Tér district of Budapest. Örs Vezér Tér should be in the Guinness Book of records for the world's most concrete tower blocks in a square mile. 300,000 people used the Metro station there every morning, which is about one sixth of the entire population of Budapest. This gave the place a feeling of constant movement. It never rested; somebody was always buying, selling, drinking, eating, or travelling somewhere.

Hungarian tower blocks were very different to those in England. For a start 90% of the population had no choice but to live in them. They were, to my eyes, quite fantastically beautiful in an ugly sort of way. I soon got used to them and all the protocols involved with living in them. For a start, as Andrea pointed out on many occasions, you had to say Good Morning/day/evening/hi to whomever else you happened to share the lift with in our particular palace. In England of course lift journeys were conducted in silence but here silence was rudeness.

"We live with these people," Andrea hissed at me, as my mumbled 'jó napot kívánok' was deemed too quiet.

Our flat was fairly normal for a tower block. It had one and a half rooms. This meant it had a kitchen and a bathroom as standard and one and a half other rooms. The half room was a little too small to be effective for anything except putting shoes in, so we lived and slept in the main room. This was fairly normal too. The sofa bed was a must-have item of furniture.

Tower blocks were also notoriously noisy. Snobs who lived elsewhere said that you could hear entire conversations from the next flat. I found this not to be true, not because the walls weren't thin but because people respected each other and kept the noise down. Once I heard an over-enthusiastic couple having sex four floors down, and the only other time I realised other people surrounded me on all sides was in the bathroom. Whenever I was in there I almost jumped with fright as a conversation would suddenly start up sounding as if it were in the room with me. After a while I realised I was listening to a conversation happening in a bathroom about four flights up and the sound was travelling down a hole behind the lavatory. I couldn't imagine why people were conversing in the bathroom, there was barely enough room for one but as I couldn't understand anything anyone said anyway I didn't let it dwell in my mind. The bathroom had another curiosity. In order to save money the tap that filled the basin also filled the bath. You simply turned the mixer tap away from the sink and it would fill the bath. The bath of course was so small that my legs were longer than it was. Most people took showers.

So having left the tower block I would stare at the twenty four tower blocks I could immediately see (there were others behind) and remembered that each of these must contain sixty flats each. I began to realise how many people lived in this small area of Budapest. Incongruously there was an IKEA within walking distance of the bustle. Even weirder was the fact that the blue and yellow monstrosity that was IKEA looked ugly and brash in comparison to the humble concrete towers.

The weather is astonishing. The digital thermometer on the corner of one of the tower blocks registered 36°C most days. I found it uncomfortable at first, having arrived from another washed out English summer, and I never really did get used to the concept of being able to almost guarantee what the weather would be like in advance. I learned quickly though when Andrea took me to the market this morning. She had woken me up with a nudge at seven o'clock.

"We have to go to the market. Get some plastic bags and be quick, we are three hours late already."

I gave her a very bemused look.

"What's wrong with the supermarket?" I asked.

"The market is cheaper and fresher and real people get the money, not Tescos[4] or whatever store is on the corner."

My bemused look stayed, but she won the battle of wills. I found myself stumbling around in the boiling sun and Andrea expected me to have opinions on different types of yellow peppers.

"What's wrong with these?" I said despairingly as we stood by another pile of vegetables only for Andrea to disappear into the melee again.

"We have to check every stall, to get the best value," said Andrea.

"But there must be a hundred vegetable stalls," I wailed.

---

[4] Of course food giant Tesco are ubiquitous in Hungary too, but we will let that go

There were, plus pasta stalls, meat stalls, bread stalls, old crones in black selling stewing vegetables, dried beans, and fresh herbs for pennies. There were cooking pot stalls; cake stalls; water melon trucks, where Andrea worked out the ripeness by bashing a few with a her fist and listening to the echo like some kind of blonde sonar device; egg stalls that sold them individually and with no egg boxes. After each stall I was burdened down with more provisions. Andrea returned from one foray with a dead chicken, still with head and feet.

"Hold that," she said, holding the chicken by the neck.

"I really don't think I can," I admitted.

"You see, you English, you have no idea of the reality of life. This is what a chicken actually looks like."

The sun was relentless; I was dressed in jeans, stupidly stubborn. I had not eaten and I was not used to the heat and the hubbub. My vision swayed. I felt weak. Andrea dived off again to compare toothpaste prices. I felt weaker; Örs Vezér Tér faded. I followed Andrea dumbly, like a robot. Andrea brought me back to life by shaking my hand. We were standing by a red Lada. Next to the car stood an old couple and a set of scales. They were selling home-made sausage. Andrea was trying to ascertain how good it tasted by some kind of mind probe. Satisfied she bought one. That was the last I remember as the world faded and I fainted. I woke up a few minutes later with a concerned Andrea holding my head and the old couple staring with interest at a rare sight for them: a fallen Englishman with the dead chicken on his chest.

I learned two things, firstly respect the sun and secondly don't go to the market without any breakfast.

Friday 29th August

There was a staff meeting organised for the afternoon. A diverse bunch of humanity sat around the table. The staff of the school came from all walks of life. There were six full time staff, two were Hungarian, two American, a Pakistani and me. Later I would find out the definition of 'full-time' was exaggerated. There were also numerous part-time staff, including a one armed physics teacher from the university, and a host of attractive female language teachers who smoked Marlboro lights furiously, all still studying at university, all hired because they were cheap and talented.

Árpád, the Headmaster stood, ummed and aahed for a while, shuffled papers for an age and said welcome and that he was sure he had the best staff available.

"Where are they then?" said the man next to me. He was a wise-cracker aged somewhere between 35 and 50 and had a very strong New York accent. He wore glasses and was dressed in shorts, baseball boots and an NYC cap.

"Welcome back Larry," said Árpád with a humourless smile which said more than his words did.

Gerry got up next. "Welcome old hands and new hands," he began with a nervous grin. "The school, as you know, is at a critical point. How we get through this year really does decide if there will be a school here next year."

"We have a lot of new staff," he continued. "I think it would be best if we all introduced ourselves."

"Introduce ourselves?" said Larry. "We don't need to know each other. We're gonna be working too hard to know each other."

"I'll start," said Gerry happily. "Gerry Ashcroft, fifty-five – retired teacher, bald, single, available," He raised his eyebrows in an attempt at flirtation. "I'm one of the governors of the school. I have some financial involvement but my main task is to provide you with everything you need to help you teach better."

"A jacuzzi would be nice," said Larry.

"Why did you retire?" asked Jessica.

"Because…and Ray will confirm this," he said looking at me, "teaching in England is no fun anymore. The government has interfered so much that it is almost impossible to teach. I was a deputy head and I was killing myself…I am not a melodramatic man…but I was killing myself. Two of my teacher friends both died of stress related illness and I thought, that's it, I'm out."

Jessica was next. She spoke through her smile. "I'm Jessica Ellis, twenty-three and I've lived in Hungary for a year. I came to Hungary because I visited it once on a Christian exchange programme and liked it. So I came over and worked in a Hungarian school last year teaching English but this year I felt like a change."

"And you wanted more money," said Larry.

"I'll be the kindergarten teacher," continued Jessica ignoring Larry, "and I'm really looking forward to it."

The man next to me stood up next. He had a confident look about him, I guessed he had worked here the previous year. "Hi, I'm Bill Fletcher," he said, "an anally retentive American. This is my second year at the school and I teach history."

"And he's my accountant and it's true, he's really, really anal," said Larry.

"I've lived in Budapest for eight years," said Bill ignoring Larry, who interjected again.

"Eight years. Let me guess, the Hungarian girl trap?" Larry was grinning.

"The what?" said Jessica.

"Oh don't say you haven't noticed," said Larry. "Out there in this city live the most beautiful women in the world. They are Hungarian women: feminine, lithe, slim, domesticated and sexy. No man is safe. They're modern day Greek sirens. Just to walk down the street you need a blindfold. I call it the Hungarian girl trap."

"I don't believe you," said Jessica. "Sure there are attractive women but you make it sound like eerie or something."

"Let's do a survey. Bill, what about you?" said Larry.

"I'm married to Orsi, and I have two children," said Bill.

"See," said Larry, " Who else? Yes, Hugh Grant over there, you…"

He was talking to me.

"Why are you here?" asked Larry.

I paused for effect. "Her name's Andrea and..."

"The Hungarian girl trap!" chorused Bill and Gerry together.

"Every foreign man in town is caught in the nectar," said Larry. "It's the only reason we're here."

"It's your turn," said Bill to Larry.

"And folks you can hear his smooth American vowels on every radio station's adverts in the city," said Larry. "The man is a walking business. Watch out Árpád he won't be with us long."

"Thank you," said Bill looking away. Larry had blown a secret but Árpád didn't seem to notice.

"So Bill how's your Hungarian?" asked Larry.

"Better than yours," said Bill with a grin.

"I speak the language of mime," said Larry. "Words are for those who cannot express themselves properly."

"That's why you get me to help you to fill out your official forms then is it?" said Bill.

"That's different," said Larry. "Anyway I'll tell you about me. I'm Larry Baker from New York. I came here to Budapest to find my roots. I'm Jewish and my family came from this area of the world. I came here via Canada, Sweden and Israel. I'm married to a Hungarian, Zsuzsa."

"Ah, the girl trap," said Árpád, catching on.

Larry gave him a look. "I teach English and P.E, but basketball is my love. I also teach at the university and I am involved with a group who go round to Hungarian schools teaching mime and acting classes. I also work with environmental groups and I give my own one man show to schools highlighting environmental problems." Larry had lost the jokes as he spoke with passion and seriousness about the things he really loved.

Nobody knew what to say.

I was about to speak next but Larry got in first.

"You don't need to say, I know the girl trap got you too."

"Yes," I said and told my romantic story. I got lots of aaahs from the female teachers.

Naima, the Pakistani woman was next but she demurred.

"No, no," she laughed. "My life is not interesting at all."

"What are you talking about?" said Larry. "We all wanna know what a beautiful Pakistani woman is doing here in Budapest. Did you find the women irresistible too?"

"Far more attractive than the American men," grinned Naima as the group laughed. "What?" she said, as Larry stared at her, a huge grin on his face.

"I like her," he said. "And for a Jew to say that about a Muslim that means a lot."

"O.K O.K enough," she said blushing. "I was invited over here to complete a PhD in 1980. I have been here ever since. I taught English as a second language for ten years though mainly to the banking community. This is my first school. That's it."

Many of the others present in the room were part time teachers, including Tibor, the one armed physicist. I looked around the room. They were a strange bunch. I didn't see how I fitted in.

"We will meet again on Monday," said Árpád. "Have a good weekend."

"The doors will be open?" said Larry. I remember last year, no-one had a key."

"And Árpád," said Naima as the Headmaster tried to leave the room, "what about a timetable? None of us know what we are to teach."

"It will be done," said Árpád, lying.

Written on Sunday 30th August

Miskolc

Punk rock should have been born here, I thought, as I saw the bleak outskirts of Miskolc, or maybe in some other East European industrial town. To a disaffected youth living here in 1976 in Eastern Hungary under a Communist regime controlled by a hated super power, the statement 'No future' might actually have meant something. When Johnny Rotten *et al* snarled their way to notoriety in the 1970's they may have meant it (man) but they also had no real idea about what they were talking about. Rotten, admittedly working class, could, for example, go on television and swear and write reactionary songs about the Head of State without ending up dead. A kid in Miskolc couldn't. A punk in England could imagine his life was meaningless but wasn't it really just a case of a kid who had his basic needs satisfied needing something else to justify his existence? Consider his life in 1976: oh no, he is forced to listen to the Eagles, or disco records that said nothing to him about his life. Oh no, his parents don't understand him, or the sense of alienation he feels, as he doesn't fit into society. Oh no, he doesn't fancy working as his father did for forty years for the same firm. Is that really 'no future'? He could think freely, if he wanted he could dress outrageously, he could vote against 'the fascist regime' and if enough people thought like him he could change the system. If he couldn't change the system he could leave and go somewhere else. That was a future. A kid in Miskolc in 1976 could do none of these. The radio would play safe music, the television was censored. This is the environment for punk music to be born if it really meant it.

Even today the harsh chords and sneering vocals of the Sex Pistols seemed to fit into Miskolc's towerblock suburbs far more than the art-schools of London. In fact, as Andrea's mother, Hungary's answer to Sophia Loren drove us through the city in the family Wartburg you could see the occasional graffito stating Sex Pistol philosophy. I pointed out some of them to Andrea.

"Most of them were done by my brother," she said with a grin. Her brother's hair turned into a pink Mohican as soon after 1989 as was possible.

I was not surprised to find that punk music was still considered relevant here, the young men went for it in a big way; that and gangster rap.

"They want to be men," said Andrea, "and as there is no work, this is how they express their masculinity.

I liked Miskolc for the very reason that to an ignorant tourist or a pretentious tourist guide might hate it. Miskolc reminded me of how lucky I am to be alive. It's ugly, say the ignorant tourists. So what, I say. How can you appreciate beauty if you don't have ugliness? And anyway Miskolc isn't all ugly. It has been dealt a hard series of blows yet its people get on with their lives without too much complaint. Maybe the good things in life are better appreciated if you have to suffer a little.

Miskolc is 180 km east of Budapest, and was a product of industrial revolution. The centre is beautiful and typical of many Hungarian towns, with candy coloured buildings along the high street and red and white trams whirring through the centre. However some time in the early part of the century a huge steel factory was built here. This factory is so enormous it takes almost five minutes to drive past it and I counted nineteen chimneys of various sizes belching out steam into the darkening sky. In its Communist heyday it ran twenty-four hours a day and the men would be called to shifts by klaxons that rang through the whole city. Every family had somebody who worked there. To cope with the demand for workers the Communists did what they did everywhere and bulldozed a lot of small houses to make way for miles and miles of identical towerblocks. If you arrived in Miskolc as we had on the express train from Budapest you would see the tower blocks miles before the station, lights twinkling from ten thousand windows.

Miskolc is twinned the English town of Corby, which to those who know that town will not come as a surprise. If it were to be twinned with an American city, Cleveland would be about right. It is also suffering from the collapse of Communism. There was no need for the steel produced in the factory anymore. The brutal realities of capitalism meant that most of the town lost their jobs when it got into trouble. A Czech firm took it over but it was still losing money. Its days were numbered.

I stared out of the window as Andrea's mother steered the Wartburg expertly through the towers. The Wartburg was considered, along with the Lada and the Skoda, the ultimate Communist car. Designed by the same East German company that built Trabants I was certain the designers considered the twin concepts of aerodynamics and ergonomics fanciful notions that had no place in Communist car design. It was an off-white brick and drove like one. I had never been in a Wartburg before and I found the square knobs, modern kitsch LED blips instead of a fuel and temperature gauge, and other ancient technology fascinating. The car was only seven years old but felt like something from the late seventies. However it got the family from one end of town to the other, even if it took most of the journey to find first gear. Andrea again sensed my amusement.

"This car is fine," she said. "We had a Dacia before, now that really was bad." Dacias, I now knew were from Romania, which said it all.

Andrea's mother was oblivious to my culture shock and navigated the million crossroads and identical towerblock boulevards with ease, catching up on the latest Budapest gossip provided by her daughter as she drove. I couldn't understand how she knew where she was, as each crossroads looked identical to the next. Outside it was still hot, even though it was after nine o'clock at night. I was surprised until I realised I had fallen for the propaganda again. We were always led to believe that behind the iron curtain the weather was always Siberian. Wrong, I had been in Hungary less than a week and the thermometer had yet to dip below thirty degrees.

We were in Miskolc for the weekend. Andrea's mother lived on the tenth floor of a towerblock. The view onto the hills was breathtaking, Diósgyőr castle[5] sitting dead centre.

"I was born in the castle," said Andrea. "My mother went into labour there. I want to marry there and I want to die there."

"So if you have a heart attack in Budapest I have to get you to hold on until I can drag you here."

"Yes. Is that a problem?" she said sweetly.

We went to Andrea's local bar, the Black Crow. It seemed to be prefabricated and contained electronic dart boards and pool tables and the same young faces were in there every night, all them Andrea had known all her life. Most were the type of cool guys you expected to see in small towns. They would hang out at the bar smoking in the way they saw in American films and beckoned dancing women to come and talk to them. Most of the women went over, to my astonishment.

"This wouldn't happen in England," I said incredulously to Andrea. "If I tried that in my local I would be laughed out of town."

Unfortunately I was unable to communicate with the guys because my Hungarian was non-existent and so was their English. The exception was a crazy man called 'the Doctor'. He was a real Doctor, brilliant by all accounts too. He wrote the definitive Hungarian book on sex, made a fortune, blew it all, now drove a scrappy Lada and drank and smoked heavily. His dark blond hair was lank and unkempt and he spent most of the time grinning deliriously as he tried to find the funniest way of saying something. He had a face that brought to mind the village idiot. It was as if he should have an ear of corn hanging from the corner of his mouth and commenting, "I don't rightly know," to every question asked of him. His English was good, but accented strongly. He also beat me at darts three times in a row, which he found highly amusing.

"This is a British pub game, no?" he said.

"So what?" I said.

---

[5] You can see the castle and a stylised view of it on the 200ft note

"No reason," he smiled, "I just thought it would mean that you would at least be able to hit the board occasionally because of some kind of latent national talent. You know the Brazilians play football, Americans talk loudly in restaurants, Bulgarians lift heavy weights, Slovaks do nothing, that sort of thing."

"What is the Hungarian talent then?" I asked.

"We have many talents," said the Doctor proudly. "We are the handsomest people, and as you can tell I am the pinnacle, and I hope you are impressed with my use of the word 'pinnacle', of this particular talent."

I laughed. "Obviously I can play darts normally," I said, trying to regain some national pride. "It's the beer; it's different from my usual."

"Hungarian beer is the best in the world," he said, "but a well kept secret. It's like Cuban cigars. They export the shit and keep the best for themselves. We let the Czechs have all the credit for beer."

"Let's toast that," I said and attempted to clink glasses. The Doctor pulled his glass away offended.

"Never ever toast a Hungarian with beer," he said suddenly serious. "Don't you know your history?"

Worried I had unintentionally offended him I asked for an explanation.

"Ah the British, you only know your own history, but then in actual fact you know nothing about Northern Ireland either. Some European history…in 1848 the Hungarians had a revolution against the Habsburgs – the Austrian ruling family – who had ruled our lands for hundreds of years. The Hungarians and Austrian leaders met and discussed things and the agreement was toasted with beer just like you did. Well after this toast the Austrians turned round and shot the Hungarians in cold blood. That is why we never toast beer. That is what the Austrians do."

"I didn't realise," I said. "Sorry."

"No offence taken," said the Doctor. "If you want to toast someone do it with wine. Another game?"

There was also a Hungarian wrestler there about to go off to the European Championships. Not that stupid American pro stuff where they pretend to jump on each other's head for an hour or so but real Greco Roman variety. I swear I've never seen such a huge guy in all my life. He must have been 6'8'' tall but built like a body builder. Andrea was amazed.

"Obviously," I slurred to her, for the beer was affecting me, "my shoulders are as impressive as his. I just choose not to flaunt my own physical perfection."

I then lost at darts again to the Doctor who was drinking Jim Beam whisky from the bottle whilst he threw the dart with the other hand. I loved the Jim Beam; its label was in Russian and must have been illegally imported from the Steppes. I still claim that the only reason I lost four times in a row was because the rules were deliberately mis-explained.

"Never mind," said the Doctor. "It was good to talk to you. My English needs the practice."

"Do you always drink this much?" I asked.

The Hungarian Girl Trap

The Doctor lit a cigarette, "What else is there to do? Besides I am at work at seven o'clock tomorrow morning."

The reason we were in Miskolc was for an Anglo Hungarian wedding on the Saturday. Richard and Laura, last seen in England, he English, her Hungarian ex au pair, were getting married and we were invited. The ceremony was to take place in a large church in the centre of town. The church was typical of the area, square and painted the burnt yellow of the Hungarian sun at sunset with pear-shaped domes sitting on two towers at the front. We sat in the gloriously ornate interior and I saw Richard immediately, looking out of place in English top hat and tails. He seemed fairly relaxed. This was probably because he didn't understand a word anybody said to him.

"Hungarian women are hard work," he said when I last saw him in England, "but they're definitely worth it!"

The first thing that struck me was that there was no organ music at all. We waited for Laura to show in a silence quite deafening. The ceremony was in Hungarian but the old priest managed a few words of English for Richard to say 'I do' at the right time. There were no hymns but they did have a singer up on a balcony. There was a holiness I hadn't encountered at an English wedding for quite a time.

Outside in the heat Richard's top hat was removed as it was completely over the top for such weather. There were no official photographs and we all got onto a shabby bus to take us to the reception in the hills.

It took place in the castle in Lillafüred, a town that was almost alpine in its appearance. It marked the gateway to the Bükk hills and blew away my stereotypes about Hungary being flat. The hills were lush and covered in birch trees, a lake glistened in the distance covered in little red dots of colour, presumably little sailing boats. The castle, now a hotel was magnificent and dominated the skyline like those seen in Transylvanian horror films. However all that was in the atmosphere was warmth.

After a cognac or two, dinner started at six p.m. It didn't finish until about midnight and consisted of about five courses. Just when you felt you could eat no more food then the waiters arrived with more platters of edible matter or with jugs of good local wine.

The speeches were familiar but slower because they all needed to be translated from one language to another. The father of the bride spoke, followed by the best man, who decided against the traditional speech and went for simply translatable platitudes. Then the father of the groom stood up and managed to alienate the entire Hungarian population by making comparisons between the wonders of the British and the Austro-Hungarian empires. I could feel the atmosphere chill in the Hungarians around me.

"It wasn't a bloody empire," hissed Andrea. "It was an occupation. It is like saying to an Irishman 'are you proud of the British Empire?'"

Nobody pointed out the *faux pas,* and the wedding continued. At midnight the more traditional Hungarian aspects came into play. Laura changed out of her white wedding dress into a red one. The band, who had been playing rock'n' roll and easy listening favourites, started playing a gypsy melody and what looked like a local village wag arrived and started bashing a bed pan with a wooden spoon. The bride danced alone and I watched as the guests went to the man put some money in the bowl and then went and danced with the bride

"What the hell is going on?" I asked Andrea.

"It is traditional for the guests to pay for a dance. Off you go," she said giving me some money.

Finally as I thought every guest had danced with her three of the males appeared and kidnapped her to the applause of the guests. Richard followed uncertainly.

"If he wants her back," explained Andrea, "He has to drink champagne from her shoe."

Soon Richard was back, Laura over his shoulder, her shoe in the other and a large grin on his face.

"She's mine," he yelled and he forced the shoe to his lips. The champagne dribbled down his chin. I watched amazed.

"Now I know he loves her," I said.

"I hope you are watching darling," said Andrea. "You will do that one day."

Monday 31st August

Today I dressed in sandals and T-shirt and my head was used to the weight of the sun on it. Andrea and I went to work. She, at an American firm, where bilingual secretaries earned good money. I was going to school for the first proper day. I was still fascinated by the seediness of Örs Vezér Tér and drank in every site.

The first place of interest was a large square edifice, which contained only a shoe shop of quite enormous proportions containing shoes easily beyond my price range let alone the average Hungarian. In the mornings a fat, grizzly man was always cleaning it. This guy brought his old dog along with him who was either barking at passers by or fast asleep in the corner. At night the shop always had people in it. Whether they were buying shoes, simply browsing or keeping out of the sun I never found out. It was true that Hungary seemed to have more shoe shops per head of population than any other place I had been. Imelda Marcos would have loved it here. Andrea explained that Hungarians bought one good pair of shoes a year and they lasted because they were high quality. That still didn't explain the disproportionate number of people in the shop.

Next to the shoe shop in an identical square block was the worst clothes/material shop in the world. I had never seen anybody actually go into this shop. The window display consisted of rolls of bad cloth and even worse clothes. There was a revolting purple felt suit for sale at about £25 which caught my eye every day and usually provoked me enough to make some sarcastic comment about it.

As you crossed the road to the Metro you could see the Buda hills shimmering in the distance. Most people ignored the hills, probably never looked up. On the hills lived the rich of Budapest, the American businessmen, the Mafia money and those who had done well in the last ten years. You could see them from here but they were a world away in reality. The Görög Büfé, which I passed next, always reminded me of the financial divide. Translated it meant the Greek Bar but what it had to do with Greece always escaped me. It was without doubt the least salubrious drinking establishment in the universe. It was the last standing corrugated iron shack of a once long line of similar corrugated iron shacks. It hung forlornly just off the vertical in a similar way to most of its patrons. It was disgusting. It was also full when we walked past it at seven o'clock in the morning. There were guys in there happily downing beer and palinka chasers at that early hour. It was most impressive. I checked the opening hours board and was astonished to find that it opened at 5.30 in the morning. Andrea explained that Hungarian men traditionally liked to have a shot of the hard stuff before going off to operate heavy machinery in the work place, so they had to open early. I had a secret desire to, just once, have a beer in there but Andrea banned me from even thinking it, saying that I would not come out alive. She was probably right.

On the path to the metro station's subway was always chaos, no matter what time it was. Örs Vezér Tér was at the end of a Metro line and the start of tram, bus and trolley bus lines. The entire Roma[6] community of Hungary seemed to be gathered there to sell fruit, vegetables, women's underwear, or super glue and screaming "Tessék! Tessék!"[7] followed by the name of their product should the passers by not have noticed what it was, even though it had been waved in their face. The Roma sat in the centre of the path causing us to make a zigzag pattern to the subway. There were more Roma inside the subway but here they sold everything from sweet yellow peppers to lottery tickets and socks to bicycles. One annoying bastard sold only alarm clocks and set one off every five seconds to show they worked. Another arrived every day on an ancient bicycle, dressed as a clown, playing a radio very loudly and with the word "Open" written all over his clothes. He then sold hair bands and hair clips. He was Andrea's favourite. There were also newspaper sellers yelling out witty remarks (apparently they were witty, they were lost on me) about the day's news. The tattier the publication the more extreme were the politics. The rubberised floor in the corners of the subway was always burnt away where homeless people had desperately lit fires in the winter and under the influence of harsh liquor had not thought of what the heat would do to the synthetic floor.

---

[6] The official term is 'Roma', the Hungarians call them gypsies. Both terms will be seen in this book

[7] "Here you are?"

Then, after a hard day at work the Hungarians finished their twelve-hour shifts and came home to see the subway full of tramps selling the contents of bins and skips. Worse was the people clearly selling their possessions from a blanket for almost nothing just to buy bread, or the wrinkled old crones, skin the colour and texture of brown leather dressed in black or what I would call peasant costume selling fives roses for thirty pence or assorted stewing vegetables and refusing your insistence that they should keep the change. The worst ever, according to Andrea was when she saw some old wino selling mini skirts for 80p made from cloth clearly recovered from off cuts he had found in a skip. I thought the old sod selling chewed pencil stubs pushed him close. Add to this the cripples and the deformed holding crucifixes in gnarled hands and a money pot in the other and you had an interesting neighbourhood. Even more curiously there was no hassle at all. They were very polite.

Finally there was the overspill from the Greek bar who urinated anywhere at all (the Greek bar doesn't have toilets) or sunbathed where they fell. I was most amused to discover a man collapsed on the grass by the railway lines naked from the waist down and fully clothed above the waist. I spent a happy few minutes trying to work out what the hell he could have been doing or trying to do.

"What's supposed to be happening?" asked Jessica as I arrived.

"Nobody knows?" hissed Ági, an old hand. "Just keep smiling." She was Hungarian, twenty-eight, taught maths, eminently sensible except for the typically Hungarian microskirt and apparently thought the school was fantastic, probably because of the Western money.

I looked around and saw that the Churchill International School of Budapest was not a big school. The entire population of the school plus a few parents could fit quite easily into the largest classroom, which was where we all stood waiting for Árpád to arrive. It was five past nine; the welcoming assembly was supposed to start at nine o'clock. The teachers stood at the front of the room grinning inanely waiting for something to happen. As I waited I counted about thirty children. A few of the children from last year were back, but many were new. Where had the old students gone?

At quarter past nine Naima, the Pakistani woman in charge of English teaching, dragged the Headmaster out his office and pushed him into the centre of the room.

He welcomed us all in English, then read out a Hungarian speech, then the Chinese teacher Sue did the same for the Chinese parents, then it was supposed to be Russian but the Russian interpreter was not there, so Árpád spoke in Russian. Finally he introduced all the teachers.

"Miss Jessica Higgins is the new kindergarten teacher. She has come all the way from America to be here."

The gathering applauded. Jessica smiled her biggest toothiest smile.

Dr. Hussein is in charge of English," continued the Headmaster and Naima did a little bow in her sari.

Larry Baker is in charge of P.E and..." he faltered as he realised Larry wasn't there. "Well he is not here at the moment," he finished.

Mr. Fletcher is in charge of History," said the Headmaster pointing to Bill in the corner.

When he came to me he introduced me as, "Mr. Dexter, he will be teaching Science, Geography and..."

I must have taken a step back and my mouth dropped wide open. Geography? Geography! This was the first I had heard about this. The last time I studied geography I was twelve. I could feel waves of panic and anger flood through my body as I smiled to the expectant faces in the crowd.

I decided to question Árpád about the geography issue immediately, but there was no time and we moved straight into a tutor period. A 'timetable' for the day's lessons had been posted on the board three minutes earlier. It consisted of five torn out pages from the Headmaster's diary and listed the classes for today and tomorrow. You found out if you were teaching by locating your name on the relevant period and that was the subject and the class you were teaching. I was teaching three lessons today and four tomorrow, including geography.

As I walked back along the corridor I noticed that there was a discussion between two Chinese students, Sue the Chinese teacher and Bill Fletcher, who seemed to assume the role of deputy head, or Dean. There was translating going on and all I heard were the American's words.

"So let me get this straight. He is sixteen and lives alone in the city. She's seventeen, going into the prep class of ten year olds because she speaks no English, lives alone too and her absent parents think it would be best if she lived with one of the teachers... I think we need to talk about that one!"

I taught three science lessons and tried to grab the Headmaster at break time but he had organised for Tibor, the one armed physics teacher, and I to go to see another school's science department on the other side of Budapest.

"About the geography..." I began.

"Oh it's very basic," he said. "Just to the prep classes," and off he went, reminding us to not be late at the other school.

Before we went Tibor and I wanted to see if we could get into our science room. Our school rented a wing off another Hungarian state school, which was closing down. I had yet to be allowed into the shared science room. The room was in the other school's domain up four flights of steps and after the staff meeting earlier I had to ask an old cleaning crone for the key. She spoke no English, I had no Hungarian but I gathered from her body language that I would have to kill her to get the key. It was time to try again with the help of a native speaker.

We climbed the four flights of stairs and found the other school's staff room. Tibor did all the talking but I could read the body language. They weren't going to give us the key. Tibor confirmed this.

"They say no contract has been signed so no key."

"What contract?" I asked. This was news to me.

"I don't know."

"But they don't use the room anyway," I said. "We only want to look in."

"I said the same," said Tibor. "But this is Hungary," he added, as if this made things clear.

I understood a little. These teachers saw this new Western private school taking over the building and feared for their jobs. America and its puppets were the new invaders. This was their way of stopping the progress.

"But we were going to let them use the equipment too," I said.

Tibor shrugged. "We may get into the room by the end of the year," he said hopefully.

"You do realise then," I said, "that at this present time, the entire science department resources consist of some paper 'atoms' I cut out of some scrap paper this morning, a Periodic Table dishcloth I was given as a leaving present from my last school, and a book of red litmus paper I just found in my pocket?" I was also going to point out that the department couldn't even manage a full quota of limbs but decided that Tibor knew he was missing his arm.

"You think you have it bad," said Tibor with a smile. "I'm down to teach I.T tomorrow and we don't have any computers."

I laughed out loud.

I liked Tibor instantly. He was an academic, a world-renowned expert in the field of superconductors, supplementing his meagre university salary teaching our students basic physics, however his idea of 'basic' physics differed somewhat from my idea. He was in his fifties but looked much older, fiercely intelligent and had the ability to say in one sentence exactly what he wanted to say – a rare quality. He had a greying beard and a cheeky smile and one could feel decades of frustration coming off him. Maybe it was his disability, maybe it was fighting a system but either way he now coped with it by smiling with his mouth and apologising with his eyes. Tibor drove us to the other school. I was assuming, by the way, that with only one arm he would have an automatic car at least, but no, he had a shift stick and simply changed gear by removing his hand from the steering wheel at appropriate moments. It made the journey over the cobbled streets of Buda more invigorating. He told religious jokes as we drove. On the Elizabeth Bridge, which took us from the peace of the Buda hills towards the chaos of Pest, he pointed to the Danube below us.

"Don't say anything about it not being blue," he grinned. "Every single English speaker makes that comment and think they are being original."

"Is it really the Danube?" I said. "My Hungarian girlfriend calls it the Duna. I didn't realise."

Tibor gave me a strange look. "I thought you were teaching geography?" he said.

"Don't you start," I grimaced.

Tibor shrugged and changed the subject. "We call it the Duna because it is the Duna. However in English it is called the Danube. I recommend you call it the Duna though."

We parked outside an imposing building.

"This is a school for people who want to work in hotels," said Tibor, which didn't explain why its students appeared to be only girls in a black and white school uniform.

"And why are we here?" I asked.

"Our Headmaster knows a lot of people. His address book is thick. He knows this Headmaster and he will order us some chemicals."

"Why can't we order our own chemicals?" I said.

"Because we don't have a safety licence and are not registered as a school."

It got better and better.

We met the Headmaster; he was a well-built bald man. He looked like a cross between Benito Mussolini and Alfred Hitchcock. We shook hands.

"Call me big Joe," he said in very faltering English as he showed us the laboratories.

"His name is Nagy Jozsef," explained Tibor. "In English that means Big Joe."

Big Joe introduced us to the science teacher and then disappeared. The science teacher seemed most agreeable and said she would order everything that she considered necessary to teach science.

As I looked at her laboratory, essentially an old lecture theatre with a demonstration bench I wondered what that would be. What kind of science did hotel employees of the future need?

I returned to the Churchill School for lunch. It was a small portion of meat soup, served with good Hungarian bread. The canteen was sparse and two old ladies served the meal with stern expressions. I was free in the afternoon so I sat in the staffroom and read through geography books…well that was the plan. The Headmaster rushed in and said,

"What are you doing here? You're supposed to be teaching maths to the prep classes?"

"I am?" I said. "My name is not by the period."

"Yes, because I could not fit your name into the box," said the Headmaster.

"So how was I supposed to know that?" I wailed. "You said nothing about teaching maths."

"Just go and sort them out," he said.

Fine, I thought. I was a little mad. Mathematics as well? This was getting crazy. I walked in and introduced myself. I was met by blank looks and amused chatter in Chinese and Hungarian. Very quickly I realised that none of the kids could speak any English at all. Well thanks for telling me, I thought again. In this classroom, known as the prep class, were thrown students of all ages, united only by their inability to speak English. Sixteen-year-olds, eight-year-olds, seven, nineteen, all of whom knew not a word. Many could speak Hungarian but the rest couldn't. I had no books, no experience and no common language. It was time to think very quickly. I drew the four simple mathematical signs on the board, followed by the equals sign, noting that this simple task used up half a piece of chalk and left a huge pile of dust on the floor. I pointed to the signs, said the names of the mathematical symbols, and was very amused by the sound of assorted foreigners repeating the words back to me in perfect impressions of a Home Counties English accent. Pleased with this success I proceeded to teach the students the numbers up to one hundred.

Afterwards I asked Ági, the young Hungarian woman and the school's official maths teacher what the best approach to teaching maths to a mixed ability, mixed age, mixed sex, mixed nationality class with no grasp of English. She looked at me and said with a smile, "it's impossible."

I went home so mad at the lack of communication I failed to appreciate the beauty of Budapest, my new home. There was no timetable available for tomorrow, there were no instructions, no guidance – nothing.

September

Tuesday 1st September

I arrived at school pleased to see that no last minute changes had been made to the 'timetable'. However to counter balance this good news there were no further days forthcoming.

I asked the Headmaster's secretary if there was any 'Blu Tak' in the school so I could stick my dishcloth Periodic table to the black board.

"No," she said.

"I beg your pardon?" I said. "Do you mean there is no 'Blu Tak' or that I can't have any?"

"The previous science teacher used to put a lot of posters up with 'Blu Tak' and left a lot of marks on the walls," explained the secretary, with a hard stare.

"Yes, but he is not here anymore so it is hardly relevant is it?" I said.

The secretary looked at me and shook her head. I was guilty by professional vocation.

"But I just want some for thirty minutes," I said, but in Hungary a no is a NO. You cannot get past pointless things like this. In the end I stole some from a poster in the staff room and carried on regardless.

At break time, Bill Fletcher the history teacher had had enough.

"How can I teach history to a class who don't know the past tense?" he moaned as he arrived from teaching the prep class.

I laughed, I had never thought of that.

"Listen, Hugh Grant, you weren't here last year," said Larry, the New Yorker. He spent most of his life looking for utopia and to escape America but his innate Americanness ran through him from head to toe. He wisecracked, shouted and cursed the world for its un-American attitude. He also told great stories and used any opportunity to tell one.

"We opened the school at nine o'clock last year," he continued. "At eight thirty there's one of the Hungarian money guys saying 'Have we enough children? Maybe we shouldn't bother opening?' Then Gerry yells 'you can't just close a school like that. It's not the same as a business.' We go into the building and there are no desks and no books at all."

"I don't believe you," I said.

"I swear," said Larry. "Árpád and I had to go over to that shed over there." He pointed to the far side of the playground. "That's where the other school keeps all its broken tables and chairs and find something for the kids to sit on. I'm thinking, some Russian sucker is paying $8000 for this!

"And also there wasn't a single book, there were no teachers hired. I spent most of the first term taking the entire school for impromptu P.E lessons outside. We didn't have access to the gymnasium at the time. Oh it was much worse last year."

"Why aren't our kids allowed in the playground?"

"Because the other school doesn't want us to. We are tenants. That is why you don't have a lab and why I can only use the gym twice a week."

It explained why the kids hung around in the corridor looking lost.

Wednesday 2nd September

Walking through ÖrsVezér Ter I managed yet another ironic comment about the purple suit in the worst clothes shop in the world. It was truly a awful garment and I gleaned much pleasure for a while convincing Andrea that I was going to buy it until she worked out I was joking and took me in the shop and told the assistant I wanted to try it on.

"You see," she said sweetly, "I can be as funny as you."

The school's population was diverse. Over one quarter of these were Chinese, most of whom formed cliques which they enforced by speaking only Chinese. The majority of the other students came from the former Soviet Union. There were four Russians, three Kazakhstanis, two Estonians and two Ukrainians. The rest were mainly rich Hungarians and solitary Israeli, Dutch and Egyptian children. There was one American girl. She was very quiet and had been stuck in a class consisting almost entirely of Chinese students who wouldn't speak to her. There was also one English boy, a four year old who seemed to be incapable of any speech at all.

I taught my first geography lesson to the prep class. This was a very disconcerting experience, as there was no link between the children except that none spoke any English at all. There was the seventeen-year-old Chinese girl, plus a few others. There was also a Ukrainian girl, who I was sure was older than me. There were also crazy nine-year-old Hungarian boys and a lost Israeli boy. We went through a few words like 'mountain' and 'sea' by using mime – have you ever tried to mime a valley?

Science with the prep class was also fun. As I stood there pointing at various parts of my anatomy and telling them what it was called (i.e. "KNEE…KNEEEE." And all the kids saying "KNEE!" back to me in a bizarre parody of my English accent) I wondered what the hell I was doing with my life.

One of the Hungarian teachers asked me if I wanted to have a private student for science. I said, "why not?"

The Hungarian Girl Trap

Thursday 3rd September

Andrea and I were invited out to dinner with Gerry. He took us to a restaurant called 'Jules Verne' on Váci Utca[8]. It had a nautical theme and Spanish guitarists. Andrea was amazed at the lavishness of Gerry's ordering.

"We'll have the finest wine you've got," said Gerry to a rather inattentive waiter and then ordered a huge starter consisting of prawns, frog's legs and smoked salmon. Andrea and I were very good and ordered a simple soup.

Four bottles of wine later plus main courses and desserts and Gerry paid the bill of 13000 forints). Andrea was shocked, as this was just under a week's wages for her. I was too drunk to care and Gerry and I swapped "Spoonerisms" and anecdotes about school life in the UK.

"I will not allow this school to fail," said Gerry as he left he left us. "It will succeed."

Friday 4th September

I taught atomic structure to a class and they understood first time. They may be foreign but they're sharp. Maths with the prep class. I was reminded that there is only one job in the world and that is teaching and I love it. I had misgivings about being a teacher of English language, I have no training in such a thing, but as I taught Xin, a tiny, Chinese girl with no English or Hungarian how to say the numbers up to one hundred I felt a sense of achievement I had never felt before.

Saturday 5th September

We call the Hungarians Hungarians in ignorance. The ancestors of the people we call Hungarians were a nomadic people who settled in the basin formed by the Carpathian Mountains in the ninth century. Other tribes already in the area were of the mistaken belief that these nomads were descendants of the Huns, and there is some evidence for this: the name 'Attila' for example remains very popular in Hungary. Hungarians call themselves Magyarok, the country is Magyarország. The name 'Magyar' came from the tribe that eventually asserted itself over the others in the group. Oh and don't go round pretentiously calling Hungarians 'Magyars' just to show how clever you are (you know who you are, you call Florence 'Firenze' don't you?), you'll pronounce it wrong and anyway you don't call Germans 'Deutsch'?

Árpád was the leader of the Magyar tribe, and he set about conquering more territory and establishing the group in the area that is pretty much where modern Hungary is today. All Hungarians know and love tales about the seven tribes who and all romantically believe they are descended from these Eastern tribal people, yet the number of blue eyed blondes in the country tends to contradict this. It's irrelevant of

---

[8] The main tourist shopping thoroughfare in Pest. Jules Verne is at number 60

course; being Hungarian is a state of mind, not genetic, as I was told on numerous occasions. The Doctor, a blue eyed blond, was typically, the most assertive in expressing this view.

Hungary was established as a Christian kingdom in 1000AD when István, a descendant of the original Magyars was crowned. He forged a strong kingdom, by cunning choice of bride, thus cementing his position, forging links with German kings and using his new strength to withstand attacks from other tribes and passing crusaders. Árpád's descendants continued to rule Hungary until 1301; from then on the Kings (or Queens) were foreigners, some were great, and some were terrible. The Hungarian empire was enormous at this point and stretched from the Black sea to the Adriatic. However in the background the Ottoman Turks were lying in wait.

Ulászló II was a very weak king and allowed noblemen to effectively rule the kingdom. There was a peasants' revolt and as central rule disintegrated the Turks took their chance and destroyed the Hungarian army at Mohács in 1526, killing the King in the process[9]. The Turks soon occupied the central plains and isolated Transylvania from the rest of the country. Hungarians looked west to counter the occupying force from the east and chose Ferdinand I, a Habsburg, brother to the Emperor of the Holy Roman Empire, to be their new king. The Habsburgs, who ruled in Austria, were keen to acquire the crown because the Holy Roman Empire was merely a political entity at this stage. They were less keen to remove the Turks from all the country though and the two invading powers seemed to have co-existed for a couple of hundred years with a kind of 'live and let live' policy being undertaken. The only fly in the ointment being uprisings by native Hungarians, which were put down with considerable force.

Between 1718 and 1780 the Ottoman influence had subsided and the Habsburg rulers consolidated the ravaged country. There was great reconstruction and new immigrants from what we would now call Austria, Germany, Slovakia, Romania and Serbia arrived. I guess the Habsburgs real plan was to absorb Hungary into the great Habsburg Empire. Effectively Hungarians felt they had to fight their own kings! The French revolution of 1789 would have given inspiration to Hungarians who had had enough of the Habsburgs. The Hungarian revival movement was born.

Finally on March 15th 1848 there were mass demonstrations and insurrections throughout the kingdom. The rebels declared autonomy within the Habsburg Empire, Kossuth and Batthyány (every town has a road or something named after these two) being in charge. Civil war followed, perhaps caused because of all the non-Hungarians now living in Hungary who didn't fancy Hungarian rule at all. Austria accepted the terms, mainly because they were facing revolution at home too; however a quick change of ruler to the stronger Franz Joseph, and quashing their

---

[9] The Hungarian crown disappeared after this battle, to reappear four centuries later. The crown, with its battered cross on top is very important to Hungarians and it image is seen everywhere.

home revolution made the Austrians change their mind and further war followed[10]. Astonishingly Hungary won initially, but the Austrians brought the Russians in and they invaded Hungary too.

Crushed, but not beaten the Hungarian people entered a period of passive resistance. Eventually in 1867 the Compromise was reached, which turned the Habsburg Empire into a dual monarchy, or the Austro-Hungarian Empire as we know it. Essentially both countries had separate governments but were under one Emperor. All foreign policy, military and economic policies remained common. The period between 1867 and the First World War was a golden age for Hungary. Many of the great buildings were created, the language was revived, nationalism flourished, Bartók revived many of the Hungarian folk songs to international acclaim. Such a shame it had to go so wrong really…

In September 1914 Franz Ferdinand, the heir to the Austro-Hungarian empire was shot by a Serb assassin in Sarajevo, the capital of Bosnia. Now there was no love lost between Franz Ferdinand and Hungary, Hungary liked their comprise deal, as it had given them their first freedom for many hundreds of years – up to a point, but they still considered the Austrians as an occupying force. Nevertheless the Austrians declared war on Serbia, and Hungary had no choice but to be involved. Russia sided with Serbia, Germany sided with Austria and Britain and France, keen to settle scores, joined Russia against Germany. World War I began.

At the end of the war the Austro-Hungarian Empire was on the losing side and the empire collapsed. Hungary declared itself an independent country, but at the same time, seeing their chance, Romanians, Serbs, Czechs rapidly took over large parts of the country. By 1919 Béla Kun had established the Hungarian Soviet Republic. Initially it had success, but they tried executing people who didn't agree with them and they lost political support. Besides the Hungarians never trusted the Russians after 1849, or after their lack of support in World War One and Communism was a very Russian idea.

In 1920 the biggest bugbear for the modern Hungarian happened in France. We know it as the treaty of Versailles. Hungarians know it as simply "Trianon". There the victors in World War I (or just the French in the eyes of the Hungarians[11]) awarded huge tracts of land the Hungarians considered theirs to form the new countries Serbia, Croatia, Czechoslovakia and Romania. Two thirds of Hungarian land was lost and, irrespective of the claims of the land on both sides, Hungary had lost its natural borders (the Carpathian Mountains) and a lot of its natural resources. Ten million Hungarian speakers were left outside the borders of Hungary, and were not exactly treated well. The situation remains similar today, although exactly how many still speak Hungarian is not clear to me at the time of writing. Certainly Transylvania in Northern Romania is still extraordinarily Hungarian.

---

[10] See the Doctor's comments about beer earlier in the book
[11] Fortunately for me and Englishman living in Hungary!

The Hungarian Girl Trap

The period between 1920 and 1939 is one of further movement to the political right. Hitler used an irresistible mix of: promises to returning the old territories, economic pressure and threats of military intervention to compel the Hungarians into supporting his policies, including those related to Jews. Hungary *did* get some of its land back at the start of World War II for playing along.

Hungary of course had no choice but to side with the Nazis when World War II started and so suffered when the Soviet forces fought back against the Germans. The Soviets crossed the Hungarian border in 1944. There followed a brutal battle as the German forces retreated, destroying everything on their way. By April 1945 the last German troops were forced out of Hungary, but the country was almost totally ruined.

After the war Hungary, on the losing side again, signed a peace treaty and lost all the territories the Nazis had help them regain. A Communist party was set up soon after. And it remained that way until 1956, which I will deal with later.

Hungary never fully integrated into the Soviet Union's little empire. It was always more prosperous, more western thinking, unSlavic I guess. In 1989, very quietly, the government adopted a democracy package. To everyone's relief, with Gorbachev in charge in the Soviet Union and *Glasnost* the order of the day he offered little resistance, and the Soviet's signed an agreement to withdraw Soviet forces in 1991. The Czechs, inspired by Hungary's success instigated their own 'velvet revolution' soon after, and the open border crossing that was established between Austria and Hungary directly influenced the falling on the Berlin Wall in 1989. So many East Germans were travelling to Hungary and crossing the border that eventually the East German government could see no point in having the 'anti Fascist protection barrier' any longer.

Today Hungary is free for the first time in almost seven-hundred years. This is the best time to be a Hungarian. And I think they know it, although many are nostalgic for the way of life they had under Communism. Many truly believed in the Socialist ideal, and ignored the reality that it didn't really work economically. Capitalism is so much crueller. There will always be issues with the old borders too, but things could be a lot worse. They do live in fear that they will die out though; that they will be forgotten, or assimilated into some big Euroland culture. They hold onto their traditions and history, their foods, their language in the same way a child holds onto a treasured toy.

Sunday 6th September

An explanation of salaries. I'd say that salaries are about 10 times less in Hungary than in England. However food is only about half price. Therefore in real terms food is five times more expensive than it is in England. The cost of living is relatively huge too. So many Hungarians are very poor. Many have second jobs. Teachers don't get paid during the summer, which is shocking. Of course there is the other side. I met my private student today. Her name is Petra. She lives in the Buda hills and it could be Beverley Hills. It is the most expensive house I have ever visited. Petra's father is some kind of arms dealer. There is a lift inside and it's only a three-floor house. They have a Porsche and a Range Rover. Petra's study is bigger than our flat. Petra's nice, with a well-fed look about her you rarely see here. She has an American accent, which I am trying to get her to lose. It is an easy £6 an hour (I would have charged more if I had known how well off they were) to just help her do her IB biology homework. Andrea is not so sure about Petra because she is a sixteen-year-old girl. Andrea gets a little possessive, but I pointed out that if she was using me for sex I'd charge an awful lot more than £6 an hour.

Monday 7th September

I was as gloomy as I can ever remember being on a Monday morning. It was raining and cold. Where had the weather gone? I arrived at the school and was delighted to see that we had a timetable for the rest of the year. I was not surprised to find that my twenty-three periods a week were four periods more than anyone else was doing. I had come to expect that. The Hungarians tend to moan and complain and the British just get on with it.

Something else sensible had been done. They had rearranged the prep classes (full of kids who theoretically don't speak English) so that those that do are moved into their correct year. This made life an awful lot easier. I can cope with mixed ability kids who don't speak English but I found mixed ability, mixed age, mixed sex, and mixed linguistic ability a little strenuous. It was O.K for the English as second language teachers; they could just talk, but I was supposed to teach them something more than English. My miming skills are becoming rather good..

Talking of the lab, the Headmaster showed me the timetable and pointed out when I could use the laboratory. Still no key of course, so it was all theoretical. He then said that the other school had decided to charge us for whenever we use the room so could I use it as little as possible

Some chemicals were ordered today but they won't be delivered until we have a poisons licence. I told the Headmaster this and he seemed very reluctant to get one. I could not understand why. He thought that as the other school must have one then we wouldn't need one. I was pretty sure that we as an institution would need our own. I said I was not letting the kids do any experiments until this licence was in my hand because it would be me who got in trouble if anything went wrong.

The Headmaster said, "Why don't you let them use them but warn them they are poisonous and be very, very careful?"

I gave up at this point.

At 2.30 all the kids go swimming. I was working on some GCSE Exam board business and two other Hungarian teachers (female) were sitting chatting. Larry, the American P.E teacher asked if anyone was free to help bus the kids to the pool, as it was the first time. Now I was busy and had no idea where the pool was, so I was out, but the two women claimed they were far too busy to go and pleaded with me to go. I did because otherwise Larry would have been stuck. I'm glad I did because a Hungarian worker at the pool attacked him over some sandal incident I didn't quite follow. Nor did Larry. Larry was so mad he threatened to kill the guy next time.

Tuesday 8th September

Still angry about the pool incident Larry and I walked into the office to speak to Árpád, the Headmaster and the secretary about what happened. Larry told the story in his usual way, with lots of mime. However he was being too funny and Árpád and the secretary were used to him joking and didn't realise how serious he was.

"If it happens next time," said Larry. "Then I will do this," and he mimed a stabbing motion. He was dead serious but once again Árpád and the secretary giggled.

"Can't you call up the pool and get this guy fired?" asked Larry. "It is dangerous having kids there."

Árpád did eventually call the pool and reported back that it was difficult to get the staff these days and that it would never happen again.

My mood deepened when of course the cover timetable appeared. It was compiled by one of our female Hungarian teachers and surprise surprise even though I teach more than anyone else I was (somehow) the one who had most spare cover periods too. This was because they had compiled it including times when they didn't want to be in school (if they had a free morning) but had not done the same for me). Plus others did other jobs so 'couldn't' cover then.

Teaching however was fun because the kids have never seen anything quite like me. If I am demonstrating gravity I will jump out of the window, that sort of thing. I don't think my colleagues do the same sorts of things!

Wednesday 9th September

I taught a lesson of brilliance today to a third form class. Physics can be a little tedious, especially if the department is too well resourced. Equipment flattens things. I taught the solar system without resources. I started the lesson by teaching them formally that the Earth was flat, and drawing it so. I was waiting for someone to say anything. The 'Prussian' method of teaching employed so widely in Eastern Europe means quiet classes and students who don't dare question what the teacher tells them. So I drew four elephants under each corner on my Earth.

Finally someone said. "That's not right."

I looked at the board confused. "Aaaah," I said. "Sorry yes. These are Indian elephants and they should be African!" I drew the ears bigger

I then laughed and laughed at the class's ludicrous Earth is a sphere theory forcing them to think about how they knew that. It was brilliant.

The department's resources increased by 100% when I built a model ear using a yoghurt carton, some cling film, some salt and a tape recorder. It was superb too.

Next I did the solar system using a basketball, two tennis balls, two Hungarian coins and various chalk granules and instructing the students to stand ludicrous distances apart. Then I had to plead with the secretary for her to lend me her lamp to simulate the sun. She wasn't happy and I had to blackmail her to get it. "Don't worry, it's only their education suffering and I have no resources anyway!"

Bill the American History teacher has worked out the way of getting things. He has avoided the Headmaster completely and ordered his books via Gerry, the Director of the School in England. Ági, the maths teacher is furious because she gave her book order to the Headmaster and he, of course, is questioning the cost and has hidden the order under a pile of paper work.

I watched Bill earn £35 for two hours work as he returned some English documents to a very grateful woman he had proof read for her. It looked the easiest money in the world.

Thursday 10th September

There are two rules about Hungary, neither of which I have shared with Andrea: everything is possible in Hungary and everything is impossible in Hungary. A slight oxymoron but what I mean is that if you try and do something you will be stopped but if you want to bribe someone you can probably get there. I find the whole thing ridiculous of course. I have actually had two of the finest teaching days I can remember. But this is probably because in the classroom I can do what I do best, which is enthuse and entertain and teach. O.K so I only have chalk dust, miming skills and a yoghurt pot but it is amazing what you can do.

Outside the classroom things are pretty bad, but I choose to ignore it. Tibor, my one-armed physics colleague didn't show up today for his classes. Nobody knew why until the Headmaster said, "Oh yes he is in America for a week for a university seminar." Well thanks for telling us! Tibor made the mistake of telling the one person who he shouldn't have told. Of course the cover timetable sprang into action but nobody knew this guy wasn't here so nobody covered the class.

Bill revealed that he would be away for ten days from next week. Because everyone in Hungary has two jobs they get clashes, compromising the running of the school. Bill also works for a company that runs summer camps all over Eastern Europe. The chaos is unbelievable. One of the female teachers then worked out how best to cover his classes and I was not surprised to find that I was the most convenient teacher to use. I made the fatal mistake of saying "No problem I was planning to take years 9 and 10 to the zoo anyway," which should have eased the problems but seemed not to.

The Hungarian Girl Trap

Friday 11th September

I went to Petra's, my private student, house today. I helped her with her Venn diagrams for an hour and she gave me £10. She said, "How many private students do you want? I can get you loads."

In the evening we were invited to a party of one of Andrea's American bosses at The American Firm. Predictably the house was in the Buda (Beverley) Hills and had such status symbols as security guards and swimming pools. The man had hired the city's finest cocktail barman to serve the free drinks and a Mexican theme was supplied by transferring entirely a local Mexican restaurant staff and all onto the lawn. It was quite fun in a too much money and I'm showing you sort of way. There was also far too much office swanking and I was glad I had nothing to do with such things. I was also a little jealous, but who wouldn't be?

Saturday 12th September

We were invited to one of Andrea's colleagues wedding. She is of course marrying an Englishman (the second Anglo Hungarian wedding of the year – do I detect a trend?) and it was held in the castle in the city park[12] on the Pest side. The last Hungarian wedding I went to I was a little overwhelmed. I had only been in the country three days and was thrown into the thing. This time I was a little more prepared and took on the role of Hungarian expert for the British guests. I explained the history and the important things, like how to order a beer (roughly "edge shirt care-eck"[13]) and not to clink glasses with beer. I was worried about meeting some British people from home (I have bumped into some English who live here now of course but that's different) because maybe they would be ignorant and embarrass me and also would I become horribly homesick? In the end I had a whale of a time.

The wedding was superb, conducted bilingually by a priest called Gábor. He was magnificent, sang all the psalms and had wise words to say. There are not really sing-along hymns at Hungarian wedding, which was a relief having endured the weak singing at British weddings recently. Then the guests were piled onto a London bus and driven over the Danube to the reception restaurant deep in the Buda Hills.

As the drink was free the party rocked. At the last Anglo Hungarian wedding the British best man told no traditional humiliating stories. This time the best Man did. To make it funnier a British man of Hungarian parentage was interpreting and kept making horrendous mistakes, breaking the ice between the two nationalities. The Best Man said:

"I would like to thank the bridesmaids for their help. I am sure you agree they are very beautiful," said the best man

---

[12] Vajdahunyad Castle, near Heroes' Square. It is an exact copy of one that is now in Romania after Trianon.
[13] Egy sört kérék

The Hungarian Girl Trap

The translation apparently mistranslated 'beautiful' to 'chair' (Szep and szek). Fortunately the translator found it funny too and enjoyed the Hungarians helping him out.

I got drunk with the British. I have missed the English sense of humour, which I employ of course but nobody else does. It was refreshing to just laugh out loud at nonsense. It was refreshing to speak in normal slang without having to speak slowly, or deliberately, or mime even. So we laughed at the Hungarian word for cheese (sajt – pronounced shite). This led to us saying 'shite' instead of cheese for all future photos and crying with laughter. We also laughed at the Eddy Grant, UB40 song "Baby Come back" which apparently in Hungarian sounds like "Baby suck it", and how the context of the song is completely changed. We laughed at the f word and how versatile it is, we laughed at the 'Generation Game' style folk dancing with full wine carafes balanced on the heads of the ladies which the British leapt into with gusto, but a Hungarian guest refused to saying "I will not dance with gypsies" (the dancers were in Roma costume).

Monday 14th September

Two new students arrived today, both from the Russian school that has closed after some unnamed person ran off with the money.

Larry was irate because his car had been stolen from the street outside his house. One of the Russian boys overheard the rant and sidled up to him later on.

"I am sorry to hear about your car," he said. "It will be put right."

Tuesday 15th September

Larry's car was back in its parking space this morning, the Russian car theft network suitably chastised at having the temerity of stealing from a high-up member's teacher.

I hear rumours of chemicals. I am not allowing myself to get too excited but apparently they exist. In my excitement I nearly forgot that we have no contract, no licence, no safety glasses. Experiments are still a long way off. Also remember I still have no work permit.

Wednesday 16th September

The chemicals arrived today; or rather I went to collect them. In the first week Tibor, the one armed physics teacher and I had gone to big Joe's school to see their facilities (minimal) and Tibor and a female chemistry teacher had prattled away in Hungarian for a while.

On the way back Tibor had said, "She will order chemicals for us. You will collect them next week."

"Great," I said. "What was her name?"

"Oh I didn't ask," said Tibor apologetically.

"Does anyone speak English there?" I asked.

"No," said Tibor.

"So how will I find her again?" I pleaded.

Tibor shrugged his shoulders.

Big Joe's school still seemed to only cater for pretty sixteen-year-old girls in black mini skirts.

"Are there many girls schools in Budapest?" I asked Tibor.

"Oh, this isn't a girls school," said Tibor.

"So where are all the boys?" I asked.

"This is a school for the children of people in the hotel business. They must just have had girls," said Tibor with his familiar shrug.

"?" I said.

After doing a lot of miming and thanking the Lord that the word chemistry was almost identical in English and Hungarian I was given a wide variety of chemicals including one kilogram of borax, which I am struggling to think of a use for.

Thursday 17th September

I was teaching all lessons today thanks to the cover timetable. I got the kids to make devices that slowed down an egg's rate of descent when dropped from five metres. I did taste experiments with the rest. In the fifth form class the Headmaster and an American woman interrupted me.

"Oh, carry on," said the Headmaster. "I am just showing her around."

I was not introduced so I carried on.

"Can I stay for a while?" said the woman.

"Of course," I said, assuming she meant for five minutes. I had no idea who she was.

While the kids worked I went to talk to her. She said she was a teacher and was very interested in the examinations taken in the school. I still didn't ask who or what she was. After fifty minutes I nipped out to get some more chalk (Hungarian chalk lasts one lesson) and asked the Headmaster exactly who the woman was who was still in my room.

"Oh it's the mother of Shama," the American girl in the school.

"What?" I said. "Shama's mother? Why couldn't you have told me?"

Suddenly the woman's presence was very intrusive.

Andrea and I met a year ago today. We planned to spend it in a Chinese restaurant owned by one of my students but Andrea's ex-fiancé chose today to get himself arrested. He is in jail, he is an orphan and rang up Andrea's mum with his one phone call. Anyway Andrea has returned to Miskolc to help sort it out. So I am left in Budapest. It's rather ironic considering that it's our anniversary and I intended to propose marriage. As the Hungarian's say "Az élet nem habas torta."[14] I asked her hurriedly before she leapt on the train. She said "yes"

Friday 18th September

Not only am I covering half the known cover periods in the universe but Naima has been put in charge of the cover timetable and she has no idea how to do it. It came to period five and she suddenly said "I have no-one to cover the next period."

I had to cover by merging two classes together and made up a geography lesson. The thing that annoyed me was that two of the full time teachers taught only on Friday mornings and had gone home. Why couldn't they call them back in? The large amount of part time teachers means they have different priorities.

Sunday 20th September

Miskolc.

We went walking with Andrea's friend Zsuzsa and István, her intellectual boyfriend. István is an intellectual because he scowls at the alcoholic fools around him at parties, and he has heard of obscure camp U.K rock band *The Fall* (I let him use my credit card to buy U.K music stuff). The man wears a *stereolab* T-shirt for crying out loud. We found a mutual interest in football, Woody Allen and obscure films. We picked mushrooms in the kind of forests that disappeared from Britain a century ago. It was wonderful.

I returned alone on the 7 p.m. express. I had a drink on the train. As I sipped my Coke I watched the hordes in the bar drink masses amounts of beer and smoke themselves stupid. I liked it. You don't get such a convivial atmosphere on a British train. It's all pork pies, expensive beer and polythene sandwiches. Here you could buy whole meals for a pound and a beer for 40p. Oh and the train was as modern as any I have been on.

Monday 21st September

Oh the joy of it all! I arrive in school to find that I have been asked to cover one class on Tuesday afternoon when I am already covering two. This is effectively the whole school! I assumed the lady in charge of cover has nobody else so was really desperate. I had decided to take the two original classes to the zoo on a trip for maximum twenty students. I thought this was a rather neat way of solving the problem.

"Why don't you take the other class to the zoo as well?" said Naima.

---

[14] "Life is not a cream cake"

I refused. I told her that if there was no one else available then we should send them home.

"Oh there are other people," she said.

"So why are you giving three classes to me then?" I asked as I walked out of the door.

I spoke to Larry. He is a good man. O.K he teaches English at an English school and cannot spell but we'll let that go. He read me a letter he is sending to the Governors/Trustees. I corrected the spelling for him. Larry also works for the University Wing of the Churchill operation with the same Trustees. He gets on well with them. He says they speak "Jew to Jew".

In the letter he thanks them for letting him work in the school and then makes an analogy (spelt analygy) with a quality restaurant, with the finest chefs (the staff), and the highest prices. The owners of the restaurant though ask the diners to bring their own silver cutlery. Would people go to this restaurant? Of course not. He asked the Trustees whether they could expect people to pay $10,000 per year for a school with no computers, no science laboratory, no gymnasium, no primary school resources and no library (we have a room called the library but no books can be found in there).

He is right. He says they will either fire him or something will get done. He says he spoke to one of the Governors who said a) he would not send his children to the school and b) they were concentrating on the university wing of their business anyway and the Churchill could just chug along. This outraged me. The bald fact is that the year elevens will not pass their GCSEs because the teachers do not understand them (except me) and they will not pass science because none of them have ever seen a single piece of laboratory equipment. How can they sit a practical exam when they have never seen a measuring cylinder? I have warned the Headmaster of this but still nothing gets done. A 0% pass rate will stop other people sending kids here and the school will die. That doesn't bother me but will bother others. So I will continue to mention what will happen. I am past caring. To me I am using it as an educational experiment. Can you teach science well without equipment? Here, all we have chalk and paper and mime!

To cap it all after school the Headmaster organised for me to meet the science teachers from the other school where we were going to look around the lab and discuss how we could share resources. I went up to meet them at the allotted time. Guess what happened?

"Oh sorry," said the teacher. "You can't go in there today. There are books everywhere!"

The lamest excuse I have ever heard. I can't believe the Headmaster let it go. It was clear stalling and time wasting as far as I could see. I don't care. I have my own educational experiment to do now.

The Hungarian Girl Trap

Tuesday 22nd September

I find good days annoying because I feel I shouldn't be enjoying myself and I worry I will be lulled into a false viewpoint and consider staying in this crazy school. I don't know why today was particularly good. I think it is because the prep classes (the two classes containing beginners in the English language) finally understand where I am coming from and they smile. I don't think they have met a teacher like me and could not cope at all. Now they are happy after we have gone through the comedy performance of them speculating as to which of the subjects (geography, maths or science) I am teaching them today.

I took the years 8 and 9 to the zoo in the afternoon. It was fun and we all enjoyed ourselves. My strategy of only taking two classes worked because now the rest of the school wants to go and I can use that to my advantage. The cover problem was solved in a fairly unique way. The woman who couldn't make it who teaches "Leadership Skills", that well-known National Curriculum subject (she gets teenagers to assert themselves and declare their feelings), is a bigwig in the Government and she sent her Personal Assistant over to take the class. The woman, a young Russian girl, looked highly bemused about the whole thing. I taught her the art of classroom time wasting and filling up the time before the bell (not that we have a bell of course!)

Wednesday 23rd September

Tibor the one armed Physics teacher was back from Palm Springs and his seminar.
"How was America?" I asked him.
"I don't know," he said. "I was talking to scientists all the time," was his crazy response.
I was sorry to tell him that no new computers had arrived. Predictably he just shrugged.
"So I teach them about the history of the operating system then," he said.
"But the class is full of ten year olds who don't speak English," I protested.
"What do you want me to do?" said Tibor. "Build my own computer and program it with my own operating system?"
Over a meagre lunch of chicken and rice Tibor and I shared a laugh at the latest Headmaster idea. Accused by Larry, the New Yorker of running a "ghetto school" because we have no computers the Headmaster announced proudly that he was going to get us ten computers and "have the internet as well but not all day because it is very expensive."
The thought of him spending £10,000 minimum was funny enough even though the other teachers were impressed. Tibor and I, who know a fair bit about our silicon chipped friends, giggled at how easy the Headmaster thought it would be to install all this. If he wants Internet he should have a network and a network needs to be managed. If he doesn't get a network the thing is compromised as a resource

straight away. Our Headmaster seemed to think we could plug them in one day and off we go. The fact that the art room was the chosen place for them was strange anyway. It would take some time for the workpeople to put in the phone lines and the tables and all the plugs needed. I can see this being a cowboy job. Surprise surprise.

In science, the entire fifth form scored over 80%: top score 97%, not bad for a boy who can barely write English. Unfortunately they will all fail because they cannot do the 'alternative to coursework' paper because they have never been in a lab.

I invented a great end of lesson activity: find out a different phrase in the class's languages. For example "What?" we had in French (Quoi), German (Was?), Hungarian (Mi?), Russian (Stor? Phonetic spelling), Chinese (Samar? Very phonetic spelling), Estonian (Mis?) and English. We did this for 'chicken', 'how are you', and 'good morning'. It was great fun. I might be able to add Kazakhstani to this lot tomorrow.

Thursday 24th September

Hollow laughs from the Budapest Sun, the English language newspaper here in BP. Aside from the fact that they could do with a proof reader (they do not know when to use "due" and when to use "owing") it is a fairly limp publication. However it lists the films on in the cinemas in English and we get complementary copies at the school, so we all fall on it when it arrives. Anyway…

1)   In a *vox pop* article on what Hungarians think about racism in their country, a certain Sandor, 22, a Budapest student said, "There is no racism in Hungary…but we do hate the gypsies."

I laughed long and mirthlessly at this.

2)   Scanning our school's advert in the paper I was very amused to see the sentence, "We specialise in mathematics, languages and personal development."

This was news to me, especially as, a) over 20% of the maths classes in the school are taught by a man with no expertise in the subject at all and has not taken an exam in the subject since 1986 (me). This essentially means the Headmaster's doctorate is in maths.

b) Language 'strength' is by default. They could hardly say 'we have no native speakers at all and the English teacher can't spell too well'.

c) Personal development is a mystery. There is no PSHE at all. The top class get leadership skills where they talk about their childhood and assert themselves with a

The Hungarian Girl Trap

Welsh woman called Jackie, who is the Headmaster's neighbour, and who turns up irregularly, but that is it.

3)   A letter I wrote responding to what must be the tenth dumb tourist since I had been here, who had been stung for all his money. A Brian Holzer had written the following, in disgust a few weeks ago and I couldn't let it go.

> Be on the alert
>
> As an American citizen I feel obligated to alert your readers to the fact that there are scams going on in this city which, if not in collusion with the police, are definitely condoned by the police.
>
> Last Tuesday night around 9 pm two women approached me and began a conversation. I asked them why they were talking to me since I was so much older than them - at least by 20 years. They said they liked Americans and enjoyed speaking English and they simply wanted to interact with someone different. Furthermore, one of the women told me she was an elementary school teacher. Within five minutes they suggested that we all have a drink at a hotel bar, because there was live music there. It was only 50 feet away from Váci Utca, there were lots of people around and it didn't seem dangerous. So the three of us went inside a glass elevator to the third floor and went into a bar with a one-man band. The waitress came and I ordered a beer and the women ordered drinks too. When the waitress returned with the drinks, I sensed something wasn't right and requested the bill from her. She returned within one minute with a bill for Ft43,500 (approximately $171.00)! I was charged Ft3,000 forints ($12.00) for my beer and the two women's drinks came to Ft18,200 and Ft22,300. I said I didn't order drinks for the women. The waitress said yes I did. The situation seemed dangerous and I knew that there must be some thugs in the back of the bar who would literally force me to pay. I was right, two big guys appeared and marched to the nearest ATM machine and forced me to draw out the money. Once I had paid I was pushed away.
>
> Within a minute I encountered two policemen and told them the essential facts. They asked me, "Where?" I

pointed to the hotel where the incident had taken place.

They said, "No speak English, go to police station." This was too much for me. I was disoriented and confused and I just returned to my apartment.

The next morning I did go to the police station. As I began relating the story to the official police translator, she asked me if it was a glass elevator. I said yes.

Then she began asking me other questions so I said, "If you know about the glass elevator then what happened to me must have happened to other people too."

She nodded her head in agreement. I asked why the police were allowing this to happen. Why hadn't the place been closed down by the police? She only shrugged her shoulders.

I did continue to make an official complaint. She told me it wouldn't do any good and I wouldn't be getting my money back.

Altogether it took me some six hours to received a signed and sealed copy of my complaint, which I have enclosed.

I had no intention of having sex with either of these two women, I didn't realize they were professional criminals, I only wanted to share some light conversation. Please warn your readers about this situation.

This was my response:

"I read The Budapest Sun regularly and I am becoming increasingly bemused and irritated by the almost obsessive mentions of thievery, trickery and being ripped off in Hungary by your columnists and readers.

Are they all incredibly naive? Have they lost all the skills that made them able to survive in their native land? Maybe they couldn't, which is why they moved away. Why do they assume that the people of one nationality will be any different from another?

Of course there are thieves and con-artists out there and let me tell you one thing - a thief is a coward who will always go for the easiest, most lucrative target.

And everyone who has written in is an easy target. Here is some advice.

1. Don't go round shouting at the top of your voice in English; be subtle and if you have to shout keep your eyes peeled.

2. Don't use credit cards.

3. Signing any forms? Get a Hungarian friend to check out the small print for you. You do know some Hungarians don't you?

4. Why do you need to take a taxi in Budapest? The public transport is wonderful.

5. Learn some Hungarian and try to use it in shops and restaurants

6. Don't carry your passport around with you. A photocopy will do surely.

7. This is my favorite (sic). If you are male and unattractive to women in your own country, do not expect Hungarian women to find you attractive. So if you find yourself to be suddenly very popular with sexy women in bars around Váci Utca, believe me the dumb person is you, not her. Run now or lose a lot of money.

So be ruthless and make yourself a hard target. And if you are really unhappy, go home and watch Hungarian tourists being ripped off by your own country's thieves.

Ray Dexter"

Larry was back on form today. He suggested we form a union in the Staff room today. I went along with him but, once again all the Hungarians either left the room or changed the subject.

"What's wrong with them?" said Larry. "Oh I know, they get scared when you mention unions. Ten years ago they would be in jail for saying what I just did."

He continued, "How many science, geography, math, I.T, English, basketball teachers do you think there are in the world, let alone in Budapest? They'll listen to you."

I agreed but still found the idea of the strike amusing. It would be frighteningly effective but would probably destroy the school once and for all. I couldn't be party to innocent people losing their jobs (the cleaners, the secretary, the canteen staff) over Larry's job dissatisfaction.

"Look," he said. "I campaign all last goddam year for some basketballs, I get 'em finally this year but I've got no fucking pump to pump 'em up with. I ask for a stopwatch and we can't afford one. I'm told to use the other school's pump but it's in their p.e teacher's room and he won't let me in there until a stupid contract is signed. How am I supposed to pump up the balls? Shall I fart into them?"

I was laughing, but it was a bitter laugh. The Hungarians had gone home already. It was past 3.30 p.m.

I followed Larry into the Headmaster's office to voice complaint but, as usual, because Larry is such a wise-cracker he was not taken seriously.

I had a look around the markets on the way home. There is the Chinese market: a sea of people flogging stolen and forged sports clothes and electrical goods. It is huge and if you like "Panoasonic" (sic) hi-fis and "Adiads" (sic) trainers then you are laughing. The other markets are slightly grottier. The trinket markets are full of Ukrainians who take the bus from Ukraine (four hours away) every day to sell crap. Every Eastern European nation is represented in these places. Finally there are the various down and out markets where the dregs of society have raided bins and are selling anything to get enough money for bread. I don't know about you but I don't want to buy three pencil stubs, one left sandal, size 42, or three pages from a pneumatic pornographic magazine. It's at times like that that I realise the poverty of the place. So many people are on the edge.

Our native speaker Shama left school today. Quite rightly she found the English class a little laboured. Why no one could put on a special class for her remains a mystery. If the Headmaster is so desperate for native speakers and will do anything why didn't he do something?

Friday 25th September

There are a few other changes in children. The slightly eccentric Ukrainian girl who appeared to speak no known world language has left. It was my fault I guess. I suggested to her frustrated teachers (who simply ignored her in class) that she drop down into the primary class where they are learning to speak really slowly. The Headmaster thought it was a bad idea, but then he didn't have to teach the girl. I spoke to Jessica and she thought it was a great idea. So I told her teachers to put the girl into the primary class every morning when they do English and get her back in when the primary kids start making things out of clay and papier maché. We did this and everything was great. The girl was happy, learning things, and then suddenly the girl did not arrive one morning. It was so annoying as we had made progress. I don't understand what the parents wanted. As soon as she starts to learn they give up. Neither of them speaks English either.

Our only native speaker now is a four year old English boy in the primary class (although the joke in the staff room was that with his grasp of the language he should go straight into the fifth form). However Thomas does not really count as he cannot actually speak yet.

We have two new students, both Hungarian, both male, both about twenty-five years old and both are in the prep class. One is called "Norby". Norby looked at the maths I gave him to do and was not impressed.

"Oh you didn't believe that advert in the paper did you?" I said. "The one about the maths specialism?" Fortunately Norby didn't understand.

Larry has found out more bad news from the governors. They won't even spend money on the university wing of the organisation. Larry asked them where his students should research topics and was told "use the Internet". He is writing to the American University that supports them to complain.

"I don't care," said Larry. "They need us more than we need them."

Tibor was in a wildly optimistic mood today.

"The Headmaster will buy the ten computers," he said with a beaming smile.

"You didn't hear the end of the sentence," I said.

Tibor looked confused. "The Headmaster will buy the ten computers in the year 2018," I said.

Tibor laughed out of politeness, but there was a nervous look in his eye. He was imagining that I was right and he had to spend the next twenty years lecturing monolingual Chinese children on the history of the disk drive.

Xin the lost Chinese girl can now say "very good" in English as well as all the numbers. That was a constructive way for her parents to spend $800 dollars last month. Considering I taught her the numbers in 40 minutes three weeks ago I am impressed to see that it has taken the rest of the month for her other teachers to teach her collectively "very" and "good". At least she isn't scared of me now. Now she just laughs every time I look at her.

"She thinks you're smart," explained another Chinese girl.

"Sartorially or intellectually?" I asked for no reason because I knew the girl had no idea what I was saying. She meant intellectually.

Sunday 27th September

After the return journey from Miskolc tonight I am simply glad to be alive. Oh the melodrama! The reason for my anxiety was that we did the journey in a Trabant, those typically Communist 'cars'. The car that came in any colour you want as long as it was blue. Normally we took the nice new Express train back to Budapest, which takes one hour and fifty-five minutes to travel the length of the country. It costs four pounds, which is an absolute bargain. However you must book it in advance which is difficult because there is one phone at the station and anyway Andrea always prefers the freedom of getting a lift back. Hence the Trabant journey.

I can't remember the name of the guy but he had a voice like Fozzie Bear. I have probably been introduced to him but I have forgotten. I was initially very excited about the journey: my first Trabbie! However the joy wore off when we got into it.

"It takes about a day to get used to it," explained Fozzie. "Especially if you have driven another car before."

"I've driven a Wartburg," I said. The Wartburg is the 'posher' car manufactured by the same company.

"Luxury," muttered Fozzie.

I saw what he meant when we stopped at a petrol station.

"You can fill it up with petrol if you like," said Fozzie, with an evil grin on his face.

I knew there was a catch but I played along. I picked up the fuel pump and searched the body of the car for the petrol tank orifice. I searched the whole damn car, including underneath but there was no hole anywhere. After five minutes of humouring the guy I gave up. He opened up the bonnet and there above the engine (small) I saw the tank. You effectively just poured the petrol into the engine.

"Now I need to see how much petrol I have," he said.

"Didn't you look at the gauge in the car?" I asked.

"What gauge?" said Fozzie still grinning. "You're not thinking Trabant!"

He pulled a dipstick from out from a pocket in the bonnet and stuck it in the tank.

"I have ten litres left so I must buy ten more."

I was completely speechless.

We got going. I watched amazed as a ferocious roar came from under the bonnet and saw Fozzie listening intently for the right moment to engage first gear. When the moment arrived we shot off at an arthritic 25 km/h. The noise was enormous, the speed pathetic. We struggled up every hill and Fozzie was clearly embarrassed at the car's performance.

"I've never had three people in it before," he explained.

"Still that bloke on a bicycle has just overtaken us," I said.

"Oh it takes fifty kilometres before it even starts to get going," said Fozzie.

So the first thirty kilometres were embarrassing. I found out that Fozzie had an excellent grasp of Anglo Saxon swear words. We hit the main road when the second problem occurred: the light switch jammed. Fozzie had the choice of blinding everybody or not being able to see a thing. More F-words were muttered as he fought with the switch.

"This hasn't happened before," he said cheerfully over the din.

On the motorway three things happened. One we stalled.

"It's the carburettor," said Fozzie.

"Yeah," I said, "you probably need to change the filter."

Fozzie looked at me again. "Filter?" he said.

Later he cheerfully pointed out the high technology of the Trabant. It was a series of five LED's that told you how much fuel you were using up.

"If it goes into the orange lights you're in trouble," he said.

"My father's BMW has something similar," I said bleakly.

"There you are then!" beamed Fozzie.

Of course at this point the LED's flew straight into the red and refused to come down again.

"That's strange," said Fozzie. "It's never done that before."

Add to this the strange whirring sound that started up half way home.

"It sounds like the fan belt," I said. "It does have a fan belt?"

"Of course," said Fozzie indignantly. "However it is more likely that it is the engine falling out." He paused for dramatic effect. "When I bought it I was told the engine mountings would only last 1000 kilometres and to replace them immediately. Of course I didn't get round to it."

"I see," I said.

Then there was the mysterious case of the oil on Fozzie's hands after we stopped at some services. He put his hand on the wheel, fiddled with a few mysterious knobs under the dashboard and his hands were covered in oil.

"What the f..." he said.

He never did find out what it was.

We finally arrived in Budapest at midnight, three hours later than if we had taken the train.

Monday 28th September

School is no better of course. Larry keeps telling me more horror stories. He quit last year but was persuaded to stay on. He told stories about the ineffectual headmaster. How clear bullying had gone on but nothing was done. Aaaah!

I went to see Petra, my rich private student and that always cheers me up. It is so refreshing to listen to a rampant capitalist who has no complaints or problems. I laugh more with her than I do with anyone else. We did some standard deviation and she gave me ten pounds. It is far too easy a life.

Tuesday 29th September

I signed up for Hungarian language class today. Andrea had been nagging me to death to go. I finally found one that was reasonably priced (i.e. not in dollars) and was at times I wanted to study. Most, and there aren't many, are crash, intensive courses, every day for a month. I can't do that of course. I went along to the language school and was treated like a king. They seemed almost excited to have me sign up. I don't think many people learn Hungarian.

I met up with Andrea in the evening and we went to the cinema to see a cheerful film about the glory of war which involved seeing lots of gore portrayed in an arty way. I didn't eat before we went in, there was no time. After surviving the film we went home and I ate some ravioli that was in the fridge. If I had known what hassle that ravioli would cause I would have gone to bed hungry.

The Hungarian Girl Trap

Wednesday 30th September

2 a.m. Violent sickness and other unpleasant intestinal explosions cause me to have a sleepless night. I think the ravioli was disagreeing with me. I was very ill. I made it to the morning with little improvement and decided school was out for the day. We had no medicine, so I felt it better if I laid low for a day or two. Andrea had other ideas and told me to phone the number I had for English speaking health care that came with my school organised medical insurance. I refused, citing the British attitude that a few days' rest and you'll be right as rain. However, as I found out, the Hungarians take health a lot more seriously than the British do. Andrea called the number anyway and they promised to send someone round. This 'someone' turned out to be an ambulance. I was very embarrassed. The drivers spoke no English so I couldn't explain that really some diarrhoea tablets and that'd be fine. They carried me out to the ambulance and I felt a right bloody fool. I was treated like a frail pensioner.

"Finom!" I said desperately, thinking in my delirium I was saying, "I'm fine". Unfortunately I now realise I was saying "delicious"!

In the ambulance I noticed that the ambulance man's attempts at English sounded German so I chanced my arm and said "Sprechen Sie Deutsch?"

He spoke enough to get by and we communicated at last. He cheered up straight away because he had thought I was American. I explained my symptoms and he listened. We even talked about football as we went past the National Stadium.

Once we got to the hospital I was seen by a doctor, who looked at me, took my passport and said "three days" to me in German. I assumed I misheard. I was taken upstairs and told I would be in room 332 after I had had a blood test. A very pretty nurse with one brown eye and one blue eye and no English took some blood and sent me to the room. There was an old man in there. He introduced himself as Jozsef.

"Forgive me, I haven't spoken English for fifty-two years," he said whilst various tubes came in and out of his body.

It turned out that he was eighty-four years old and had learnt his English whilst he was in an American prisoner of was camp in 1945. The Hungarians fought with the Nazi's against Communism.

"How long are you staying?" he asked.

"About half an hour, I hope," I said.

A Doctor arrived. "Excuse me are you English?"

"Yes," I said.

"That's what I heard, good. This hospital is attached to the International Medical School. We teach many international students medicine here and the common language is English. They rarely get a chance to speak to a real English patient so could they come and see you?"

"Sure," I said.

There were nine of them. They asked me various questions and I gave jokey answers. One chap practised blood pressure and said it was very low (it was normal), causing much mirth from his colleagues. They thanked me and left. My Doctor then arrived; she spoke excellent English and asked the same questions the students had. The ravioli was the main interest. I was feeling much better.

"I will be back when the blood tests are here," she said. "Catch up on some sleep."

I tried to, but another Doctor disturbed me. "I have some more students who would like to practise on you because you are English. Can they come in?"

"Why not," I said.

"They are practising pneumonia at the moment so they might want to see if you have it."

In filed the students, mainly Greek, Italian and American.

"How's the Queen?" drawled Leroy, a very laid back American.

They asked me the same questions and practised form filling.

"Any venereal diseases?" asked one.

"Now that is not the first question you ask a patient Alannah," said the Doctor/lecturer with despair.

They too concluded I had food poisoning. But their Doctor wanted them to practise the pneumonia drill so I removed my top and let ten students tap my back for half an hour. By the end I knew the drill better than they did. I liked Leroy's bedside manner best: "Now I'm gonna put this here metal thing on yer. Don't y'all now worry about a thang."

He meant a stethoscope. I was laughing despite my illness. Leroy was also the only westerner I have met who spoke any kind of reasonable Hungarian and he prattled away to Jozsef, my roommate.

"I've been here four years and I like to talk to people. What am I s'posed to do, mime?" he said reasonably.

They left and I was alone but for Jozsef.

"You speak German yes?" said my companion.

"A little," I said.

"You have nothing to read. Here take this," he said in German and he handed me a book by Albert Schweiser.

I thanked him but pointed out my German was a little rusty to cope with such a book.

Two hours later my Doctor returned.

"The blood test shows a little infection, probably food poisoning. We will keep you in over night just to be safe."

"What?" I yelled. "But I am fine!"

"Don't you worry," said the Doctor and left.

Supper came round. I looked up hopefully. I learnt the Hungarian for "Sorry you are a 'nil by mouth' patient," very quickly. The nurse must have seen the disappointment on my face because she blew me a kiss as she left.

I had no pyjamas and the hospital did not supply the patients with loo roll. I used the staff lavatory instead using the old rule that if you look like you know what you are doing people will not question you.

Andrea arrived at seven tearful because reception said I had to be in three nights and assumed I was dying. I pointed out I felt fine and my Doctor said one night. I also said that I was so pissed off at having to stay that if it wasn't for the fact that they had my passport I would have walked out already.

"If you had not called the Doctor and I was home now I would have gone to school tomorrow. Instead I am here with all these ill people!" I said stroppily.

Andrea relieved my boredom by lending me her Walkman and I listened to terrible Hungarian radio stations until 9 p.m. (lights out).

October

Thursday 1st October

I woke up feeling very well indeed. Today's nurse was auburn haired and in a tantalisingly near see-through white uniform. She was very cute indeed and asked me using childish Hungarian the kind of personal bodily fluid questions I wouldn't even ask myself. I said 'no' to all of them regardless of the question and then tried to fake the thermometer reading that read 36 degrees. I wanted it to read 37. I couldn't force it any higher but she was very pleased anyway. 36 appeared acceptable.

The food hell continued. A Communist shot putter of a nurse ignored me and handed out breakfast to everyone else.

"You can have cold tea," she explained in Hungarian.

"Yippee," I said in English.

"At 9 o'clock my Doctor told me I could go home this afternoon once the Professor arrived to sign the papers. I was very excited and transferred myself into the lobby to wait. It was a long wait.

At two o'clock I had explored the whole hospital and still no papers. I started to pick the plastic off a paper clip.

At three o'clock my Doctor looked apologetic and introduced me to another eight students whom would like to practise. That made twenty-three students in twenty-four hours. We went back to my bed and we went through the routine again. I was tempted to make up some symptoms but decided against it. This lot were Swedish and Norwegian and they were very funny. One Swedish girl, who looked far too glamorous to be a Doctor, had learnt her English in Hastings and caused me to be very surprised when she pointed out she had been to the 1066 pub in Battle, which was my old local.

At four o'clock I was getting annoyed and rang Andrea to complain that I was in prison and I was leaving without my passport at six o'clock and bugger the consequences. I went outside to see the world and felt very tired just walking. I went back to the lobby and disguised my exhaustion for fear of being kept in another night.

At five o'clock the Professor arrived looking flustered and unshaven. He looked like Alan Alda but with eyes that bulged more. He was a good man.

"Ten minutes," he promised. "I have to write it in English."

It took half an hour. Then the computer would not print. He called up the computer people and they fiddled for twenty minutes.

"I should have called Bill Gates," joked Alan Alda. Finally at six twenty he got his copy and he handed it to me.

"My passport?" I asked.

"Ah," said Alan Alda, "that is in the main office. Come back tomorrow and collect it."

I decided that I was cursed never to leave the place. I went home and ate soup.

I think the problem with private health care is that Doctors know insurance is paying so they make a lot of fuss about nothing because they know the insurance company would pay. In England the uproar caused by me wasting a hospital bed would be amazing. There was no need for my incarceration at all in my opinion. My very cynical opinion is that as I was the first English patient in there for ages they kept me there to give their students a chance to examine me.

Friday 2nd October

I had to go back to the hospital again today to get my passport. It was relatively problem free and I was pleasantly surprised. It is raining hard and I tested the system by eating a McDonalds cheeseburger. I got a call from the school saying 'don't go to Mátra if you don't feel up to it.'

Monday 5th October

Mátra

So we are to take the whole school on a trip to Hungary's Mátra region. It is mountainous and beautiful apparently. The meeting place was at the bus station behind the National Sports stadium, a place just a little less salubrious than other bus stations I have visited the world over. Therefore it was full of swarthy types trying to sell you knives or exchange money. To make matters worse our coach wasn't picking us up from there but from the even dodgier car park behind the bus station. Here Romanian coaches barely capable of leaving the car park surrounded us. I tried to work out which decrepit bus was ours. The car park was also full of Romanians who were so swarthy they made the previously mentioned swarthy Hungarians look like supermodels.

A new teacher introduced himself. Steve (American) is to teach dance: yes I know, this is a higher priority than computers and library books. He was wild and wacky and played court jester all week. The Headmaster was late. He had put his car in for a service that morning (how sensible). Fortunately the coach, a pink heap, arrived even later. The driver was a droopy moustached chap who, I noticed with relief, was only slightly swarthy.

We set off. The coach made grinding noises every time the driver turned the wheel.

"Now it didn't make that noise when it left the factory," I remarked nervously.

As we drove the cloud lowered and the rain fell. It was the perfect weather for a walking and view-experiencing vacation. Slowly we wound our way up the mountain to our hotel, a stone building designed by someone who used to design

The Hungarian Girl Trap

British workhouses in the 18th century. It was forbidding. At this point I saw what the Headmaster was doing. He was taking all us capitalist types back in time to the 1970s to really appreciate the delights of holidaying in Communist Hungary. The hotel was built with trade union money in the seventies and there had been a waiting list to get in. Now it was empty save for us and I was not surprised.

The Headmaster had negotiated for the pool to be open. It wasn't. It opened between 7 a.m. and 3 p.m. Very useful times for those who go out during the day as we had. We had taken the kids to one village and marched them along a high ridge until they reached the next village: a 10k walk. The Chinese girls wore platform shoes and everyone was in jeans. The climb was steep and in the rain, slippery and wet. The views did not exist owing to the fog. Hold a piece of paper in front of your eyes to see what we could see. Subsequently the two hour walk took three and a half-hours.

Supper was equally weird. Here is a list of the events:

The Headmaster, who has negotiated the economy meal for us all (I suspect) wanders around and takes the soup order. Jessica and I, the first into the restaurant, order 'meat soup.'

Other people arrive and order their soups.

The waiter arrives with large amounts of fruit soup. He tries to place it in front of us. No, no we say, meat soup for us. Our companions gladly accept the fruit soup. Where is our soup we ask the Headmaster. "I am waiting for mine too," says the Headmaster. "Meat soup?" we say. "Yes," says the Headmaster.

Mushroom soup arrives. We reject this as well. Meat soup please. All but Jessica and I have soup now. Even the Headmaster who said he was having meat soup. We scream at him and he denies ever saying he would have meat soup (this happens a lot). Jessica is getting agitated. "I don't care what soup I get as long as it is not liver," she said.

Main courses start arriving. Once again we reject them. I decide this might be a mistake. Everyone else starts their main course. We get some Hungarian speakers to get us soup.

Soup arrives! We tuck in. It's liver soup. Jessica rejects it with an angry snarl. I wolf it down. I have learned the first rule of dining in darkest Hungary. I eat hers as well.

Desserts start to arrive. We reject dessert. "Main course" we plead.

Main course arrives. Hooray

The Hungarian Girl Trap

Dessert arrives. Hoorah.

We order cappuccino. Mine is hot, Jessica's is not. She gets very cross indeed. I've now recovered from my strop and collude with the others when she storms into the kitchen, by hiding her cappuccino and pretending the waiter took it away.

The Headmaster goes round again to order the soup for tomorrow. "Does it bloody matter what we order?" I ask.

Later in the evening Steve the new teacher discovered the joys of teaching kids with no grasp of English as he attempted to have a bit of a barn dance. Most amusingly the Headmaster was the most inept of all. I kept finding my partners were the tiny seven year old girls and having to dance on my knees. After all this a beer was needed. The hotel bar closed at nine p.m.

"Is there another bar in the village?" we asked.

"Yes," said the receptionist and gave directions. We set out for it as it drizzled. The rain got harder. It was pelting by the time we got there. It was closed. We trudged home miserable and went to bed at 10.30.

Tuesday 6th October

Welcome to former Communist Hungary! It should be a theme park, or maybe it is a theme park. I discovered my bed was dome shaped in the night. No matter how I lay down on it my backside was in the air and the rest of me was sliding towards the floor. I fell out of bed once, something I have never done before. As I lay uncomfortably this morning I noted the lamp fitting in the centre of the room (a sort of wooden chandelier effect manufactured with no interest in aesthetic design) was identical to the one in our tower block in Budapest.

Breakfast consisted of ersatz orange juice (orange squash with unidentified 'pulp' at the bottom), various pickled vegetables, tepid coffee, cheese and sniffy waiters. The Headmaster had negotiated for the pool to be open when we got back today. The sauna however would cost fifty pence and you must wear a swim hat at all times (available for rent at 18 pence each).

First stop was the highest peak in Hungary. You could tell it was high because, once again the fog enveloped us. Fortunately there was a snack bar so the kids kept the owners in business through the winter by buying everything they had. Next on the Communist tour was a trip to a glass factory. We were thrown out of the showroom immediately by officious officials. I was not perturbed, it was full of some of the most hideous items I have ever had the misfortune of seeing. So we went into the factory instead to watch real people working in a real factory. They were really blowing glass. It wasn't for the tourists at all. The workers looked a bit startled as they sweated away in vests and shorts.

"Perhaps they can blow me some glassware," I said cynically, and a little too loudly.

Next was one of the most chaotic lunches I have ever witnessed. The Headmaster stopped us at a lay-by and went off to compare prices in various hotdog kiosks. He selected the cheapest and ordered nineteen hot dogs and nineteen hamburgers. He then formed two queues for the kids who wanted either delicacy. Of course it took so long to cook them all that the first kids came back for seconds taking the burgers off those who hadn't had any yet. So we just ordered more, scuppering the Headmaster's stinginess. I didn't care because he played an unforgivable trick on Ariel, our Jewish boy.

"Is there ham in the food," he asked shyly.

"Oh there isn't ham," said the Headmaster. "You can eat it." He then turned and winked at us all. "He didn't ask about pork," he grinned. I went and bought the lad some fish.

Next we went up to some fantastic castle ruins on a hill. The Chinese girls mutinied at the sight of the hill but they missed a treat. You could see for miles and it cost nothing (trust the Headmaster). Finally we went to an old Communist Labour camp where innumerable Hungarians had been taken by the old regime and made to break rocks or get shot. Now it was sanitised and our kids couldn't get to grips with it. I watched as a group of boys, two Russian, two Estonian, two Hungarian, one Chinese, an Egyptian and an Israeli, had a jumping competition next to the memorial and in the shadow of the preserved watch tower. They played happily together, as they would anywhere. Considering these kids' nationalities I couldn't decide whether this play was grossly ignorant of their respective past/present or a sign of great hope for the future. In the end I decided I was pleased. They have their whole adult lives to worry about things like this. Let them play free and in ignorance and let old guys like me draw analogies.

Back at the hotel I declined to swim, feeling tired. No maid had been near my room. Supper passed by relatively incident free. We did stock up on alcohol before the bar closed though. I coached Jessica in how to talk English English. She proceeded to sound absolutely ridiculous. Do we really sound like this to Americans? Anyway we all got a bit drunk and conversation flowed. One particularly bizarre conversation involved one female teacher and an American teacher arguing over a comment I had made at the labour camp. I had remarked whilst I was alone watching the boys jumping, that freedom was something that is only appreciated when it is taken away. Now the woman argued with the man over exactly what I meant by this. I wasn't allowed to get a word in edgeways. The conversation had moved away from me completely.

Wednesday 7th October

Last night's alcohol meant I was feeling a little rough. The breakfast ersatz juice was not 'orange' today. It was more yellow and tasted vaguely citrusy but it was no more identifiable than that. I also noticed with horror that the 'coffee' I had been drinking of the last two days was not coffee at all. It was a chicory based brown substitute. I could not believe I did not notice yesterday.

The hotel tried to fiddle the bill but Árpád, our Headmaster, who could haggle for Hungary spotted it and got it changed. The hotel had such a strange attitude. You would think they would be glad of the extra revenue but no we were simply an inconvenience.

I had a slightly queasy, hangovery trip to the historic town of Eger. Eger is one of those truly great towns which, if it were more central in Europe would be way up the must see tourist lists. Why? It's got a great castle, a great cathedral, it nestles on the other side of the Bükk hills from Miskolc, it has the most northerly minaret tower in the world. This is as far as the Turks got, although the Hungarians, under Istvan Dobo made a great effort to stop them taking Eger. It is the centre of a fine red wine region, the famous Bulls' blood wine is made here. And the valley where the best wine cellars is called something like the 'valley of the beautiful women' so you can't go wrong. All this culture was of course lost on our students. We went to a blind exhibition where you were given a white stick and led through a series of blackened rooms designed to be like every day situations (market place, road, bar, forest) with suitable sound affects. You could see nothing at all and were completely at the mercy of the stick you had and what your ears were telling you. It was a strange experience: terrifying, dizzying. I also felt confusion and annoyance and wanted my sight back. Afterwards we went to a typically Communist self-service restaurant and ate bad food like fried cheese and pasta with jam. After an exhausted trip round the castle and nip up the Turkish minaret we went home. Everybody was completely shattered and if democracy was in place there would be no school tomorrow.

Thursday 8th October

Back to the old routine. I noted with interest that I hadn't been paid yet. I should have received my first salary last week. I went to check and was not surprised to find out there was a technical hitch. I eventually received dollars under the table for only one month when I had been promised two.

I went to my first Hungarian class tonight. It was good fun to be on the other side of the classroom. Most of the students speak English so there is a lot of side-chatting. I conclude that the only foreigners in Hungary are either students, refugees from poorer Communist countries or guys like me who met Hungarian girls. There are businessmen here too but they go to expensive corporate courses paid for by their companies.

I went for a drink with the guys from the course afterwards. There was John, a strange Geordie. There's also a couple of Russian speakers (guy with gold teeth, troll-like girl), another hopeless American called Ritchie, a Croatian, an Albanian and a pair of Italian lovebirds. Finally there was Jake, a completely spaced out American pilot who was probably in 'Nam judging by the way he was utterly…lost is the only way I describe it.

"I followed a girl here," he said, "but she went to Japan so I thought I'd stay anyway," was one of his more coherent thoughts. He had been here a year and had no idea how even to pronounce Hungarian. I chatted to him about Berlin as he was based there with the army for a while.

Meanwhile I subsidised the Albanian's orange juice, as he really couldn't afford it

Friday 9th October

Suffering from a cold like virus but went in anyway. Rule number one in Hungary: never tell anyone anything. I had let it slip that I had lived in Germany and so I was asked to take the German class because Réka, the regular teacher was sick. Secondly the Headmaster proved what a bastard he can be. When there was a covering crisis a few weeks ago (because a teacher went to a Moscow conference for ten days) the cover teacher said I would be paid extra for the extra classes (nine). However the Headmaster applied a special equation. Firstly doubling up classes didn't count and that left six classes. Now the Headmaster decided that as this was over a period of two school weeks (Thursday to the following Sunday) therefore it was only three periods for each week, therefore he would only pay for over three periods a week. Rather convenient, I thought. The Headmaster then told me off for ordering science equipment from England. I pointed out that Gerry ordered it for me and it was nothing to do with me.

"I'm sure we could have got that cheaper in Hungary," he said

"I don't see any around, do you?" I said. "If it can be ordered why hasn't it been? I can't order it. You give me no budget and I can't speak Hungarian."

I was furious.

Sunday 11th October

Miskolc

A gloriously cultural day. Andrea drove me along what she called the wine trail road, which isn't really but it heads to Tokaj. It's already one of my favourite roads in the world for a variety of reasons. Number one it seems to be dead straight and single carriageway, which gives me an opportunity to observe mad Hungarian overtaking at first hand. Szerencs is the first town on the road, it seems unique for Hungarian towns because it seems to have some kind of civic pride, with coordinated flower beds and hanging baskets full of flowers on every lamp post. Once through Szerencs the Tokaj wine region starts to be more obvious. Lines and lines of vines on the hills. Every so often beautfiul wine houses tempt you from the road. For those who don't know Tokaj is probably Hungary's nearest thing to a French 'Appelation

Controllée'. And Tokaj wine is famous around the world. Why haven't you heard of it? The British aren't great dessert wine drinkers, but I guarantee that if you go to your local big supermarket there'll be a bottle of 'aszú' there priced rather expensively. We were there in harvest season, not that I could see them picking off the grapes that had the noble rot, the 'botryis' which is used to make the wine. Tokaj itself is a startling town. It stands below a hill rather appropriately called the Great Hill at a point where the Bodrog and Tisza rivers meet and it seemed such a peaceful cultured place. So pretty. Why doesn't everyone live near wine regions? Andrea is lucky enough to live near two as Eger is the same distance away in the other direction.

Next is Sárospatak, the so called Athens of Northern hungary but I am not sure why. Very nice castle, it's on the 500ft note. We didn't stay long, we had dawdled in Tokaj and we were running late for our lunch appointment in Sátoraljaújhely. Now first of all I apologise for the name of the town, totally unpronounceable I know. It's the last town in modern Hungary. Slovakian hills were easily seen over the border and automatically gave the town an exciting feel. I liked it immediately, as it had the bustle of any border town, albeit a recent one. We were there to visit Andrea's Godmother and family. Both her and her husband Béla were local judges and were very hospitable. Béla in particular seemed particularly pleased to see me, as he lived with his mother-in-law as well and lacked male company. So the brandy, the palinka came out immediately. His English was pretty good and we passed the time of day. The big surprise was that Andrea's father was also there. The big mistake the women made was to send the men off to get some vegetables. Off we went and please bear in mind I was little tiddly before we started off, so maybe I should have pointed out to them that it was clear to me that we had passed at least two greengorcers. Of course Béla led us to his favourite bar instead. A double "vilmos kőrte" (pear schnapps) was put in front of me as well as a pint of beer and we sat down and talked about the local area.

"Ray, this is a very important place Tokaj," said Béla. "Perhaps the wine here is the best in the world?

"Easily," said Andrea's father.

"Did you know that when the Pope takes mass in the Vatican," Béla continued, 'he uses Tokaj wine?"

I didn't.

"Did you know that the chairman of Ferrero, you know Ferrero Rocher..."

"Ambassador you spoil us," slurred Andrea's father.

"He," continued Béla, "flies his helicopter in every year to get his supply of the aszú."

It was clear I had been missing out on something my whole life, but I didn't ask why we weren't drinking it now if it was so good.

Another round was ordered for and I began to understand why Hungarian men behave the way they do in pubs. They always seem over friendly to the poker-faced barmaids. Our one, a perfectly pleasant young lady, was starting to resemble a supermodel. Making a flirty comment was beyond my Hungarian though, so I left them to Andrea's father. I also realised why all Hungarian barmaids have poker faces too. Imagine being slirred at all the time! We talked about the essentials for a good wife (breasts were mentioned), and Manchester United's chances in the Champion's league. I was falling off my chair and I decided enough was enough, but was it rude to refuse drink in Hungary and what about the vegetables? Anyway we got up to pay but surprise surprise Andrea's father ordered *another* double Vilmos for the road. Although it is polite to chink glasses, say 'Egészségedre!' and look your fellow drinker in the eye by now I couldn't hold my hand up and I could see three different versions of Andrea's father.

We staggered home, me wondering what bizarre twist of fate had led me to be walking arm-in-arm through an obscure East European border town with the local judge and a world reknowned architect three sheets to the wind. Béla, showing remarkable fortitude, was still managing to say 'hello' to almost everyone in the town, and managing to get his form of address right too, *szia*, or *csókalom*, or *jó napot kívánok*, depending on their age and his relationship with them. Andrea's father, as is his way, was also greeting everyone warmly, though he knew nobody. The only sign that he was drunk was a slight reddening of the nose and a more confused look in his pale blue eyes. At one point Béla pulled me into a plain looking building, a bit like a warehouse. It turned out to be a Tokaj wine distributor. Béla took me to the end with the good years, some were over two hundred pounds a bottle. He must like me too because he bought me a slightly cheaper bottle, which I immediately decided needed to be drunk at a later date.

Miraculoulsy Béla remembered to get the vegetables though I have no idea if they were the ones we were supposed to have bought. More surprising to me was that none of the women complained, well Andrea did, she seemed to think I should have stopped them! Lunch was excellent and unworthy of my attempts to eat it. I slumped in front of the television in the afternoon and Eurosport rather cruelly decided to put the world ballroom dancing championships on. To say that Béla, Andrea's father and I paid rapt attention would be an understatement.

The hangover came on the way home and Andrea had no sympathy at all.

Monday 12th October

Final week to half term and Jessica is up in arms over her new books; of course they are useless. They are books designed to be used by parents at home to complement school education. As about £100 has been spent on them Jessica is very annoyed. She complained to the Headmaster that all she wanted was a maths book for primary schools with lots of examples. The Headmaster claimed that they do not use maths books in England. At this point I had to butt in and contradict. I told Jessica to go to Foyles in London when she is there at half term and take photographs of the books there. Here the Headmaster changed his tack and argued that this might be the case but they are much more expensive than if you go direct from publishers the school gets a discount from.

"Hang on," I said, "a minute ago these books didn't exist!"

"But the books from this publisher are useless," pleaded Jessica, "so you are wasting money."

"I was in a primary school in England," said the Headmaster knowledgeably, "and they did not have maths books. They used their own resources. They never used maths books."

"Yes but they took those resources from lots of books to make a perfect set," said Jessica.

I went off to class at this point because I saw no point in arguing with a man who is the living embodiment of the saying "Penny wise, pound foolish." The thousand sticks of chalk bought cheaply at the start of the year are almost exhausted. In the class I went to I handed out books, one between three.

"Why haven't we got one each?" said the class.

"Yes I know the school promises school books but I only have four. Tell your parents," I said. I suppose I should have felt guilty.

I also learned that Bill, the American history teacher and Dean of students is leaving ASAP (he has another job) and Larry, the other American is in the process of getting out, or so he says, I feel he is a habitual resigner. This means that as Jessica and I will also depart in June that all the native speakers (staff and students) will have left.

The cover timetable was complete, then the Headmaster noted that the dance teacher could stay a bit longer so, without telling anyone he changed the cover timetable, removing himself from a maths cover (he is a Doctor of mathematics) and putting the dance teacher in for extra English. Naima, the cover teacher was very upset, and, as usual, I made a remark:

"If it's your job to do the cover then you should be the only one allowed to change the timetable. If he wants to do it, tell him to do it all," I said bolshily.

Where has this attitude come from?

Later I walked home with Jessica and we agreed that all the Headmaster had to do was give us teachers a small budget to buy what we need to teach. Instead he controls the purse strings and, in his pursuit of the bargain, we wait and wait to get useless equipment.

I tried the Tokaj wine! It is very sweet and an acquired taste.

Tuesday 13th October

The Headmaster asked me for my food poisoning medical report from the hospital today.

"Don't you believe I was there?" I joked.

"No," he said, "but you had blood tests and for your work permit (yes folks I'm still illegal) you need blood tests. To save money I thought we could use these results. It's very expensive and not covered by your insurance."

"But these results will show I am sick as a dog," I protested.

"You didn't have any x-rays did you?" asked the Headmaster.

"No," I said, "I was in for food poisoning."

"Pity," said the Headmaster.

Jessica and I decided we were going to see the Governors in person after half term. We want to look them in the eye so we can see with what we are dealing with. Jessica is going to see Gerry, the British Governor when she is in England.

"He is going to hear about it," said Jessica.

"Remind him he promised I would be paid from August the fifteenth and I wasn't," I said.

Hungarian language class. Jake, the Vietnam vet was spotted before class disappearing away saying, "I can't face it today man!" Obviously the class reminded him too much of the hellish skirmish in Ciao Leung in '72 and he was having flashbacks.

Wednesday 14th October

Larry agreed to come on the visit to the Governors.

"It won't make any difference," he said gloomily.

This evening was a parent's meeting. I was expecting that I would actually meet parents but no. The Headmaster took all the parents into the big classroom and spoke to them for forty-five minutes. This would be fine but he is not a forceful personality and his speech was somewhat rambling and pointless. At one point he said in English:

"Some of you parents don't speak English, so if you need this speech translated put your hand up." Nobody put their hand up.

There followed another staff introduction, and a ski trip announcement. Then the dance teacher got up unannounced and explained the story of his life. Finally the parents were told they could meet the teachers but he had gone on so long that only two bothered to come and see me. Considering I teach all forty-five children I was not best pleased.

Thursday 15th October

Tibor, the one armed physicist insisted that ten computers would arrive today. They didn't. I was in a gloriously cynical mood. When one part time teacher arrived today and asked how I was, I responded with "mutinous."

Actually I was in a thoroughly good mood. I felt I was used to being in Hungary. I also sent my CV off to the big spending, big wages American school today just for the need to do something proactive with my situation.

In Hungarian language class the ugly Russian girl was acting very strangely. Apart from speaking in English, not Hungarian when prompted she kept turning round to look at me this evening and pointing at my leg. The whole class was quite amused by this. Finally she asked if she could move to sit next to a Bulgarian woman. The teacher agreed and everyone gave me an amused look (remember the class is full of men who are here because they met Hungarian women and are mostly bumming around drinking beer).

Later in the pub she walked in whilst we were having a beer and immediately left again.

"What were you doing mate?" asked John the witty Geordie.

"I think my aura was touching her, because I certainly wasn't," I replied.

Friday 16th October

The ten computers arrived today. I was almost disappointed. I haven't seen them yet and I fear the worst for when I asked Tibor what they were like he replied, "they're fine for school use."

Translated into English that means they are very old indeed. I fear I will see the name ZX Spectrum on the side of the things. They are alleged to have Windows 95 but I am not sure. I am pretty cynical about the e-mail as well as I have not noticed many workmen putting a phone line into the art room downstairs.

The Headmaster ignored it all. He was slightly distracted because he was already thirty minutes late for a maths class he was covering (they are forty minutes long) because he had decided to do his photocopying just before the lesson. The photocopier (a cheap one) knew this and fouled up enormously. The Headmaster ignored his class and stuck his head in the machine for thirty minutes. I have remembered this for future reference because we must try to emulate our superior's superior teaching techniques.

Friday October 23rd

On this day in 1956, millions of Hungarians rose up against the Soviet influenced government. The revolution began with student demonstrations in Budapest and grew to include much wider parts of the population. They achieved initial success in driving out the surprised Soviet occupying troops, and for a few days it looked as though they had succeeded in liberating themselves. Hungarian flags flew over Budapest with the hateful Communist emblem cut out of the middle.[15]

---

[15] Romanians did the same in their 1991 revolution

Then, on November 4th, the Soviet army reentered Hungary and crushed the revolution. In the aftermath, the Soviets murdered over a thousand people and dumped their bodies in unmarked graves. Communist rule in Hungary continued for thirty-three more years. Many Hungarians emigrated in the immediate aftermath.

The revolution is still remembered. I watched on TV as children walked the streets carrying paper flags with holes in the middle. Though the ceremonies were solemn and heartfelt, I could tell that already the Hungarians, years after the final and peaceful overthrow of Communism, were beginning to treat it less as a day of sorrow and more as just another national holiday. This is good: a relaxed attitude toward history is a mark of felt freedom.

Sunday 25th October

Half term was relaxing and pleasant. I kept myself preparing for the visit of my mother. It was quite cool because we could play tourists and I could impress her by ordering coffee in Hungarian, and asking for the bill.

It was nice to see Budapest through her novice eyes too. She had never been to Eastern Europe before and believed it was a uniform shade of Battleship grey, populated by miserable turnip eating peasants. It was good to see the amazement and delight in her eyes as she discovered a beautiful, cosmopolitan city.

Of course the Hungarian side of the family pulled out the stops too and Andrea's mum "just happened" to be in Budapest when mother was here. She also "just happened" to have flowers as well. Andrea's father, that great, great bear of a man, was also around on Sunday and had been brushing up his English in his usual, slightly warped way.

"Here is the woman who broke up the family," he said, as he introduced his current fiancée.

We had a good time, ate out every night and I enjoyed the English supplies mother brought over from the U.K. Chocolate cake and Branston Pickle are being lovingly consumed in a part over Budapest's tenth District that will be forever England.

Today Andrea's father took us all to the opera (well ballet actually). The Budapest opera house is arguably the most beautiful in the world and it has the second best acoustics in Europe after the Scala in Milan. It really is stunning. Also opera is a bit more entertainment for the masses so the best seats (a box) will cost you about £8. We were in the stalls; barely ten rows back and our seats here cost £4. I think the best seats in Covent Garden would set you back £160 and it's better here believe me.

We saw "Giselle" and to say it was one of the most startling performances I have ever seen understates it. I have not been so stunned by anything in a long time. The set design, the orchestra, the dancing were all quite, quite sublime. The dancers took thirteen curtain calls and I joined Andrea's father applauding loudly in the aisle. Magnificent.

The Hungarian Girl Trap

Monday 26th October

I returned to the shocking site of the ten computers actually being installed. Tibor, the one armed physicist, was supervising the installation by a longhaired guy who, of course, is the friend of a brother of a maths teacher. I even heard rumours of a network and I was furious because I might have had to eat my words. Was the school actually doing something right? How disappointing!

However…I should point out that the things don't have speakers, CD ROM drive or any of the accoutrements that would mean we could invest in sexy multimedia packages. None of my software will run on it so I will continue to use my laptop. Therefore these computers have been bought for word processing and spread sheeting. This means they will be used six periods out of 35 a week. I personally think they are a false investment for so few periods considering we have no science equipment for 23 periods a week. But computers look impressive when the parents come around I suppose.

Also, I hate to be the boy in the Emperor's new clothes tale but am I the only one who has noticed that the computers are in the art room? Am I the only one who has noticed that there are six art periods a week and six I.T classes a week? Guess what, they are timetabled for exactly the same time in exactly the same room! That should be interesting. What will happen is that two classes will be in the room at the same time and like it?

Tuesday 27th October

Gerry, the English governor is back in town and he's brought some cronies from the state school he used to work at in England. I'm being harsh; the woman is very positive and helpful to the ESL teachers and genuinely loves teaching here.

Gerry has spent most of his time walking into classrooms unannounced and observing lessons. He loved my prep school work, entitled "Science in English to non-English speakers" – have you ever seen anyone mime a galaxy before? He was more concerned with the fifth form and felt I was flying above their heads. I showed him their test scores and contradicted him. Just because he doesn't understand DNA structure doesn't mean the class doesn't.

Lunch was pasta with icing sugar and raisins – what a bizarre idea!

The farce that is Hungarian customs meant that today, two weeks after it arrived in Hungary, the filter papers and funnels ordered from England are in the school. The Headmaster had to make four trips to the customs office with invoices; bank statements and another form promising that the school will include these filter papers on all future inventories. The Headmaster kept giving me looks. I knew what he was going to say – "I could have got this much cheaper in Hungary."

He did as well. "Well why didn't you then?" I retorted. Either he buys the stuff I need or I get it myself, or we do nothing. It is his choice.

Gerry saw me at lunchtime to check I was happy. I was my usual diplomatic self. Gerry asked:

"Do you regret coming to Hungary?"

"Nah," I said. "You've got to do crazy things sometimes or life gets a little routine."

Experiment on 'touch' in the afternoon. Amazing what you can do with 18 pencils and some sticky tape.

It has been a day of Dexter *faux pas* too. I was introduced to a prospective pupil.

"This is (foreign name) and Mrs. Foreign name," said Gerry.

I looked at the child, a fat teenage girl with greasy hair. Charming, I thought.

"He will probably go into the prep class," continued Gerry.

"No SHE will," I said correcting Gerry. I mean this was a fat girl right?

Wrong. HE was a very fat boy with a heavy metal fixation. I made my excuses and left quickly.

Then, in Hungarian language class in the evening I spent an entire dialogue trying to buy a skirt instead of a pair of socks (well 'szoknya' and 'zokni' sound pretty similar believe me!)

Wednesday 28th October

The Headmaster has finally decided that Jessica and I not having work permits is a very bad thing.

"It could get us all into trouble," he said. "If the police come for you you must say you have just arrived in the country."

He had organised for the necessary medical tests (blood, electro cardio somethings, x-rays etc) to be done on Friday. Then we will have to go through the ridiculous bureaucracy of the Hungarian government. Larry was full of horror stories about his problems getting his work permit. The details of your accommodation, proof that your landlord IS the owner of the flat you live in, the monthly returns to the police where upon waiting for three hours he is told to come back at the same time next month. Jessica and I cannot wait. We have decided we will not go to the police alone and want a native speaker with us.

Then the Headmaster threw his next bombshell. He has decided that the inevitable absences from school that we will have because we have to do the paper work is 'our' problem. OK I am putting words into his mouth but the staff are allowed five days per year paid 'sick' leave. So if I am sick I will still get paid provided I am not sick more than five days. If I am sick more than five days I still get paid (in theory) if I can provide a note from the hospital. Anyway the Headmaster has decided that these days we spend at the police station will be counted as part of these five 'sick' days. Jessica, Larry and I are up in arms about this because we are on school business, we don't want to be there and if the damn school had got their act together in the summer then this would not be an issue at all. I angrily retorted in a staff meeting that "if this takes five days and then I am ill next year, then I won't get paid. Now if the reason I am going to the police is in order to legally work at the school then I should not be penalised."

The Headmaster still did not see this, "we can't afford unlimited sick days," he responded.

We shall see what happens.

Today was significant because I finally got hold of the keys to the laboratory. Tibor, the one armed physicist, unlocked the door and saw an Aladdin's cave of science equipment, covered in dust and arranged in a highly random order. It was a mess. Tibor disappeared into the cupboards to look at the physics equipment. Clouds of dust appeared at the door.

"Well?" I said when he reappeared.

"It is all in need of repair," he said with a shrug, "but it is life, no?"

The chemical equipment was limited but something can be done. I am looking forward to getting things sorted.

Thursday 29th October

I wandered around in a state of disbelief today. I took a class into the lab. I will repeat this sentence, just in case you didn't get it – I took a class into the lab. O.K we did nothing much but talk about lab rules but still – I took a class into the lab!!!!

At the language school things are getting funnier. Jake, the life weary Vietnam vet last seen going AWOL before class, was back! He was told to sit next to Grigori, an elderly Russian builder with a set of metal teeth that James Bond's adversary Jaws would be very proud of. Grigori likes Jake but Jake isn't so sure of Grigori. It didn't help that Grigori started a dialogue with Jake with the words "Excuse me Madam!" to the hysterics of the more linguistic and giggly members of the class. I know I can talk after asking for a skirt on Tuesday but that is not the point. It's funny when Grigori does it.

After class a drinking cell has formed with the four guys who are dating Hungarian women: Nenet from Croatia, John from Newcastle, Jake from spaced out world (and the USA), and me from the South. We frequent the bar next to the school and are very loud. John ordered an üveg (bottle) of wine when he wanted a pohàr (glass). As it only cost him £1.50 he didn't mind. Jake told the funniest ever story told by a guy dating a Hungarian girl to three other guys dating Hungarian girls.

"When I met my girlfriend in the States I went up to her and said 'Hi Honey'. Do you know what she said to me?"

We shook our heads grinning.

"I hope you like to travel!"

We fell about with laughter.

So us well-travelled guys all in Hungary pass the time of night until we look at our watches at 8 p.m., panic because we will be late and rush off to our respective beloveds! It is a hard life.

10 p.m. I was rung up by a strange American woman. I hate this because Andrea does not like me being rung up by any women. Fortunately this woman had good reasons.

"Hi I'm Brittany," she said. "I have just accepted a job at the Churchill International School..."

She may have said more at this point but I do not know because I had fallen off the bed in hysterical laughter. When I recovered five minutes later I said:

"Congratulations."

It turned out that she wanted to join Jessica and I at the hospital tomorrow to get our medical stuff done for work permits. I told her I would identify her if she just wandered around looking lost for long enough.

Friday 30th October

Of course the medical tests were quite bizarre. Brittany turned out to be a pleasant enough girl, stuck in the Czech Republic teaching English in a Czech School. Do not be fooled by the sophistication of Prague, the rest of the country is dire compared to the heaven that is Hungary. She is being paid $100 a month and lives in a small town where no one speaks English and everyone knows she's American. There is no supermarket so she has to shop in the butchers, the bakers, the grocery store, etc. In every store they try to rip her off because they think she is rich. Plus she hates the Czech pollution. I had sympathy, the Czech Republic, like the former East Germany burns tonnes of lignite, or Brown Coal as it is known. It is foul and makes the air grey. Hungary seemed to use other methods of heating their houses. So Brittany was quite happy to be here.

It was also funny to notice that the Headmaster had arranged for the medical tests to be done at the children's hospital. He knows the director and can get them done for free. Unfortunately it took quite a lot of explaining to get this point across. And you know how good my Hungarian is. Soon it was sorted out. However after a few giggles: ludicrously oversized receptacles for urine samples ("I think seeing each other's urine is a bit intimate for our first meeting," I joked to Brittany as we walked back to the lab with our flasks in our hands. Fortunately she laughed) and my electrocardiogram producing alarming flickers until they realised an electrode had fallen off.

I am off to go and see Deàk Bill play at the weekend. Bill is a twenty stone hard drinking, bearded blues man who happens to only have one leg. A stomach operation that went wrong put paid to his left leg. Only in Hungary! I hope to get legless too – or is that in poor taste!

November

Sunday 1st November

Forgive me for going on a bit now if you have no interest in the Blues, but I must write about Deák Bill.

Blues singers are very important to me, but being a bit of an anorak I like to try and categorise and I do ask myself the question, who is the greatest white blues singer? Answer: Janis Joplin, no question, but she's dead, so who is left?

Of course on Saturday I found the answer to this question. Deák Bill is the greatest living blues singer.

The man is a Hungarian legend. He looks like a huge, violent, twenty-stone professional wrestler, with shaggy grey hair and shaggy beard. He has one leg and stands on stage supported by a black crutch. He wears a huge tent of a Jim Beam whisky T-shirt and just belts out the blues.

Chuck Berry (who knows a little bit about the blues) saw him eight years ago when he was in Budapest and said that Deák Bill was the nearest he'd heard a white man get to sounding like a black man. That is some compliment. If Deák Bill had been born in Louisiana not a suburb of Budapest, the one legged genius would be as famous as Jerry Lee Lewis.

We arrived at the club, a garage like back room in the outskirts of Budapest. It's the kind of club where the band changes in the toilets and sits by the stage before they go on. This meant that Andrea had the pleasure of sharing a bench with Deák Bill's buttocks (or perhaps buttock – I don't know where they cut the leg off). Then, out of the blue, Judit and Zsolt joined us. Judit had been in Andrea's primary school with her. They did not even know they were both in Budapest. Zsolt was a guitar player and lived next to Deák Bill in some tower block somewherein Kőbánya suburb. He shook hands with Bill and chatted to his guitarist. I avoided being introduced to Bill, too scared. Then I casually mentioned that I too played the guitar and Zsolt was very pleased and I had to decline the offer of a jam with him and Deák Bill sometime. I pointed out that I was really not that good a player and I was not going to embarrass everyone. I am the Mick Jagger of bass players. I just impersonate, mimic.

Anyway it was time for Bill to play so he hopped on stage and the audience of 200 went wild. His band (old fogey rhythm section, young bucks on guitar and harmonica – the way it should be) were excellent but Deák Bill's voice was astonishing. He roared and he whimpered. His range was incredible. One minute it was like Hendrix without the velvety edge that Hendrix had, the next minute he was crooning like a Bing Crosby, then he was roaring like Joe Cocker at his very best. His songs were in Hungarian and sad (apparently). The audience worshipped him, Bill pumped his arms up and down (you can't really dance on one leg) and we pumped them too. He played for three hours and when he finished I turned to Zsolt and said simply:

"Chuck Berry was right."

Legendary and local. He plays twice a week to pay the rent, usually at the Old Man's Music Pub near Blaha Lujza tér metro station[16]. He is magnificent. There is a Faustian aspect to the Blues. The story that the blues is the devil's music is mythical now, but the great Robert Johnson made no bones about his Faustian pact with the devil. He sung many times about meeting the devil at the crossroads and selling his soul and I don't think Johnson read much German literature in Mississippi. He was sure his pact gave him his awesome ability to play the guitar and that ghostly voice. Johnson was dead within two years. Did Deák Bill make a pact too? Did the devil return and just take his leg? Is this too morbid? So what, Deák Bill is the best.

Tuesday 3rd November

After my Hungarian language class this evening the gentlemen repaired to the pub. I like it in there enormously now, probably because the barman has memorised our order and brings it to the table. It feels like we belong. Plus we probably keep him in business. Anyway we were telling a few rather off-colour urban sex myth catastrophe anecdotes (all are far too rude to even begin to tell) when we noticed that there was a moustachioed bloke at the bar who was crying with laughter as well.

"You must be English mate," yelled John to the guy. "Come and join us."

He was English and I had him down initially as a West Midlander because he introduced himself thus, "Err Trevor's the name," which, taking the moustache in to consideration guaranteed he was a Birmingham man. Unfortunately Trevor blew away my logic by coming from Dartford in Kent. Still you can't win them all. He too was married to a Hungarian woman (there must be something in the air) and is studying in the more advanced Hungarian class. He told us all too familiar problems about bureaucracy and red tape. He is a stone mason and cannot get a work permit because there are a thousand million stone masons here. Now English, science, maths, and geography teachers are harder to come by so I have no problem…except of course I haven't got one either. Anyway he is a nice man and a good addition to the gang of husbands. He also alleged to have once been in the French foreign legion.

Thursday 5th November

Language class again. Stefano, the Italian, is having problems with Tamara, the other Italian student who he lives with. They came to the course together usually, but not tonight. They are finding that student tensions in their flat are driving them mad.

"She is a witch pig," bellowed Stefano before class, and before Tamara arrived.

---

[16] 13 Akácfa st, Pest

Tamara duly turned up, beatific smile on her face and made it absolutely clear what she was doing as she came and sat next to me. She usually sat next to Stefano.

Teacher arrived and asks about homework. All of us have done it except Stefano.

"Was there a problem?" asked the teacher.

"Yes," said Stefano bitterly. "I was trying to do it this afternoon and I asked…her... Tamara to help me but the telephone rang… and it always for her…and she always spends twenty minutes talking…nyaaa nyaa nyaaa (Italian term for gossip). So I try to interrupt her conversation and ask for the homework but she won't give it to me. So it is her fault." He folded his arms defiantly.

The rest of the class snigger. Tamara just smiled sweetly.

I must say that Tamara was quite delightful company and was not a 'witchpig' at all. She laughed at all of my jokes and she was such pleasant company that in fact if Andrea had asked who I'd sat next to I would have had to have lied and told her I actually sat next to Grigori, the gold toothed Russian – if you see what I mean.

On the way to the pub John casually asked Stefano, "so you and Tamara aren't getting on too well then."

"Pah," snarled Stefano and lengthened his stride cursing Italian females all the way.

"It's because Juventus lost really," muttered Nenet, the Croatian. "He just has to blame someone else."

Friday 6th November

It has been a good week actually. I have settled into this life a little. It is amazing what one gets used to very quickly. Even the school has been less crazy than normal…oh no, hang on…

The I.T/ Art room fiasco came to a head today, as it was the first time the timetable actively clashed. Nobody had noticed but I noticed Tibor coming out of the class shaking his head hopelessly.

"Problems?" I said, knowing what they were. "I just thought," I lied, "that art and I.T are in the same room at the same time. How can you cope?"

"It's impossible," he shrugged.

I went to see the art teacher, who was being stereotypically highly strung. "HELP! HELP!" she yelled.

"Have you told the Headmaster how impossible it is?" I said.

"Yes, he said there was nothing he could do."

"So even though there is an empty room upstairs, he still put the computers downstairs?" I said cynically.

What they'll do is simply get on with it and more education will be compromised.

Larry, the New Yorker resigned today. Keep a count, this is going to happen a lot. He has had enough and will quit by Christmas. We only have seven full time staff for heaven's sake. Surely something screams out to people here? Where are they going to find an English/ P.E teacher from before Christmas?

The gas does not work in the laboratory. Not that we have Bunsen burners but the illusion that I could have them if I wanted them has gone.

On the positive side I have become impressed with the progress of the non-English speaking kids. I can have conversations with many of them now, with only a little bit of miming. Of course the problem will be that we will admit more non-English speakers and we will be back to square one.

This leads to another problem, namely there are some kids in the prep classes who make great progress and get promoted into the normal school. Unfortunately the Headmaster made no provision for this in the timetable. We have no year seven, no year ten and classrooms designed for twelve. Now and eighteen year old and a fourteen-year-old are ready to be moved and neither really have a place. The Year ten/eleven class are gearing up for GCSE and these kids have studied courses for fifteen months already so they can't put them in there. And year nine is full already. The only option is to make a new year ten but this would mean rejigging the entire timetable and they couldn't staff it properly. So these kids get a compromised education too.

I am happy here under crazy circumstances. I have conquered the school in a way. The kids are used to me. This pleases me, as you never know if skills and humour translates to other schools/countries. I am happy with the progress of all the classes and wish the very bright Russian Chinese kids I have could have the benefit of laboratory time and decent facilities. We don't even have curtains for shutting out the sun when a video is playing. To be honest I would love to organise a *coup d'etat* and become Headmaster myself. I know it sounds crazy but this little school has a lot of potential and, if you could just invest in it instead of penny pinching, if the teachers could simply be allowed to teach, then we could be in business. No chance of that.

Sunday 8th November

The weekend was curious because we went back to Miskolc to do our laundry. My eyes were opened to the reality of non-intercity rail services in Hungary as we were forced to sit in the most disgusting, hazardous looking carriage I have seen since I back-packed into Romania in 1991. Then my travelling companion wrote that the curtains on the Romanian train were "unfit to wipe one's bottom on, but judging by the state of them, somebody already has." That train also had the exit doors that swung open as you went round a corner, oh and it was the place where I saw Romanian border guards practically bayoneted our seats as we left Romania to ensure no one was trying to escape.

No this train wasn't quite as bad but it was fairly appalling, but it only cost £2 to go the whole way across the country so I shouldn't moan.

When we got to Miskolc I had to go through the routine of asking permission from various family members as to whether I could marry Andrea. In the back of my mind I was remembering that scene from "Summer Holiday" where Cliff Richard is in an Eastern European peasant village and wants some bread. He grabs a local peasant girl, consults his dictionary and asks her to marry him by mistake (Nebgyester I believe was the word he used). The whole village subsequently charges out to offer congratulations and a three-day party ensues. When Cliff tries to escape the men folk bring out their guns. Fortunately the Hungarians were much more relaxed and just grinned a lot as I dished out flowers to all and sundry as a token of friendship. Andrea's brother was the funniest,

"What do you wanna marry her for?" he yelled.

The other thing about the marriage is that for years I have wittily remarked that all a chap has to do is turn up in his best suit with the ring and cough up for a honeymoon in Bognor Regis. We guys get the easy option as the bride's family pays for it all. Not in Hungary. I will give you no prizes for guessing who pays for the wedding in Hungary, yep the groom.

"Right then," I said in my most miserly voice to Andrea, "so we'll have five guests and share a tin of pilchards."

Andrea gave me the kind of acid look I want to avoid receiving in our married life. It could have been worse; she didn't know what pilchards were.

The reception is to be held in Andrea's castle. Diósgyőr castle stands about a kilometre from where Andrea lives and by a quirk of fate she was born there, therefore she wants to married there too. I think it is a lovely idea and we have a contact (the magic words in this country). Fortunately, Andrea has done the sums and we can cater for eighty people, buy a dress, and hire everything etc. for about £1000, which is the kind of bargain that will probably send every bachelor in England, heading this way.

Although I am quite used to Hungarian life now, the constant soup eating, the social conventions of saying hello to anyone vaguely alive, the greeting of "Csókalom"[17] to every old lady you are introduced to, I cannot get used to the way Hungarians live on top of each other. Flats are very small; we sleep on a sofa bed. When we stay in Miskolc Andrea and I have to sleep in the same bed as Andrea's sister, Gabi. Anyway this bed sharing, as you can imagine, I find very strange. To Hungarians it is as normal as having breakfast. Firstly Gabi and Andrea could be twins, they share each other's clothes, they have the same hair colour, figure etc. I live in constant fear of making romantic overtures to what I think is Andrea's back and then find that on her turning round it is not Andrea at all but Gabi. So I have a policy of no tactility at all unless a) I have my glasses on, or b) I have my glasses on. A mistake could be the height of embarrassment to this Englishman.

---

[17] "I kiss your hand"

So anyway I have to sleep with both the sisters but of course I insist on sleeping on the very edge of the bed, practically falling out, Andrea next to me. I then feign sleep until both of them have got up (it's simpler believe me) no matter how long this takes. The only problem, apart from falling out of the bed a lot is that Berta the dog, for some bizarre reason, likes to sleep next to me too. So I wake up at 4 a.m. and the bloody dog is next to me on the duvet, trapping me completely. I am cocooned in. If I move the dog, she will whimper, waking up everybody else. I dread sleeping there now and will probably migrate to sleeping in the bath in the near future.

Monday 9th November

So what have we got this week then? We have the mysterious case of the boy who broke his arm at school on Friday. Did the Headmaster order a taxi? He did not; he sent the boy home on the bus to save money. He then asked us today why we did not send the boy to the hospital in a taxi. When someone tells him off he seems to get complete amnesia. Tight fisted fool.

Tuesday 10th November

Jackie, the Welsh woman who advises most of Eastern Europe's government how to operate properly, and who teaches Leadership skills here, sent the senior class round with a questionnaire to get all the teacher's views on the school. I went on a bit; as did the other teachers then we panicked as we wondered how confidential they were. Jackie is a shrewd woman; she also lives next door to our Headmaster. I wonder what she is up to.

Hungarian class post class drinks were very funny tonight. Jake, the Vietnam vet from Florida had not shown up for two weeks. We guessed he was out of it again. At 7 p.m. he turns up at the pub grinning, steaming drunk and knowing far more Hungarian swearwords than he knew last time I saw him.

"I just got back from Stuttgart," he beamed, "and I missed you guys so I thought I'd come along."

"What about class?" we said.

"Yeah, I got lots of that!" he said.

"No, Hungarian class."

"Oh, this is more important," said Jake.

"Now Jake," I said, "be honest you did not come here straight from Stuttgart did you."

Jake adopted the guilty look of a naughty schoolboy.

"No," he said.

"Your train came in a long time ago didn't it?"

A nod.

"You've been to other bars haven't you?"

"No!" he wailed.

"Jake, you have beer in your hair. Now how many bars have you been to before here?"

Jake sheepishly held up four fingers. He was very drunk. We found out what he was doing in Stuttgart and why he was so pleased with himself. He had partaken of a large amount of marijuana and slept with his sister-in-law on far more occasions than is probably healthy.

"Was this wise?" asked Nenet.

"Shit no," said Jake. "I'm dead when my wife gets back from Japan and I haven't put the wallpaper up yet. She goes away for six weeks. I have one job to do and I haven't done it."

"Well whatever you do," said John, "don't do it tonight when you get in or it might be a little lop-sided."

Jake fell off his stool laughing. Some kids never grow up. Whatever happened in 'Nam I never want to find out.

Wednesday 11th November

I went to see Petra, my private student at the American School. I like helping her with her biology and maths, but she is typically seventeen in her attitude to life, which is quite refreshing. She spends most of the time laughing at my grey hair and trying to convince me to work at her school. Then she drifts off for a while and wants to practise her English accent. I don't care, she now pays £15 an hour.

Thursday 12th November

The Hungarian class gentlemen decided on something gloriously suicidal today. We went for two beers BEFORE class. So Jake, Nenet, John, Stefano and I giggled away in the pub, cribbing each other's homework. The problem was later in class when nature inevitably called. John lasted twenty minutes before he had to nip out to the bathroom (serious giggle suppression), next went Stefano (puce in the face) twenty minutes later and then off went Nenet. I was giggling so much that I had to interrupt the teacher to ask a particularly pertinent question about Hungarian post-positions in order to regain control. I went next and Jake managed to hold on for a whole hour before he too had to rush out of the room. Jake is a hard man.

In the pub again after class Stefano revealed that he had been desperate to go and was about to stand up when John stood up instead. He then decided he could not go at the same time for Italian homophobic reasons, so he held on for what he considered to be a reasonable time. Then we talked about war for a while.

The Hungarian Girl Trap

Friday 13th November

It is Friday the thirteenth so I was not expecting miracles. Firstly Andrea and I had a very polite conversation on the Metro concerning her belief that I was in the wrong about the school and actually they had been extremely helpful and kind to do all the work to get me the laboratory. I disagreed strongly with this comment and was in a black mood for the rest of the day. My thoughts are that my fiancée would rather I stayed in Hungary slowly dying at this school than go back to England and do a job properly. The fact that I get paid no money here, have no pension, work permit (I am working illegally still and could be thrown out at any minute). Why can they not even organise a work permit? Andrea and the Headmaster's advice if the police catch up with me is to lie. She also explained (I can't believe I didn't see it) that the reason the Headmaster does not give me the money to spend is because I haven't got a clue about money and I would waste it all. This assumption is based on the fact that I have no money in my English account. But of course this is because the school did not do what they said (again) and pay me my salary into my account. I have $1600 dollars in my sock draw, which was conveniently ignored.

At school I went on the case of the mystery of the missing safety glasses. Remember the lab is part of the other school who were not keen on letting us in there. It took eight weeks to negotiate a contract to allow us in there and we 'share' equipment. This means in reality that they have locked their chemical cupboard, and they have locked the cupboard that contains the gas tap and we don't have the key. The teacher who had just been using the gas lied outrageously when I asked him for it and he said he did not know where it was. Anyway I went up there to tinker with things when I noticed that the safety glasses I had bought for the school had been moved. Now as I was the only Churchill teacher who had been in there I knew it wasn't me so I guessed the other school's teachers had used them. I searched the prep room and the lab to no avail so I asked the Headmaster to ask them for me (they don't speak English). The response was, and I quote, "Oh yes I think we borrowed them and we locked them in one of our cupboards. You can have them on Monday."

Saturday 14th November

I went with the Headmaster to collect some chemicals today. A friend of a friend's mother was a technician in a hospital and they had a room full of chemicals they wanted to dispose of. However to dispose of them costs money so any I could take off their hands saved them money. So I finally got the chemicals I needed rather than ones other people thought I needed. The hospital was another dingy affair with porters smoking cigarettes in the foyer.

We went to the Old Man's Music Pub in the evening. This is a cool place for a night out. First of all it is free but you are guaranteed to have live blues and jazz every night. Afterwards the dj plays old disco records until the early hours. And for the ladies out there who hate night clubs in the U.K because of the appalling meat market atmosphere present in them you will be pleased to hear that I saw no boorish, drunken behaviour, I saw no women being hit on. All I saw was people dancing and having a good time. Now I am sure there are some pretty dodgy night clubs in Budapest too but the point is that there are very few places like the Old Man's Pub in England where you can go, listen to live music for free and have a good dance without any hassle.

Monday 16th November

Jessica informed the Headmaster that she was off at the end of the year. She cited her reasons as being unable to pay off her university debts on her salary. The Headmaster offered to pay off her debts for her and she could pay them back to him but she was adamant.

Tuesday 17th November

The first ever experiment performed at the Churchill School happened today. It was a simple filtration/crystallisation of a water/sand/copper sulphate mixture but the kids absolutely loved it. Sasha, a rather naughty Russian boy refused to go to Russian school and stayed to complete his evaporation. I don't know if you have ever tried to evaporate water using alcohol burners but it is a harrowing task. First, any spillage catches fire and these burners are in such a state they encourage spillage. Secondly they are slow and need refilling after ten minutes but you can't refill them because they are too hot to touch. However somehow we got there.

Brittany, the girl who is to replace Bill arrived today. She has been teaching in the Czech Republic and has a few stories to tell. As hers are probably more interesting than mine I plan to steal them at the earliest opportunity. She still seems a bit straight to work here. You have to have a hard skin, really believe in what you do (she is just taking a year out of life to visit Europe) and have a bloody minded determination to succeed. I have these 'qualities' which is why I am still here, damned determined to teach science the proper way. I can't fail you see. I spent sleepless nights talking to a drowsy Andrea about how this bastard school was not going to beat me. How I was going to do experiments etc. I am still standing and it's nearly all in place. I don't have sleepless nights anymore. I am the one everyone asks advice from (whether it's disciplinary, or how to unblock the photocopier).

Wednesday 18th November

I expect to be appointed Dean of Students soon. Because Bill, the American, is leaving there is no-one else male here to do the job. Maleness is not a pre-requisite, except in the eyes of the Headmaster. So I am in charge of student discipline and other matters. I am in theory the deputy head (ha haaaaaa). Now if I can just knobble the Headmaster then my plan is completed. I will rule the school (hahhhhhhhhaaaaaaaaa!!!!!).

The dance teacher quit today. I don't know if this is permanent or not but not enough kids want to dance after school and then he couldn't find the tape player so he walked out in a creative huff. I hope he comes back. He's a photographer too and I have ordered a copy of his famous "Great Hungarian Moustaches" calendar. If he goes I will have to think of different Christmas presents. Facial hair is significant here. Although this is an unfair survey, thirty percent of the men who passed me in the Mamut shopping mall yesterday while I was waiting for Andrea had some kind of beard, goatee or moustache.

The weather has become rather nippy. The Siberian wind has kicked in and snow is in the air.

Melanie, an old German friend arrived for a visit today. I am skiving off school on Friday provided I don't get sick. There is a terrible flu going round. Andrea had it earlier in the week and instructed me to kill her at one stage the pain was so bad. Actually having been to the pharmacy to collect drugs for her I think killing her would have been faster. There was a kind of three queue system involving receipts and keeping the maximum amount of people employed in this closed business. You can only buy medicine in these places. You can't even buy cough medicine or aspirin or vitamin C capsules in a supermarket or 'chemist'. You have to go to these places.

Some bright spark has thought it a good idea to make one member of each class a 'prefect' responsible for chalk supplies, chair putting on desks and window shutting. The kids were very reluctant until some fool told them they could put teachers in detention too. So I have been given a detention for leaving the school premises to buy chocolate, forgetting to put my chair up and stealing an orange off a student in the corridor (I deserved the third one), I was very naughty indeed,

Thursday 19th November

Melanie is here! It is strange her being here. So far she is very impressed with the way the Hungarian's change their plans all the time. Tonight we were supposed to be going to the cinema but instead we went to the ship pub[18] and then onto another pub.

Friday 20th November

Feigning a toothache I showed Melanie around town. It was cold but we had a good time. I showed her the sites I am now very used to.

---

[18] "Columbus", Pest side, near Elizabeth bridge

The Hungarian Girl Trap

Saturday 21st November

Miskolc

Miskolc is even colder. I refused to even take my hat off for the entire time. We went shopping in the morning, Andrea deciding to go to the cheap shops. There are many expensive looking shops in Hungarian towns now but there are also the old style pile 'em high sell 'em cheap stores. They smell of cheap glue and the garments come exclusively from Chinese sweat shops. I like them because they are packed with people and because of the terrible English written on them. Chinese clothes manufacturers believe that the rest of the world loves English, and festoon their clothes with terrible phrases like 'vital spirit of sport', or 'adventure way of life'. I find it very funny and Andrea frowns at me a lot for smirking at these phrases on friends' clothes.

"Why can't Hungarians have Hungarian on their t-shirts?" I asked.

Miskolc has also provided me with a piece of graffiti I shall never grow tired of. In an alleyway just off the high street in huge black letters is written, "never fuck in a snack bar" in English. No explanation, not even a snack bar nearby. Brilliant.

Sunday 22nd November

We drove to Slovakia today, like you do. As I am an illegal alien, in the country as a traveller, I can only stay for ninety days. That is sometime next week so I have to leave the country and return to get another stamp in my passport and another ninety days of freedom. Slovakia isn't far from Miskolc, maybe an hour to the border. Up here the villages became more and more backward. Even though it was very cold, it seemed to me that people came out of their houses to watch the car go by.

The border redefines sleepy. It was a house between two fields and two barriers. We have to wake the Hungarian guy up.

"Come back before six," he said, "otherwise this is closed."

I looked at the flimsy barrier and wondered how this border could ever be closed. The Slovak border guard was a little more alert. We drove to Kosice, or Kassa as the Hungarians know it. We had lunch in a town, which, far from the desolate hole that Hungarians had warned me about, is a buzzing little place, with a beautifully restored central area, and a gloriously kitsch waterfall that changes its ejaculations according to the musak it is playing. We had a great lunch and I bought a recent English newspaper, something much harder to do in Miskolc. The girl behind the counter spoke English too. On the way back sleepy guard forgot to put a stamp on my passport and we had to go back and ask him to do so.

Next time I intend to do this at Aggtelek, which is a cave system up the road. Apparently there is a passage in the caves between Hungary and Slovakia and there is a passport control there. This is the kind of cool thing I get very excited about.

The Hungarian Girl Trap

Monday 23rd November

Well everybody was in a foul mood today, for no apparent reason. Jessica and I, usually the most moany, were so belligerent today we even apologised to Brittany for depressing her. One of the reasons was that the Christmas party at the British embassy has changed. The Headmaster has decided it will be far too expensive to feed all the parents, kids and staff so he is asking the parents to bring food and calling it an international dinner party. This is actually an O.K idea if it was done for the right reasons but of course it is being done to save money so it stinks. The thing that made us really laugh was the letter to the parents that politely informed them that 'service would be provided free of charge by the school'. I thought this was a mistranslation for main course or something but no the Headmaster really did want to say that the teachers would serve the food to the parents for free.

After school Andrea and I went to visit the priest we want to have for our wedding. Father Gábor is a lovely man. He was the priest at the last Anglo-Hungarian wedding we went to in faultless English and provided the finest wedding service I have ever heard. As we arrived at his rooms in the church I was delighted to see the place was a pigsty: a man after my own heart. Even more amusing was that he had to remove a framed picture of Pope John Paul II from the armchair so I could sit down. We were delighted when he said he was available on the day we want (he would have just come off retreat – or something). He asked if I was converting to Catholicism and I said I doubted it. However it was fortunate that I did my teacher training at a catholic college. We have to go back next week to talk about marriage. We left feeling very joyous and I can't really work out exactly why.

Tuesday 24th November

"Budapest is the most happening city in Europe," said Slade the Leveller from the stage of the e-Klub[19] this evening. Slade, lead singer of New Model Army and long time hero of mine had paused mid-set to remind the locals of their fine city.

"We're never coming back in the winter though," he added. "It's bloody freezing."

New Model Army were a fantastic rock band. They hardly changed over twelve years and (I don't know if this is just me getting old but) I think they are the only band of the eighties who still sounded relevant and whose back catalogue has not dated embarrassingly. They played a blinding set tonight.

"Well, I guess you've had nine years to get used to that song," said Slade after the applause died down after the final chord of 51st State. 51st State is all about nasty American culture taking over a country. The Hungarians loved it. NMA were always much bigger in Europe than at home. I guess the British public all preferred Thatcherite sympathetic pop like the Pet Shop Boys ('Let's make lots of money') to

---

[19] In the People's Park (Népliget), Népligeti st 2

NMA ('Here in the land of opportunities watch us revel in our misery'). I love 'em to death.

Actually I nearly didn't get to see them and I blame Endre, one of my Hungarian pals. He had taken Melanie to the pub and then took me (after Hungarian class) to eat stuffed cabbage in a restaurant (excellent). However it took longer than he thought (I was all for grabbing McDonalds but he was insulted – 'what about all that 51st state crap you just talked about') and we were late to meet Andrea who was so cross she called off the engagement for about five minutes. I did my usual trick of battening down the hatches until the storm blew out (by the cloakrooms) and didn't remind her of the time she was 45 minutes late picking me up from Vienna airport at midnight in May. Fortunately she forgot about it after NMA started playing.

Wednesday 25th November

As the new Dean of Students I immediately asserted my authority by placing four children in detention for various little things (swearing in Hungarian in class).

The evening was marvellous. Unfortunately Andrea was working, so Melanie, Endre and I went ice skating. I had been trying to get out of this for weeks but you can only delay for so long. I went once before and found the whole thing humiliating. However the Budapest ice rink is worth seeing anyway. It is outside, next to Vajdahunyad castle and it is one of the most picturesque things I have ever seen. I don't know why but watching the skaters from the bridge over the river it reminds me of a Breughal painting.

So I stagger onto the ice, black skates, black trousers, black jacket – at least I'll look cool as I fall on my butt, I thought and so began the laborious process of teaching me to skate. It's all about leaning forward apparently. So I fell over a few times and after a while a young Hungarian lady took pity on me, and helped me for about half an hour. Her English consisted of "left", "right" and "duck quack, quack" (as in the positional requirements for my feet). She was very insistent on helping me and never got frustrated. Eventually Endre slid over to see what was going on and she left.

"Nice girl," I said. "Is she employed here to help beginners?"
Endre gave me a strange look. "No she was trying to seduce you!"
"I beg your pardon," I said. "Was she really?"
I decided I would be a hopeless Don Juan. I never have a clue.

Afterwards we went for a beer and then we went to the cinema to see a film with a happy, romantic ending that covered a multitude of sins.

After the cinema we went to Mamma Rosa's[20] for spaghetti and salad I outlined to Endre my plan to become the Woody Allen of Budapest (but with more hair). I think this means I want to eat out in restaurants and wander the streets for inspiration. Endre wasn't sure Budapest was ready for such fame.

---

[20] 31 Ostrom st, Buda, near Moszkva Ter. Watch out for the cats

"Keep us secret," he said.

We got home at midnight. I was grinning ear to ear. This is what life is all about – having days like this. How much did all this entertainment cost? In total, about a fiver. I know, unbelievable, and I hired some ice skates!

Thursday. 26th November

It's Thanksgiving today and the Americans are sulking because they had to work.

"It's a holiday," they screeched.

Actually Larry wasn't sulking. He was playing his Israeli card.

"I think Thanksgiving is the most hypocritical piece of American culture," he spat. "They thank the red people for getting them through two winters then spend the next two hundred years systematically slaughtering them or putting smallpox into the blankets they kindly gave them. Adolf Hitler read American history. Where do you think he got his holocaust ideas from?"

The Americans looked at their shoes and admitted it was true, then went on to talk about pumpkin pie again.

"I will never ever attend a thanksgiving," stated Larry firmly, then sheepishly added, "…except tomorrow because Bill is a friend of mine."

After school I went to the pub where the Hungarian class met. John, John, Nenet and Jake, the Vietnam vet were already there.

"MIT CSINÁLSZ![21]" bellowed Jake, clearly drunk already. His Hungarian is always better after a skinful.

"I missed you buddy," he said and gave me a beery hug. "You don't mind me hugging you, it's an American thing, we hug people we like. It's natural."

"I'm touched," I said but Jake was away rubbing Nenet's bald head. "It's so soft, don't you love it," he said bellowing with laughter.

"I presume you are not going to class in this state," I said. He could hardly stand.

"What are you saying man," said Jake mock-angrily. "Are you saying I'm incapable of speaking this damn language?"

He then bellowed out all the swear words he knew.

We went to class. Jake was impeccably behaved except for turning round and asking '"Mit csinálsz" repeatedly under his breath…oh and giving the teacher a bear hug halfway through the lesson.

Back in the pub after class and John revealed he had started to work at "Video mania" the English video store. He only started last week but already he has been promoted to manager.

"Blimey," I said. It was symptomatic of the Hungarian work attitude.

---

[21] "What are you doing?"

"They just do not make an effort," said John. "They want six smoke breaks an hour and present a sulky attitude at all times. A Brit turns up and wants to do his best and it's so amazing the owner can't believe it."

This probably explains why I am the Dean of Students after ten weeks too. Another example is Steve the dance teacher at the school who is a professional photographer. He needed £80 of prints developed but they weren't right so he asked for changes but the shop found it all so inconvenient they told him to go elsewhere. He was amazed. £80 is a fortune and the guy did not want the money and the future money. It was too much effort to do the extra work. He made enough; he didn't want more because it involved effort.

"Say can I work at video mania?" asked Jake.

"They don't have a bar," said John.

"That's why I need to work there. It will stop me getting drunk all the time."

Friday 27th November

Jessica berated the Headmaster over books he ordered six weeks ago that have not arrived yet. She has no books and needs them yesterday.

"It could take six months," said the Headmaster.

"But school will be finished by then," protested Jessica. "We are ripping off the parents."

"Can't you buy them here?" said the Headmaster.

"You told me I couldn't because we had a contract with this publisher."

"I am sure I didn't," said the Headmaster.

I reassured Jessica that it did not take six months to order books in England. I postulated that the Headmaster had not ordered the books at all and was just fobbing her off with this six months nonsense. I told her to check by asking the Headmaster if she could check the order form as she has forgotten what she had ordered.

Saturday 28th November

Melanie, Andrea and I went to a party at Endre's tonight. I made a slight alcohol purchasing error and bought some killer beer, which went straight to my head, so I was the life and soul of the party. I started out by translating what was said in Hungarian for Melanie (and she calls herself a linguist, she was here ten days and she cannot even say 'thank you'. She just shakes her head and says 'I cannot understand one word!') Unfortunately most of my translations involved pigs drowning so Melanie soon grew suspicious of my ability. Later a man called 'Donut' (I asked him twice because I was sure I misheard) introduced me to a rather attractive young lady who was studying Lewis Carroll and wanted to talk about him to an Englishman. So I did until I realised I was talking about Lewis Carroll and C.S Lewis at the same time (I think) so her essay is going to be confused. Also (and I don't know whether she was just being flippant because she thought dumbness was cool and thought I would prefer dumbness in a woman but…) she kept dismissing his stories as 'fairy tales' and nothing more. Before I could discuss this Andrea decided I needed to dance with her instead, which was a relief.

Meanwhile there were other shenanigans going on. Melanie was very popular and there was a queue of Hungarian men after her. Andrea's sister, who was drunk sidled up to me and said, "at first I blamed you for making my sister stop coming out and having fun, but now I realise that you like parties too and she has just changed." Then she disappeared and was last seen doing the lambada with György[22] (to pronounce this name just stick a wet finger in a light socket and say 'aaahhh' at the same time) in a ridiculously short skirt (Andrea's sister wore the skirt not György). Soon György gave up and focused on Melanie and they disappeared for a while only for Andrea to rescue Melanie after an appropriate period of time.

On the way home (about 4ish) I apparently (according to Andrea, I have no recollection) talked the most profound stuff stating my philosophy on life and happiness and what everyone should do to reach my own level of inner peace. I find this hard to believe. What I find downright impossible to believe is the assertion (by both Melanie and Andrea) that I then lapsed into fluent German for the remainder of the journey. Why can't I speak German sober?

Monday 30th November

Various rumpuses (rumpi?) at school today included Jessica and the missing books. She pressed the Headmaster for the book ordering slip but none could found.

"Was the order placed?" asked Jessica.

"Yes," said the Headmaster.

"When?"

"In October," insisted the Headmaster, "…well late October."

Jessica pursed her lips, "and my order was definitely placed?"

"Yes…well with a few minor adjustments," said the Headmaster.

This is about as positive answer as you are likely to get. Jessica is mad because she offered to buy the books whilst she was in England six weeks ago but was told they were "too expensive". The Headmaster now wants her to buy them here even though he told her not to six weeks ago. Jessica has said that she will go back to the U.S.A if the books are not here by January – and she means it. She will also write to all the parents in her class apologising for having no books and recommending they take their kids elsewhere. Jessica is a great teacher, but teachers have to have help.

Meanwhile the swimming pool water is causing the Chinese girls to get skin rashes. All gave in notes last week saying they were not going swimming again until it was sorted out. Larry, the swimming teacher told the Headmaster who did

---

[22] Most foreigners give up and prefer the Anglicised 'George', or Juri.

absolutely nothing about it. Therefore Larry has said he will not report any child who misses swimming who does not have a note.

"I'm all for kids making their own decisions," he said.

On the positive side Wendy, the Chinese teacher called in one of her contacts and the school had one of the chefs from the expensive Chinese restaurant come down and cook us school dinner of the century. Hot and sour soup, followed by kung po chicken and something else with almonds. I was very pleased, especially considering we usually have black potatoes for lunch. I am certain this will become the highlight of the week.

Evening

We invited Andrea's father round for dinner so I could do the traditional thing and ask him for Andrea's hand in marriage. He took it rather well, his eyes widened and his face went the colour of a beetroot. He said nothing but, "you're both crazy."

I took that to mean he was completely overwhelmed and didn't quite know what to say at all. He didn't finish all his dinner either!

December

Tuesday 1st December

Not only has the Headmaster not ordered Jessica's books but he has also not ordered Brittany's either. Now Bill, who left, WAS the history teacher and every day he asked the Headmaster where the books were and the Headmaster assured him they were coming. Now he has gone and Brittany is here the truth is out. This is very serious as she is teaching a history course based on a certain text book without the text book. I told her to tell me what it is and I will buy the bloody thing for her for Christmas and she can at least photocopy it.

Meanwhile the dangers of getting someone else to order and store chemicals were drummed home to me today. I needed to refill the spirit burners (do not ever use these nightmare things for anything) with alcohol and reached for a new bottle from the polystyrene box marked 'alcohol 95%' kindly provided by another school and acquired by our Headmaster. The bottles were all brown and similar and I had no reason to believe they contained anything but 95% alcohol. I sloshed some into the spirit burner and was surprised to see a bizarre coagulation going on in the burner. Concerned I looked at the bottle again. It didn't contain alcohol at all; it contained 98% sulphuric acid arguably the nastiest substance in the laboratory. One drop would cause me agony and I had sloshed it about wildly. I watched as black marks appeared in paper left nearby. I charged over to the sink before any splashes started dehydrating me. It taught me (reminded me) to always double-check everything you have not prepared yourself and to ensure I never again work in a place where non-scientists interfere with the procedures in the science department.

In the evening we went to Father Gábor's for our first theology lesson. Gábor is a good man, Catholic of course but he doesn't hold my Anglicanism against me. Having never married before I don't know how the English go about preparing for marriage but here we start from the beginning and discuss the origins of Christianity (Abraham, believing in one God and monotheism) and work through why Christians believe etc. Don't worry, my Hungarian hasn't become brilliant, this theological discussion was in English. I tell you it was a fascinating tutorial and I reminded myself that the atheist can deny the existence of God but if he does so then he denies his own culture which is based entirely on a belief in God. To take rock and roll for example, well that comes from blues and if you are into blues you reach Robert Johnson, a man who went to his grave believing the devil was after him. Rock'n'Roll couldn't happen without belief in something. To believe your life is untouched by religion is a fallacy; to live life without belief is a little pointless. As G.K Chesterton said (in 'Heresy' I believe) for someone to say life is not worth living is not really thinking (or existing at all). If the statement were true our world would be stood on its head. Murderers would be praised, firemen denounced, poisons would be medicine etc. etc.

So I know I am going to enjoy our scripture lessons with Father Gábor. I feel a fool in his presence and I like feeling a fool because it reminds me how little I know about this life thing.

As we left I told him that I disliked my job because there were certain things I morally disagreed with happening there (being told to lie to the police, the racial intolerance of lying to Muslims about the pork content of school dinners). He said, "Yes the English are much more moral than the Hungarians. I like the English. I am very saddened sometimes by this poisoned democracy we live in here in Hungary."

I turned round to look at Andrea and hoped she hadn't heard. Father Gábor would have not been conducting the wedding if she had heard such things! She hadn't.

Wednesday 2nd December

The students sent some letters to the Headmaster asking him to change some things in the school. "Your school has good teachers and the classrooms are nice," wrote Dmitri, a Russian boy, "but many students are discontented with the food." He went on to comment about the terrible swimming pool. Another anonymous pupil wrote, with the kind of sarcasm I like, that, "to have a computer room separate from the art room is a basic requirement of any school." This pupil also commented that the lab has no equipment, that a corridor was not enough space for kids to run around in break times (The Headmaster hasn't negotiated use of the playground yet). S/he also mentioned that E.S.O.L teachers cannot spell (none of the teachers of E.S.O.L are native spellers – Larry is a native speaker but can only spell in Hebrew apparently). Finally the kid wrote, "Our parents paid much money to send us here but all we can get are the worst conditions school (sic) of all the international schools. This is a shame on us and a shame on Britain."

Quite right too! So these letters came up in staff meeting and The Headmaster addressed all the points as if it was some kind of game. Where the kids English was poor he dismissed the point as "I am not sure what they are trying to say." He commented that the food was poor but the portions were adequate causing uproar from the staff. He dismissed a swimming pool change as simply impossible then changed the subject to moan at the staff for using too much paper in the photocopier. An anonymous person whispered that if the books had been ordered then we would not need to photocopy so much. We have apparently used up two years' worth of paper but as this seems to consist of about five reams I think the maths is out somewhere. The photocopier is the worst in history. It will do about five copies before giving up and sulking. Brittany and I, soul mates in untidiness but also in efficiency both photocopy all the stuff we need three days in advance to save problems later. I always blame Réka, the rather teasable German teacher. In actual fact it is Wendy, the Chinese teacher who is usually the culprit. She has the audacity to try and do double sided copies to save paper. What a mad idea.

Thursday 3rd December

Another flu virus has hit the staff. At the moment it is going to be me, Larry and Brittany running the school tomorrow. Most of classes are doubled up or I set work in one class and run off to my official class and continue the mad rush.

After school I dashed to Hungarian lessons where I realised an important lesson: alcoholics are not fun after a while. I am referring to Jake, the Vietnam vet, who, far from being amusing and innocent, is starting to cause problems. John left money for a pizza he bought in the pub with Jake last week, as John had to go home and the waiter hadn't delivered the bill yet. Jake was drunk and spent this money on some more beer, leaving John to have to fork up for some more this week when he arrived. The management weren't impressed. Today Jake was paralytic as I arrived and couldn't even walk through the door to class. It was 4.30 p.m. I asked him how much he had had.

"One beer," he insisted, denying his alcoholism.

Class passed by reasonably easily and we went back to the bar where Jake managed to severely antagonise the waiting staff with various Anglo-Saxon words. This led to the waiters trying to massively overcharge us in revenge, causing the Trevor, the fifty something, ex-French foreign legion soldier to argue forcibly with the waiters until they relented. He then bellowed "I will never drink here again." Poor John, Nenet, the Croatian and me. We just like a quiet beer in this vaguely salubrious place and now we were persona non grata. Oh and Jake didn't pay for his beers; he simply accused the waiters of trying to fiddle us and we paid for his. Nenet, John and I will have to work out a way of keeping away from these two loose cannons. They cause hassle and I don't need it...especially as I am STILL in the country illegally.

Friday 4th December

About four inches of snow fell on Budapest today. I shall try to avoid the clichés but it did make Budapest look quite lovely. I am very pleased to report that the British are far too hard on themselves when it comes to our belief that we cannot cope with a single flake of snow compared to our ruthlessly efficient European cousins who are prepared for cold weather and deal with it with the minimum of fuss. It was chaos here in Budapest. All the roads clogged up with cars so no public transport ran. The gritters and snowploughs only appeared about lunchtime and they too got stuck in the traffic jams. So all the roads were white. The snow shovellers were spending the day standing around from what I could see. I walked the three miles from my school to the nearest metro station and watched as the rest of Budapest sat in cars swearing at each other or stood forlornly at bus and tram stops glancing at their watches.

The Hungarian Girl Trap

Of course the school couldn't cope at all. The van that brings the school lunch got stuck somewhere, leaving us all starving. As we were down to skeleton staff, there was no lunch and it was a blizzard we felt the kids should start trying to get home, but we needed the Headmaster to make a DECISION. But our Headmaster simply dithers and instead he hid in his office and did a very good impression of an ostrich with its head in the sand. In end the food arrived at 2.15, Brittany gave the school a snow fight; the girls painted Christmas cards, the rest of the boys played basketball.

Sunday 6th December

Well the snow has continued to fall. We are now in a situation where I have never seen so much snow in my life, which is kinda cool. The Hungarian snow clearers only give priority to roads and the pavements have turned into ice rinks, and I do not mean they are a bit slippy. The snow has turned into a pure sheet of ice. It is completely treacherous and I cannot believe more people haven't broken limbs. I have bought a new winter coat to counter the constant minus five conditions (was I really complaining about the constant +35 degrees Celsius last summer?) and I bought Andrea an engagement ring for 7500 forints. I will let you use your powers of investigation to work out how much that is! I'm not telling.

Monday 7th December

The photocopier is dying a horrible death. Dexter, sick of it, threatens to throw an important piece in the bin.

"Why don't we rent another one?" I asked logically. "I mean we have no books so we have to use this thing. We are stuck."

No-one answered. Then Naima came in saying, "I can't work at all. What am I to do?"

"Are you asking me as Dean of Students or friend?" I said.

"Both."

"Write in every kid's diary that the reason no work has gone on this week is that the school photocopier is useless and we have no books," I said only half joking.

I found out later why we persevere with the dratted machine. The Headmaster bought it! Of all the stupid things I have ever heard BUYING a second hand photocopier has got to be up there with the best. I could see him thinking of how much money he was saving. Yet all he has bought is a lead weight to tie us down.

"All the parts inside were new," he insisted.

"So why is it always jammed?" I said.

You never buy photocopiers, you lease new ones. That way you are safe. Photocopiers jam. Full stop. This contraption has only a one year guarantee. What happens next year? The bills get bigger that's what. The guys who sold it to him that laughs all the way to the bank.

Tuesday 8th December

The photocopier has been switched off. Utterly ruined. Even the kids know about the fiasco. It has its upside though, no easy handing out of printed sheets, back to chalk and talk.

I am in serious revision mode for my upcoming Hungarian exam. If I pass I get a diploma (whoopee) and am allowed to continue next year. I am expecting the pass mark to be a bit low, because it makes no sense to stop people taking a course. So I am learning my 'endings' feverishly and panicking at the last minute. Fortunately I have enough nous (I think) to wing it. My studies have been somewhat compromised by the fact I am English and everyone speaks English to me.

Hungarian is a tough language. It also has the kind of iron logic that you would admire if it weren't so damn weird. I have said this before but most European languages have some structural similarity and we thank Latin for that. Often I dream of learning French again, so easy is it in comparison. Hungarian doesn't follow those rules. There follows a summary of Hungarian.

First of all if you were not born speaking Hungarian, forget it.

Verbs: in Indo-European languages we have the definite article (I, you, he, she, we etc). Now we have the fact that in Hungarian there are six ways of saying "You," depending on whom and how many people you are talking to. Secondly there is no way of specifying gender in Hungarian. Literally there is no word for he/she/it/him/hers/its. It is all one word or more specifically one way of ending a verb. The final logical point is that all verbs have a different ending depending on whom or what is doing the verb. In English this is not the case (I eat, you eat, he eats, we eat, they eat). See, they are nearly all the same.

Example: to go

Én megyek
Te mész
Ő megy
Mi megyünk
Ti mentek
Ők mennek

This is fine but the Hungarians have decided that as all the verbs end differently why waste time saying the definite article? Therefore they don't *use* words like I or you. The verb tells you who is doing it so no need to have it. This is a nightmare for learners because if you don't know your endings you are doomed.

The Hungarian Girl Trap

In English this would mean the sentence "I am a teacher", becomes "Am a teacher" or in reality, "Teacher am." You begin to sound like Yoda.

Finally there are numerous irregular endings depending on the vowels in the verb and the letter the verb ends in. There are no short cuts. I could mention vowel harmony at this point but trust me, it's better that I don't.

Plurals: In Hungarian you add a 'k' to the word to indicate plural (or ek, ok, ők depending on the vowels in the word). However you must also add this plural ending to any descriptive words about the thing you have more than one of. In English this would mean a sentence, "The bigs, reds, cars". No problem, you say but Hungarians DON'T put a plural ending on something that is obviously plural, i.e. 68 guns would be 68 gun because the 68 implies more than one (of course).

Endings: There are 186 different endings you can add to nouns etc. With these you can say in, on, at, into, onto, from, my, its, yours, theirs, next to, plus a lot of other things less tangible which we don't even think about in English. For each ending there are two or three different types depending (again) on the vowels in the word.

Word order: Forget conventional Latin word order. Definite article (subject), verb, object. In Hungarian the order is determined by the importance of the words in the sentence to the meaning of the sentence. This all depends on the context of the sentence and is impossible to teach. Also how you say the words changes the sentence. The nearest example would be a phrase such as "working today," or "Working today?" In English we would raise our voice at the end of the second sentence to show it is a question. Hungarian is based entirely on this principle.

Dative, accusative: German fans will be pleased to hear that both appear here with a vengeance. Non German speakers, don't worry about it.

Pronunciation: Once you have got it, it is very logical and there are very few exceptions. Unfortunately the difference between the sounds is difficult to hear. "új" – 'new', and "ujj"- 'finger' sound identical. I keep asking for ice (jég) instead of a ticket (jegy). 'Gy' is completely unpronounceable in a sentence. It sounds like a cough. S is pronounce Shhh, Sz is pronounced "s". Zs is pronounces Zhhhh, c is pronounced "Tss". All these sound the same to me. The one I make most mistakes with is 'ck'. It is pronounced "ssskk". "j" is "y", "y" is more "Yer" without the 'er' (!). Oh, and Busz (bus) must be pronounced as if you are from Manchester. If you pronounce busz in Queens English you are saying "Fuck it".

Hungarian has compound verbs like German too. I keep thinking, blimey this is just the first course. What the heck must the hard stuff be like?

The Hungarian Girl Trap

Next week: "English – what a stupid language", a critical study by Andrea Sári. For example did you know that "I am called" and I am cold" sound identical? Well it does. Whiskers and viscous are also the same word apparently. I managed to confuse year nine the other day who thought 'whiskers rock' makes up the Earth's mantle, rather than the more conventionally accepted 'viscous rock'.,

The final class before the test was interesting. Our teacher, Judit, informed us that Jake, the alcoholic Vietnam vet, had been expelled from the language course for 'repeatedly turning up drunk'. This was quite amusing as I am sure this is probably the first time anyone has been expelled from a language school. Afterwards Nenet, John and I went to the bar and were shocked to see Jake waiting for us outside, barely able to stand. He was furious and making no sense at all. We carried him onto the metro but he was too far gone. He staggered off yelling obscenities. To our right an alcoholic woman urinated in the street, the first time I'd seen this.

"This is not the country to be an alcoholic," said John sadly, freezing breath pluming in the air around him. "You fall asleep in the open here and you wake up dead – if you see what I mean."

Wednesday 9th December

Réka, the German teacher had a spectacular accident with the photocopier today. It had jammed (quelle surprise) and she had pulled out the relevant piece of machinery. She left it on top of the copier while she lifted another part. Unfortunately this caused the copier to incline and the machine piece fell to the floor with a huge crash. The staffroom went silent. This was bad. As I always tease Réka and blame her for all the photocopier jams I felt guilty so I spent a pleasant five minutes bending back the various metal parts and forcing the thing back in. Somehow it still worked. She owes me one.

The afternoon was strange. I had to accompany our Chinese girls to the dentist on the other side of the city. As you can imagine this caused quite a scene. Various Hungarians at the bus-stop, including some old codger asked me what was going on and I explained in my pidgin Hungarian that I had no bloody idea why I was entrusted with the task of taking nine over-excited Chinese girls to the dentist. The Chinese girls found my Hungarian very funny, as they all speak it like natives. Later the same old codger tried German and I was able to explain exactly what was going on. Unfortunately his German was pretty shoddy so he didn't really understand. At the dentist I had nine Chinese girls and a total of forty six cavities! Quite impressive.

Thursday 10th December

It looks as if term will drift to an end rather than finish with a bang. The Christmas party is on Wednesday night at the British Embassy. The following day, the Headmaster declared, the kids would not be in the mood to work and has declared that the whole school should go for a walk in the Buda hills – in sub zero temperatures. The final day of term (Friday) has also been declared a no-no. So why bother having them at all?

After school I went straight to the language course for some panic cramming. The test was very hard but somehow I managed 70% so I have my diploma.

I was in the pub with Endre and Andrea afterwards. Endre had Mark, an Englishman, with him. Mark was here doing business with Endre's company. I arrived late, having been at my increasingly friendly private student Petra's mansion eating her Christmas chocolate and refusing to be drawn into a conversation by her about why chocolate is a substitute for sex. (In the manner of the Richard Gordon's, "Doctor' books – in which our hero's landlady's daughter kept turning up to his room complaining of a vague leg pain that moved slowly up the leg: the Doctor gave notice when the pain reached the hip – I have decided to stop being her tutor the moment she tells me they have reached human reproduction on the IB course). So I arrived, a little flustered just at the end of a conversation where Mark admitted to actually having a Hungarian father and was actually called 'Tibor'.

"My father played trumpet on the Northern working men's club circuit," he said wistfully. "He was on 'Opportunity Knocks' too and beat Mary Hopkin on the audience vote. Unfortunately he left my mum when I was seven... He ran away to Caracas because the male/female ration is 1 to 25."

I listened to this not really believing how surreal the people I meet are.

"Apparently he lives in Budapest now so I am going to look him up," he continued.

The guy's father was a philanderer.

"When I was young I remember my father driving me across Europe to Hungary," he said. "I remember we stayed at all these aunts' houses and I remember at the time thinking, blimey these aunts are a bit sexier than most aunts. It wasn't until about five years ago that the penny dropped and I realised these women weren't aunts at all but girlfriends."

Then we changed the subject and talked about rugby to the dismay of the Hungarians.

Friday 11th December

I was in a foul mood today because Sky News has disappeared from our cable television. It is amazing how sulky it can make you being totally cut off. I have been reduced to watching Hungarian TV. If it wasn't for subtitled Fawlty Towers twice a week I would go mad. I have even considered German television but am terrified by the random pornography that always turns up on their TV if you watch it for any length of time.

Sulked all day at school and only cheered up when Naima took my maths classes away from me to throw a Pakistani party for the kids.

The Hungarian Girl Trap

Sunday 13th December

We (me, Andrea, her sister Gabi and her father's fiancée) went to the opera on Saturday. It was a quite remarkable performance of Puccini's Turandot. Turandot is well-known in England as the opera that 'Nessun Dorma' comes from, or even more colloquially, 'the song fatty Pavarotti sings that played over the World Cup once'. As such Turandot has a lot to answer for. Opera's detractors accuse it of being elitist and I answer that of course it is. Opera is performed by the most talented artists in the world, people who have trained for years to reach near-perfection. So of course it is expensive and as a respect for the talent one should dress up. So we paid our exorbitant £4 and went to see a treat.

The story for those unfamiliar with it is very simple. It is the story of a fat princess reluctant to marry and a prince set in 'legendary China'. So reluctant is the fat princess (she should be young and beautiful but young beauties can't belt out the numbers like plump old women) to marry that she sets three questions to would-be suitors, all of whom so far have failed to get them right. The penalty for failure is beheading and the stage front is adorned with ten heads on sticks. As the opera starts another one bites the dust. Anyway our trivia mad Prince (who should be about nineteen but is actually a rather portly middle aged Spaniard) decides to have a go having fallen in love with the Princess at first sight (clearly blind as well as being a middle-aged, portly Spaniard). There follows about two hours of trauma as the world tries to stop him trying, even the Emperor, dressed in gold with a tray on his head pleads with him, but no, the Spaniard is smitten.

Enter the Princess with the questions. As the opera is in Italian with Hungarian sub-titles (on an L.E.D screen above the stage) I may have got the gist of the questions wrong. The first question is how many naturally occurring chemical elements are there. The Prince isn't sure whether Technetium is naturally occurring and frets for a while (especially as it won't be 'discovered' for another 2000 years). Finally he plumps for 92. He is correct. The crowd cheer, the Princess scowls. The next question is what is the fastest land animal? Again it's a toughie. Is it the gazelle, is it the cheetah, would a Persian Prince have heard of these animals anyway? He goes with cheetah and this time the Princess throws down the answer board in disgust. The final question is trickier. Who had a number one hit in 1982 with "Shaddap a ya face"? Damn, he thinks, 1982 isn't for another 2000 years. He doesn't know. Then inspiration hits him and just as the Princess walks away in triumph he yells out Joe Dolce! He's correct. There will be a wedding.

I am kidding about the questions. They were riddles about hope, love and the Princess herself.

The Princess orders the populous to search for the Prince so none shall sleep 'nessun dorma' and it all goes tragic then happy and I am not doing it justice at all. It was the finest thing I have ever seen in my life on the stage and cannot wait for my next one. I recommend visitors to Budapest don't come in the hot summer but come during the opera season and get the best value for money in the world.

The encores were astonishing and I was reminded of the cultural differences here. As in Russia a slow hand clap indicates rampant approval yet to my ears it sounded as if we hated it. The slow hand clap is meant to sound like 'Vissza', Hungarian for 'encore': "Vissz-a Vissz-a". There were screams in the audience as the performers bowed. Wonderful stuff. Nothing is more powerful than good opera.

Monday 14th December

Back at school and everything is a bit demob happy. I don't mind because all the 'arty' teachers keep borrowing my classes for final rehearsals where the darlings murder 'Oh Come all ye Faithful' in preparation for the Christmas party.

I suggested that we have an agenda for the next staff meeting and also suggested a cut off finishing time of 4.30. I was stared at with awe by my colleagues. It was as if I had just invented the wheel such a brilliant suggestion was it.

"You mean these round things," said the voice, deep and cretinous, "if you attach them to this cart thing they will turn and make the whole thing much easier to pull? Blimey that's brilliant!"

Tuesday 15th December

Today was really farcical. Our Headmaster managed to annoy everybody. The problem is that the end of term has not been thought out at all. There is a Christmas party at the British embassy tomorrow which will end the term essentially. However the school still has two days to run. It was agreed last week that the kids should buy each other presents and distribute to each other at the party. I did the draw where the kids picked who they would buy a pressie for. However the Headmaster had never heard of this and seemed to think it was a bad idea. Fine but *why* had he not heard of it? What does he do all day? If he wants to be involved he should take the bull by the horns. If he wants to take a back seat then he should not stick his nose in later.

The Headmaster has also decided that the kids would not want to work after that and proposed a hike in the hills for Thursday. Fine, but it was the Friday that most concerned the staff. Last year the last day was a chaotic mess with nothing organised and all the staff leaving in a furious mood. This year they wanted to avoid it. However it became clear that the Headmaster planned to show the same 'Scrooge' video that was played to such derision last year. We proposed our idea of a Headmasterly end of term speech, which was initially dismissed because, "it is not the end of term really. The semester ends on the 29th of January".

I reminded him that he wasn't planning a speech for that day, was he, and he agreed he wasn't so the speech plan went through, somehow. Then Larry offered to put on a performance for an hour and somehow we managed to convince him to let the kids go home at midday. But should it be up to the staff to tell the Headmaster two days before the final day what should be done? Either the Headmaster tells us what to do or we do it and organise it.

Next he agreed with everything and then said, "A note should be sent to parents Brittany," to Brittany, although no-one was quite sure why he chose her and why the school secretary couldn't do it was unclear. Anyway Brittany did it and printed and photocopied it only for the Headmaster to suddenly pipe up, "no the students should come in later on Friday. Make the note say they should come in at 9.30."

Brittany told him she had just finished and had a class. If he wanted to do it he should do it. He didn't. We decided to take a leaf out of his book and not hear the instruction and deny ever hearing it.

Also Gerry arrived from England. Did he bring the books he promised? Well not quite. Brittany, operating since November without any resources at all was waiting on Gerry to bring the GCSE books she needed. Instead she got a primary school picture book entitled "History is Fun! Book 3, the Middle Ages". Not quite the resource she needed for teaching the Cold War to GCSE students. I told her I would buy the books in England at Christmas and if the Headmaster didn't reimburse me we would use them then burn them outside the school.

Also the rehearsals for the party tomorrow (singing, dancing, plays) have eaten away teacher's classes. Fine, but we were not told and only found out when classes told us. Only one teacher had the courtesy to tell me about the rehearsals. I hear tomorrow will be the same, well the kids know. It is simple rudeness again.

On a more humorous note I found more English words can also have different meanings in Hungarian, having exhausted the amusement of the Hungarian word for cheese (Sajt) weeks ago. I was doing some Geography with the Hungarian prep class today and drew the Ordnance Survey symbol for a church (a kind of black dot with a cross on the end). I pointed at it and said "Church". This caused hysterics from the class, and it took about five minutes to realise that 'church' (probably csörcs) apparently means a bad word for breasts in Hungarian.

Wednesday 16th December

Another day of absolute chaos and running around on the hoof because of impromptu rehearsals for this evening's party. I was pretty annoyed by the end just because a simple communication of what was supposed to be happening would have helped. At lunch I proposed to our darling Headmaster the novel idea of a daily staff meeting, but he rejected the idea for no real reason (mainly because he doesn't wander in until about 10ish). The final straw was when the Headmaster announced that he was far too busy to come on the walk with us tomorrow. As it was his stupid bloody idea in the first place and no-one wanted to go except him we were pretty mad. I stalked off home vowing not to attend the Christmas party tonight and only the realisation that Brittany and the others wouldn't know what was wrong made me go. I was glad I did in the end.

The Hungarian Girl Trap

The party was held at the rather swanky British Embassy building and consisted of all the kids dressed up to look angelic by doting parents, the parents, the teachers and other invited guests (the Headmistress of the school we share the building with, various governors (who I checked to make sure they didn't drive BMWs, etc.)) Andrea was there too and her heart was melting at the sight of all the cute primary kids dressed by Jessica as characters from the nativity. Unfortunately the autistic kid had a freak out just before, but recovered just in time to take up his role as Balthazar.

The entertainment was truly surreal. It was presented by Larry, a great entertainer. The choir sang "O Come all ye Faithful!", "Silent Night", Away in a Manger" and a Hungarian song. The year eights did a play so weird I would swear it was L.S.D fuelled. The Chinese girls sang some songs but couldn't light the sparklers to accompany the song and to be waved at opportune moments. This led to the song fading a little as they all bent around each other flicking lighters. They then performed a play about the five Chinese sisters, one could 'drink the sea', one who had 'an iron neck', one who could stretch to a great size'; one who 'could not be burned', and one had 'large breasts', which drew very confused looks from the parental audience. They then realised this was as close to 'large BREATHS' as the Chinese can get and serious suppressed giggles occurred.

Next was the year one nativity play and other songs, all of which drew severe aaahs from the audience. Unfortunately Sag Nai the child from hell was more concerned with holding his trousers up than being a tree at one point.

The Hungarian students did a story involving a ball. I'm afraid I have no idea what it was about. Then Larry severely ad-libbed a story with the primary class which was very funny indeed. Larry, an actor and performer by profession played to the audience brilliantly.

Finally there was an American square dance organised by Steve. They had great fun and although one square lost it a bit during the doci-does (sic) it went off well. I was pleased to see Steve, he owed me two of his "Great Hungarian Moustaches" calendars. He is a well known photographer in the real world and his pictures are stunning.

Next was the auction for the children's pottery, all money going to charity. Larry was auctioneer and was brilliant. Andrea bid for a rather ugly brown thing and when Larry saw her he said, "Ah so now I know why Dexter came to Hungary!"

After that we ate food provided by the parents (cheese scones and sushi). It was probably one of the least British nights I have ever been to.

Thursday 17th December

We took the kids for a walk in the Buda hills. The snow had still not melted so it was a bit slippy. I was bombarded by snow most of the time. It was good to see that Shaniel (Israeli) and Karim (Egyptian), two ten year olds in the prep class, were best pals.

"So what's this I hear about an oil pipeline between Egypt and Israel?" I said.

They held up fists to each other.

"But think of all the money it will bring," I continued.

"Aaaah! Business!" they said grinning, and shook hands and walked off arm in arm.

Wednesday 23rd December

We have decamped to Miskolc for Christmas. We aren't doing much, except prepare for what will be eaten at Christmas. My activities for today were limited to finding and purchasing a copy of the *Budapest Sun* to catch up on news from Budapest. The front page headline was that another British school in the city has collapsed.

The other job was to go to the Russian market, a rather seedy place on the edge of town where people went to sell things. It's a bit of a combination of car boot sale and flea market. I bought some long johns (in the summer I found UK clothes too warm and now I realise that UK clothes don't give any protection against the cold either), but really I was there to marvel at the different ways of life. It was -7°C, bitingly cold, hat a vital piece of apparel. Every stall sold East Asian manufactured clothes and trainers, the assorted crap stalls were manned by Ukrainians. There was an impromptu car sale in the far corner. This, I was told by Andrea was the place of the famous puppy purchase.

"A friend of a friend, said Andrea, "came to the Russian market to buy a puppy for his children. He saw a rather shaggy dog that looked particularly cute and fluffy. He bought it, took it home and then watched amazed as the thing grew and grew and grew and resembled a creature nothing like a dog. Eventually he called in the vet who took a couple of scared steps backwards and said 'that is not a dog, it's a polar bear!"

Soon my frozen feet could take no more (do you really think Hugo Boss makes bobble hats?) but they were briefly forgotten as I saw purchase of the day. It was called a 'Polystation' (sic) and it rescmbled its more famous namesake exactly – except that the Polystation was, in fact, one of those old TV game packages in disguise. It could only play 'space invaders', 'snake', and 'ping pong'. This summed up the Russian market perfectly. Crap disguised as glamour, but is so crap it doesn't get close.

.

Saturday 26th December

Most of the time before Christmas was spent in the pre-shopping madness, less frenetic than England, but the two giant hyper markets in Miskolc: Metro and Tesco were ridiculously busy. The queues went on forever as Hungarians bought up the world's supply of sausages, alcohol and turkey breasts. We spent so much money in Metro that we were entitled to a free trout from the fresh water tank. Not something you get everywhere. My main concern was with the family car, a Wartburg of indeterminate age. It chose the winter to become unreliable and over the last week its starter motor had completely given up. This of course meant that I spent most of the time push-starting the bloody thing. Fine normally, but on Christmas Day and Boxing Day about two feet of snow fell, and that kind of snow hangs around. Have you ever tried pushing a dead car on an ice rink? Don't. The amusement of falling on your face rapidly wears off, especially when the darned useless piece of GDR technology is bumped to start and it coughs into life only for it to stall immediately again.

We went swimming in a few of the baths in Miskolc, the cave baths have been refurbished so now they are even more delightful. There is a star pool now where you can float around staring at an ultraviolet stellar effect. The saunas were great too. The other baths are less ostentatious but have the added attraction of having an outside pool approximately 50 metres away from the complex. This pool is heated to about 38 degrees Celsius (that's hot) but the walk (sorry run) to it through large amounts of snow and sub zero temperatures is quite fun in a vaguely masochistic way. You can't see this hot pool of course, steam surrounds it completely. The cave pools are one of the most wonderful things in Hungary yet get barely a mention in Hungarian guides. As if tourists are really interested in 'the house of science and technology', which gets more lines about it in my guidebook.

Christmas was fun; presents are opened on Christmas Eve. I found the day strange and different but similar. Unlike in England the tree is put up in the morning. Andrea's mother appeared to have acquired the largest tree in Europe and the trunk was about three inches wider than the tree holding device. So Andrea's brother and I had great fun chopping away with an axe in an attempt to solve the problem. Once solved the tree of course was still way too big for the ceiling and its top branches bent themselves double along the ceiling. By this stage we were heartily sick of the thing so we just lopped the top off and hoped no-one would care. Andrea's father arrived around lunchtime and lunch was served. For reference it consisted of cabbage soup with bacon, and then a choice of trout or turkey with mashed potatoes. I have no idea how traditional this is but it was good. Why I was expecting an English Christmas dinner is beyond me now. Christmas is for special feasts and the roast is the English thing. After lunch (although it was nearer four) the 'children', which included me had to wait outside and sing a song about angels arriving, whilst 'Jesus' brought the presents. I don't know how Jesus has manifested himself in Hungarian culture as the present giver, but I suppose it makes a lot more sense than Santa Claus. Apart from that we didn't do much, just relaxed a lot, and used the bath products we were given for Christmas, but the rest of the family joined us on Christmas day. The relatives have bought me a language course, tapes and all, so I made a great show of studying.

The same slightly disconcerting sleeping arrangements are still in place: me, Andrea, her essentially identical sister and the dog in the same bed, me daring not to move away from the far edge of the bed – it's a lack of space thing. I have found that my Hungarian has much improved, which worries me as I have done absolutely nothing to improve it. Now what does that say about studying. I suppose you submerge yourself in the language. It is taking root at the expense of my German though. My brain is obviously not capable of handling two languages at a time.

Sunday December 27th

We met up with Richard, who married Laura in the summer and we went to a tiny village by train to have a sort of annual get-together of old school friends. We ate wild boar freshly hunted and got caught in 'the great gypsy conversation'. This is how it goes. Person from the politically correct world offers the suggestion that the Roma population are a persecuted minority and there is terrible racism against them. The Hungarian in the conversation then argues that, contrary to this belief, the gypsy has only himself to blame. The politically correct Westerner is ignorant of the true problem and should not comment about things he knows nothing about. The Hungarian will quote statistics about their ludicrous gypsy birth rate, which will mean that (apparently) there will be more gypsies in Hungary than proper Hungarians very, very soon. You will hear the following anecdotes; how he has heard how gypsies never pay for public transport tickets (although the only people I had seen in Budapest getting caught were either Japanese tourists or shifty regular Hungarians) and get aggressive if they are asked to pay. They are given huge amounts of government assistance including large houses, because of their huge number of children. They will tell the famous story of the friend of a friend who lived next door to gypsies who had been given a nice new house to live in and they were so lazy to find work that they burnt all the floorboards to keep warm during the winter (I heard this one a lot). How the gypsies aren't interested in joining in decent society, how they are stupid, disinterested and uneducated, and rejected every school they were ever expected to join. I had already got bored with the arguments and had worked out that these arguments were identical to ones you would have heard from racists in England about West Indians in the 1950s. You would then ask the Hungarian, did they actually know any gypsies and, yes they did, but the ones they knew actually happened to be quite decent, but they were the exception. I was never brave enough to quote Larry's statistic (mainly because I couldn't verify it) that of all the millions of Roma who lived in Hungary, at that time, only one was actually studying at university, which if true, probably said it all about how isolated from society they are. Why do all communities need a scapegoat to blame their ills?

The village was fascinating for us. We British are not used to serious amounts of snow and our perception of snowy scenery is hilly, mountainous alpine regions. So this quiet village in the middle of nowhere on the flat plains was a new experience. The snow 'poured' down, the wind whistled and that was the only noise my ears could detect. As we legged it through the masses of snow, wrapped up like never before (I threw coolness out the window and wore long johns for the first time) back for the last train at 10.30 Richard turned to me and said, "This is just like Dr. Zhivago!" He was right. This was seriously Russian.

Richard was getting into the Hungarian life. I blame it on him receiving a ceremonial Hungarian sword as a wedding present from his father in law. We met them in Miskolc later and he was considering buying a Russian bear hat, or may be a whole bear skin to wear.

"Imagine that in Reading!" he beamed.

Then he watched fascinated as lorries attempted to barge through huge snow drifts and slid dangerously across the road. "It's a different world isn't it. How do you explain this to people back home?" he said.

"I don't even try," I admitted.

Tuesday December 29th

Returned from a quick sojourn in the mountains. We drove up to Lillafüred (the big castle hotel) and kept going up. The snow is at least six inches deep, and, Hungarians being Hungarians, the roads have only been given a cursory sweep and not touched at all past the lake. They assume we all have chains on the wheels, but the Wartburg doesn't. The Lake is completely iced up, people skating on it in coloured tunics. The waterfall is frozen up too. We kept driving up the winding roads. The Bükk hills are almost completely untouched by the modern world, silver birches fitting in beautifully to the grey skies. Eventually we make it to Bükkszentkerest. Here really is an untouched village. The air is gaspingly fresh and tinged with the smell of wood fires, plumes of smoke coming from every chimney. There are even one horse open sleighs! The Wartburg got stuck as we entered the village and the whole community came to help out.

Eight of us were staying in a log cabin, drinking mulled wine. We took sledges to the hills and had great fun careering past the skiers, skaters, horse drawn sleighs, bin liners, plastic discs. The hills were packed but the only emotion was fun. From a distance, if you are low brow, it would remind you of that video from Wham for 'Last Christmas' (minus George Michael and the unrequited love). High brow think Breughal again, but I always think of Breughal. In the evening we watched TV (it's not that backward) and I played chess with a guy called Zsolt, who spoke German. I won the first rather cleverly, and lost the second, cockily looking for the perfect mate and made a suicidal mistake.

Wednesday 30th December

I have hit a tremendous vein of studiousness with reference to the Hungarian. To assist me in my reading I have purchased a copy of FHM magazine in Hungarian. The fact that you also got a very convenient 'babes calendar' had nothing to do with the purchase.

I also bought a Hungarian business journal to try and see where Hungary is in the grand scheme of things. Comparing things such as GNP, growth and inflation with the Czech Republic and Poland Hungary is doing remarkably well. Inflation is only 7%, which considering past history, is amazing.

January

Saturday 2nd January

New Year's Eve was as expected. It started at 5pm with a drink of palinka downed in one. I should've guessed by the hushed voices as I asked for it that it was potent. I should've been really scared when it arrived in what looked like some kind of medical flask. It burned all the way down to my stomach and affected my vision. Andrea's sister had one with me. You get a lot of home-made palinka[23] here.

There was a lot of dithering about what to do but predictably Andrea and her sister Gabi were sold on a party that their friend Bea knew about. Now I warned them that past experience showed that Bea knows everyone and will desert us as soon as we get there, and we will know no-one, but the girls wanted to wear pretty dresses and not spend all the time with their drunken pals in the local bar. I was sold on the words "the best food and only 3000 forints." Of course the best food turned out to be peanuts and everyone else was lawyers who knew everyone else. Gabi and I got as drunk as possible and tried to steal some bottles of wine in revenge but Andrea stopped us. We got a taxi back to the local party.

Andrea's friends had hired a youth hostel for the night and had free reign for two days. Unfortunately the owner in a drunken state had leased out half of it to some travelling Poles, so space was very limited. The Poles were bemused.

The drinking had started at six. Andrea's cousin Gábor had arrived with a bottle of Tequila priced at half a week's wages and did what you must do with such expensive liquor – he downed it with his pals in five minutes. He never really recovered from this and we didn't see him again until midnight. Everyone was drunk, everyone was smoking. The girls looked astonishing. Richard showed up with Laura, observing the fun and 'fun' is the only word that matters. Every cheesy song and Hungarian classic were greeted with joy, no sense of irony at all. "We don't need the West!" bellowed a lad called Levente at one point as a suitably melodramatic classic about Miskolc screamed from the tape deck. Gabi was very drunk too and crumpled on a bed in the way that women do. The Doctor, the man with the manic grin, who I had seen on several occasions over the last few months, was incredibly drunk and kept bursting into our room and saying something unfeasibly funny in Hungarian which he would then try to translate into English. As his descent into unconsciousness continued he became less and less clothed. Finally he appeared naked but for Gabi's necklace.

The air was full of cigarette smoke but it was too cold to open the windows. Music blared from the social room. I chatted to a few of the English speaking guys. "Hungary is like Ireland" sticks in my brain. If I was argumentative I would have

---

[23] Schnapps effectively, made from either peach or plum.

pursued that one, because they had spotted the divided part but had no idea about the religious craziness in Ireland. Instead I agreed.

Zsuzsa and Istvan were there. Istvan sat in the corner all night with a bemused look on his face not speaking to anyone at all. He wore his *Stereolab* T-Shirt.

"Don't worry about him making Zsuzsa miserable with that sad face of his," slurred the Doctor at one stage. "She tells me he is great in bed."

There was the traditional boy girl couple completely drunk, boy kissed girl, girl didn't really want to but quite liked it despite herself. Kissing is so addictive. They crashed out in the single bed designated for Andrea and me.

Midnight, the music stopped and a rousing rendition of the Hungarian national anthem started, the boys missing the high notes completely and large amounts of Russian champagne cracked open. Then started the "Boldog új évet" and everybody kissed each other, men on men too, whilst that dire Abba song "Happy New Year" played without irony in the background.

"I have never kissed so many men in my life" I joked. The Doctor gave me a strange look. A phone was thrust in my hand at 12.15. "It's America, talk to them," said someone. I had no idea who they were, or who was on the other end of the line.

The Doctor rang up Andrea's mother. "Who is that?" says the Doctor.

"You called me," said Andrea's mum. "How are my daughters?"

Gabi grabs the phone at the second attempt. "Of course I'm OK," she said, "I couldn't speak if I wasn't OK."

Some of the Poles ventured down in cheap suits and danced a little. They were a moustachioed bunch with an over-enthusiastic female.

Things got a little hazy after this. Mainly because I speak enough Hungarian now to speak to Andrea's brother and cousin and therefore I had to drink their whisky (I'm family you see). I was also given my own bottle of Russian champagne, which as you know is the only good thing the Russians made. So I was all over the place and ended up receiving a surreal language lesson in the lavatories by a typically cool Gentlemen who couldn't understand why I couldn't pronounce the Hungarian letter 'gy' (imagine choking on a fishbone is the best way I can describe it).

I flaked out at four, next to the newly snogging couple[24].Gábor re-appeared looking devastingly drunk. He too collapsed on the bed. As did Andrea. The room was full of people and the music was deafening. I got to sleep by recalling old pupils and where they sat. I awoke at seven to see Andrea's brother collapse under the coat pile and not move until eleven. Gabi slept on him unaware he was underneath. She woke at ten and asked "Where is my brother?" and refused to believe the answer.

They like to party.

In the morning Gábor and the courting boy awoke. The courting boy got out a fresh bottle of *Unicum* and started again. And the guys recounted the incidents of

---

[24] Much as I shouldn't come out of diary mode I would like to report that the couple moved in together soon after, the snogging continued apace for about six months until they realised they really didn't have enough in common after all.

last night to uproarious laughs. The music was still playing.

Andrea and I could stand no more and went to the swimming baths. The Wartburg wouldn't start again. The hangover induced by Russian champagne and whisky made the performance even less funny than it was before. At home Andrea's mother served up some kind of black lentil dish which apparently means I'll get rich this year. If my Hungarian had been any better I would point out that, on the assumption that most Hungarians were eating this glop today, and had done so most of their lives they must realise it doesn't work!

Monday 4th January

A new term and my mood is beyond black. I don't know what it is about returning to school that sends me into such a downward spiral…actually I do know, it is because I milk the holiday to the last second so I don't ease in slowly. One minute I am partying then I am working like mad. I got through the day somehow.

Back at the school the tiny Chinese girl Li Qin is not returning. This takes our numbers below 40 again. I got through the day somehow. The promised gas supply to the laboratory had not materialised. Now that *was* a surprise. Apparently, according to the Headmaster there is a problem with the administration at their end. Don't you just love living in a 'can-do' society.

I rang John, my Hungarian class colleague. He had some news for me.

"Oh they've cancelled our class," he said. "Not enough people want to do it in the early evening."

So I now have to go on Mondays and Wednesdays at 7 p.m.

John had some other news. "I've been offered a job in two months," he said.

"Great," I said.

"The problem is that I have to speak Hungarian so I am having to do an intensive course and take it seriously," said John.

So he won't be on the new course either.

Tuesday 5th January

"This is the most disorganised school in the world," said Brittany, our more down-to-earth American today. I was quite surprised it had taken her that long to realise this. She is having a hard time at the moment. Her boyfriend Michael who has wanted to go home ever since he came to Europe now wants to stay in Budapest for another year. This would mean Brittany would have to stay manacled to the school. So her response of "No way Buster" was unsurprising.

"He just wants to put off reality for another year," she said in explanation.

I have been inundated with desperate Hungarian teachers coming up to me and saying, "our top year will no way pass their GCSEs."

"Tell me something I don't know," I said.

The problem is the teachers have not really looked at what GCSE is all about until now and only have because I have insisted they set mock exams for the week ending 29th January. Now they realise the kids can do none of it. The first problem is that the Art and Design distance learning pack has not arrived so Bea the art teacher does not know what to do (she does not even know what coursework is). The English teachers have realised the kids cannot write essays yet. This is because Stephen, a professional photographer, whose only qualification was that he spoke English, taught ESL for three months. He was asked here to do dance classes but ended up doing English. Even he admitted he wasn't a teacher at all but he was still hired.

In the evening I waited two hours at the bus stop waiting for Andrea to go to dinner with her father. I found out later, as I shivered home confused, that she had meant I should wait at the end bus stop, not the start bus stop.

Wednesday 6th January

Ági the maths teacher, in a panic, asked the Headmaster where the hell the IGCSE maths books were he had ordered for her in the summer.

"It has been six months," she said. "What is the problem with British publishers?"

The Headmaster's previous answer to this question had been, "Oh I don't know but it always takes six months," but this time he did something else: he confessed. "I didn't order them at all," he said. "I don't think you need them."

Ági was furious, not necessarily because the books weren't ordered but because the Headmaster felt he had misled her for all that time. Why not just tell the truth? Ági feels that she is the Headmaster's favourite, another Hungarian in this mad school of foreigners who don't understand. She thought she would be looked after.

I chased up the missing Art and Design distance learning pack and found we had been charged for it. So I rang them up and was told that we had signed the paper saying we had received it. But we hadn't.

The top class teachers had a crisis meeting, chaired by me where I outlined what they were telling me and told them the consequences. Ági thought that they would fail maths, Brittany said they couldn't write history essays at all, I said science was dodgy because they had not really done an experiment and we were trying to do two years of double science in six periods of week; ESL was the same story. Art was a complete non-starter. I then said did they realise that if not one child passes a GCSE it would have dire repercussions on the reputation of this school? Would parents of native speakers send their kids to a 0% pass rate school? What would parents of current students think? The School would really be in trouble. This was very serious to the teachers because this is their livelihood; I can always come home. So they were all for going and lynching the Headmaster, who seemed to care not one jot for the school's academic performance. The other scapegoat was Jackie, the woman who came in for four periods a week and taught leadership skills. However as she works for the Government as well, and was the Headmaster's neighbour she had negotiated a contract with the Headmaster that she could fail to turn up if something more important turned up. This meant that she has been in less than she has been here. So for four periods a week the kids kick their heels. She rarely bothers to call and say she won't be here so no one knows they are not being 'taught'. Putting this into context they have more 'lessons' of leadership skills than they have of chemistry. The staff want her fired and the lessons used to teach the kids how to work for examinations.

Anyway I decided that the Headmaster could cope with mad Hungarians but not a subtle Englishman so I told them I would see him and see what his feelings are about the situation.

Thursday 7th January

Yesterday evening I went to my language class. I was delighted to see Nenet, the Croatian was there. Apart from that the class was full of those studious girl types who I dislike because they can see through a rogue like me and are obsessively interested in studying. Two were American and both had mobile phones that rang in class. They immediately ran out to take the call. Now I'm with Andrea's father on this one. You switch off your mobile phone if you are busy. It is rather rude to rush out I think. Andrea's father walks out of meetings if it happens saying, "I see I am not important to you."

There was also an English chap, an Australian man, a Chinese man called Victor (not his real name I suggest) and a half Swedish half something woman whose name also escaped me. The really shocking thing was that the class was conducted almost entirely in Hungarian and the native English speakers spoke Hungarian to each other.

"Bloody hell," I said to Nenet at one stage, "my head is exploding."
Fortunately by the end of the lesson I realised that I 'knew' as 'much' as they did, they just were prepared to try and speak. This competitive atmosphere made me say my first spontaneous Hungarian sentence in class.

"What's this," I said, pointing to a dog's tail.

It did make me realise what a terrible class I was in before. Let's consider the students. There was Jake the alcoholic who had never learned a language in his life and was usually drunk anyway. He got expelled. There was also Richie, another American who interrupted every five minutes saying, "Boecsarnart"[25], or, "I'm sorry can you tell me again," or "where are we?" and the class would wait five minutes for him to catch up. He justified not paying attention by saying, "I prefer to go over it slowly with Hungarian friends in my flat."

There was Maria a troll-like Russian girl (I am not being rude, she was tiny and really did look like some mythical woodland creature) who vaguely spoke

---

[25] "Bocsànat" - sorry

English but was nowhere with Hungarian. She communicated only in high-pitched squeaks in the manner of an excited hamster. There was also Stefano and Tamara the Italian couple who lived together and hated each other. Finally we mustn't forget Grigori the Russian with the gold teeth who did not speak English and had no idea what was going on as the course was 90% in English. It is now quite clear that only Nenet and I escaped from the class with any grasp of the language.

Friday 8th January

The Headmaster revealed that he had only ordered Jessica's books in December contradicting what he said in October. He came clean because he realised Jessica was definitely leaving (she was filling out application forms). I am beginning to understand his mind. He really does not believe no is no. She told him she was leaving before Christmas and he didn't believe it. He offered to double her salary (still less than mine) and Jessica just said no. Now he has promised to get the books in the hope this will persuade her to stay.

"If they are not here by February I storm home to America anyway so it doesn't matter," said Jessica grimly.

The Headmaster then told me that yes, the Art & Design distance learning pack had arrived and the art teacher had it.

"So why is she a nervous wreck because she thinks she hasn't got it?" I asked.

"I have the paper here," said the Headmaster, "look my secretary signed to confirm it."

"That doesn't mean the art teacher has it," I said.

I asked Bea, the Art teacher and she gave me an 'are you mad?' look. So we both went and told the Headmaster that she hadn't got it.

"Well as it's not here," I said, "regardless of where it is, it means that GCSE Art is finished for this year."

"That is very strange," said the Headmaster finally realising what we were saying. Forty-five minutes later the Headmaster returned with the Art & Design distance learning pack.

"Um, for some strange reason my secretary locked this in the safe," said the Headmaster. "I don't understand why. It's been in there for two months"

"The safe?" I said. "Two months?" I said.

I pointed out that as the exams officer it would help if I were informed when documents from the exam board arrived.

Still all I can do is my job. I have prepared an exams timetable and everyone is ready. No hassle, everyone knows what is going on. Why can't I be Headmaster?

The Hungarian Girl Trap

Sunday 10th January

The weekend was spent in a state of some inebriation, because finally Robbie's bar opened. We have been hearing about this on the Miskolci grapevine for quite a while, although I haven't mentioned it before because I never thought it would happen. Robbie was another Miskolc lad trying to make good, but he did seem to have some get up and go about him. He had spent time in America, English impeccable. The bar opened only two months late and disappointingly was not named after any 'Hitch Hikers guide to the Galaxy' people (I still think 'Slartibartfast' is a great name for a bar). Instead he has named it 'Pirx' after an extremely obscure Polish sci-fi character, created by Stanislaw Lem. Inside it is quite nice, all silver girders, silver tables in weird shapes and leather sofas. It is a very Star Wars bar (without the aliens) and it was filled with types who would have been called Beatniks in the 1950s (so my father tells me) – all intellectual airs and unreachable coolness. It is a bit Miskolc though and seemed to be congregated entirely by Robbie's mates from Miskolc. This was confirmed by one guy who came in, looked around and said, "Blimey it's Miskolc Chinatown!" (This does not show my Hungarian language prowess by the way, what he actually said was 'Francba, Miskolci Chinatown!" – I think anyone could've translated this!)

Robbie hung out on every table and Andrea got drunk for the first time in twelve months, she knew people you see. I splashed out on a bottle of 'champagne' costing £2.50 which was very agreeable, then I lapsed into German (shock horror) with the non-English speakers, then had to lapse into Hungarian (double shock horror) when one guy didn't know what *hässlich* [26] meant in German.

So all in all Robbie's bar is pretty cool. It is pretty close to my ideal bar: uniquely themed by an individual not a corporation, beer is cheap, a clientele whose attractiveness (bar me) can be only be described as 'ridiculous', a cocktail menu just asking to be tried (What is a 'Ford Prefect'?) and music by The The. If you haven't heard of the The The (and there is no reason to feel bad about this, they have dated terribly) imagine a driving back beat and a singer who has read the Marquis de Sade's prison works and was convinced the world was doomed, having worshipped the paintings of Hieronymus Bosch. It also had toilets which were marked only with those strange male/female symbols with arrows and crosses. Now I always forget which one I am (not gender – SIGN) and have to stand outside guiltily waiting for someone else to go in. Weirdly there are often ten guys doing the same thing and then a woman comes along and knows immediately. Its only weakness was that it was maybe one kilometre too far out of the main sprawl of Pest, on a side street, and would attract no passing trade at all. I wondered if it had a long term future.

I spent Sunday with Petra, my private student, whose father I found out last term was one of the world's biggest arms dealers. I admired the new Mercedes (his fourth) and I wrote Petra an essay on the Weimar Republic (don't say I am not

---

[26] ugly

versatile). Finally I was introduced to the Head of the Hungarian army who was at the house as well (presumably to buy some extra hand grenades for the weekend).

Monday 11th January

There has been some kind of Chinese rebellion. One of the Chinese girls has defected to a Hungarian school and another is missing. This has seriously panicked the Hungarian teachers as they now believe all the Chinese will go. It turns out that this girl lives alone (aged 14) and has simply decided to change schools because she 'does not want to lose her Hungarian'.

Also we have a new photocopier, except it is not new, it is an identical but older model of the last one. So far it is working fine though, mainly because it has no provision for double sided or document feeding, so little can go wrong.

I have been press ganged into writing a letter to the top class parents to explain why their children will fail GCSE. I am trying to find the words that don't imply it is the school's fault when it clearly is.

Still two new students started today, neither of whom speak English and are six months behind their predecessors. This makes teaching them impossible of course because the classes are way above them. Upon complaining to the Headmaster, Naima our Pakistani English teacher was told "haven't you heard of differentiation?" I pointed out that for the Headmaster to even accept them without being able to adequately teach them was unethical and they should have waited until the end of semester (Feb.) when a new class could have been formed for beginners. But who listens to us when taking money off gullible parents is involved?

Jessica said that she lived next door to the two American girls on my language class. Apparently they were all round at Jessica's on Saturday and she showed them some school pictures and they recognised me.

"I told them you were horrible," she grinned

Language class was productive again. Is progress being made? The whole class went to the pub afterwards. The girls talked about turkey basting (!) and the gentlemen talked about why we were there (Hungarian girl trap). There was an English guy called James who works in the casino, which is rather cool. We told him anecdotes about the previous class (Jake and Trevor and knife brandishing in the pub). Still the new pub is most convivial and a pint costs 50p. The staff are used to English and don't raise the prices every week.

Tuesday 12th January

Owing to a misjudgement by Andrea involving a taxi and a forgotten meeting, I ended up £6 poorer and on the wrong side of town with twenty minutes to get to work. I was late for the first time in my professional career. This meant I missed the first assembly ever held at the school. It was meant to last ten minutes but Larry took over and 40 minutes later it still hadn't finished. He started telling anecdotes (I listened from behind the door) about how the only man-made thing you can see from space is the Great Wall of China (which isn't true by the way). So period one disappeared completely.

At 11.30 I had Naima, a fifty-two year old Pakistani woman wearing a sari almost crying on my shoulder over the Headmaster and his alleged stooge, Ági the maths teacher's schemes.

"I keep hitting a brick wall," she wailed. "She questions everything, she is lazy, forgetful and resentful. Am I a bad person Ray? I rely on you you know."

I gave re-assuring noises and Larry helped out too. She was really upset and swore, well she said 'bloody' twice, which for a woman of her background is astonishing. Then she said, "that woman, I think she is autistic or something! She forgets everything!"

Unfortunately I agreed and disagreed, Ági is very jobsworthy and rarely puts herself out. But she thinks the Headmaster is a fool as well. And as for forgetfulness…later that day I asked Naima if she needed the video room in the afternoon. She said "No" but was in there and oblivious when I took my class to use it. I put it down to her stressful day.

Jessica tried to interest me in working in the States for a year, having seen an ad in the TES[27] (she was stealing information for a discipline essay). I saw that one of the States involved in the scheme was South Carolina.

"Well I'm not going there," I said. "I wouldn't be able to teach evolution down there," then left very quickly because I realised that devout Christian Jessica doesn't accept evolution either. Whoops.

"I believe elephants were created old," she insisted.

Gerry, the Governor is no help either. I gave him a list of past papers to order at Christmas and they came up in conversation on the phone today after I'd called him to point out that a fax number he gave was not for our sister school in London but for an Indian man in Southall. Gerry had asked me if there was anything I needed and I replied, oh only those past papers.

"Oh…um…" he hesitated, "What were they again?"

I reminded him but it was pretty obvious he knew nothing about them. No surprise, half an hour later I got a fax saying "THE BOARD HAVE NO IDEA ABOUT THESE PAPERS, SILLY B________s, CAN YOU SEND ME THE DETAILS AGAIN" which I took to mean 'I have lost them and am blaming someone else.'

Wednesday 13th January

It is my birthday and every Hungarian I have met has pulled my ear lobes for some utterly inexplicable reason. I received presents from some of the kids (chocolates and

---

[27] Times Educational Supplement

a silver pen and writing paper). I faxed the paper details to Gerry but he has one of those combined fax phones and picked it up. I told him to put the phone down.

"Listen mate," said Gerry, "do you need anything because I am coming out to Hungary on Sunday now."

"No nothing," I said, exercising my great gift for suppressing surprise. Why was he coming all of a sudden?

I was teased today because of my birthday. Brittany's extra question on a year 9 history paper was: "How old is Mr. Dexter?" which, of all subjects (history) was the most cruel. A man feels bad enough at thirty anyway. Gone is his youth. All that is ahead is mortgage and death. I also neglected the Hungarian tradition of bringing in a cake to celebrate with your friends. But I did solve the ear pulling conundrum. Hungarians pull your ears and wish your ears to grow long (!) as an old person always has long ears. Rather cute I think.

Thursday 14th January

I finally published my exams timetable today. It passed without incident except that I have the GCSE students down to do three maths papers and the maths teacher thinks they have to do only two. Whoops.

Andrea and I went round to Bea, the art teacher's flat to have dinner and for me to explain GCSE and course work to her in a more convivial surrounding than over a ten minute lunch break at the school. Bea's flat is wonderful. It is on Váci Utca, the Kings Road of Budapest and the ceilings are almost five metres high and book shelves run around the room at head height. She also has some of her own work lying around (she has regular exhibitions all over the world). She offered me a whisky as soon as I arrived.

"I don't drink," she said, "but Gerry always brings bottles of it with him."

I noted that there were quite a few bottles of single malt. I declined the offer. It's amazing what happens to deputy heads when they leave schools.

As his name had come up I asked if Bea had any idea why Gerry was spending £250 to come to Hungary for two days (my conclusion — something pretty bloody serious) when Bea said:

"Wait a minute did you say Gerry was coming this weekend?"

"Yes," I said.

"Shit," she said.

"What's the problem?" I said.

"Well Gerry takes over my flat when he is here and I move out. He pays me a month's salary so it is worth the hassle but I had no idea he was coming."

"Hang on," I said. "In the Budapest Sun last year they had an interview with Gerry in their 'people' section where Gerry talked about HIS wonderful flat on Váci Utca and how great it was to live 'right in the heart of things'. But it was actually your flat."

"I know I was furious and really upset," said Bea. "It is so much hassle when he stays. I want to say no, but I need his money."

After a very good paprikas chicken we set down to business. Bea told me that the Headmaster had told her to postpone Art until November.

"Oh no," I said. "Who does he think will do the exam in November?"

Bea, who had been relieved at the let off said, "Well he said that our students would carry on to do A level…"

I stopped her there. "Bea," I said. "The Headmaster knows nothing. I hate to be so blunt but I have told him one hundred and twenty times that this school does not have the facilities or the space to do A level but he never listens. I don't think he even knows what an A level is. These kids will not return next academic year. If the school wants GCSE Art it runs in June or it never runs at all. A level will not happen."

"But is there time?" asked Bea.

"Yes," I said, not really sure but knowing this was a better option than November.

Why can't our Headmaster ever listen? We currently offer GCSEs in Science, History, Art, English as a second language and German/Chinese. The A levels we could offer with our facilities/ students are art and maths. Brittany says they can't pass History and Science has no equipment. They could offer business studies I guess but the school needs more students. We will have three taking GCSE this summer, hardly a justifiable sixth form.

So I sorted Bea out and she was delighted.

Friday 15th January

I spent a pleasant morning floating around the IGCSE switchboard being sent to various random people who kept telling me it was the receptionist's fault because she didn't seem to know the difference between GCSE and IGCSE. Finally I got through to a very nice sounding girl called Kerry who answered all my questions about Art IGCSE in a rather flirty manner that made me forget how annoyed I was. Memo to Cambridge board: all exam board people should answer questions on the phone in the manner of Kerry the Art & design officer – or is this the first sign of my mid-life crisis?

"You've solved all my problems," I told her after I'd asked some extremely facile questions.

"Not all of them surely," she said.

"So you've heard of this school then," I said.

Then I asked to be transferred to the publications department where I ordered some maths past papers on the Headmaster's credit card: a very pleasant experience.

Meanwhile received a phone call from the Israeli family saying they were withdrawing two of their children from the school. That's four this week. Also another boy's parents are considering doing the same. The school is sinking fast, yet the Headmaster was cracking jokes. He fiddles as we burn. It does make it very difficult to give a damn about the school when Tibor, the one armed physicist and I spoke to him about the fact that we needed more periods a week to cover science at GCSE. We currently had six. This was a serious request and the Headmaster treated it at a joke and pointed out that the deadbeat school in inner London where I did my teacher training managed with six.

"What do you want your school to be like?" but the question was unanswered as something else had grabbed his attention (a speck of dust if I remember correctly). So we still have four periods of Leadership skills a week and only two periods a week of physics. That's sensible. I have stopped caring.

Sasha, the school's resident naughty boy, sidled up to me today looking guilty.

"I am very sorry I have not bought you a birthday present," said Sasha, genuinely upset.

"No problem Sasha," I said.

"No, it is unforgivable. I will bring you one on Monday," and he walked off. Oh no, he likes me. I hate it when bad kids like you because you become their only hope.

Sunday 17th January

I had a weird experience at the weekend. We were back in Miskolc relaxing and marvelling about the fact the pre-Christmas snow is still on the ground. The weirdness was because I had a conversation with "Uncle László" at last. Uncle László is not an uncle, he is the significant other of Andrea's mother. He is an architect of some repute with a moustache so fine I need only say the following words to give you an idea of what I am talking about. The words are 'handlebar' and 'Lech Walesa'. His moustaches are magnificent; you can imagine Attila the Hun charging over the Hungarian plain with a similar set. László used to be a colleague of Andrea's father but I guess he moved in when Andrea's father moved out. This will cause wedding problems as Andrea says her father will not attend if László goes. So László won't be there. Apparently they came to blows in an office over this 'betrayal' – well I don't know this but in my head Andrea's father went in and decked László, followed by lots of feverish grappling. I think László and Andrea's father are similar beasts you see: brilliant, creative, passionate and bloody stubborn.

I think I like László on principle even though we appeared not to share a language. In fact when he came round in the early days I had so little idea of what the family conversation was about that I used to concentrate on counting how many cigarettes he smoked in an hour (five) to stop myself drifting off. This works out at sixty a day or one every twelve minutes. He lights one about five minutes after the last one has finished and I kind of perversely admire such a ridiculous addiction. He did try to make conversations with me but the only English words he knew were

The Hungarian Girl Trap

Beatles song titles, so he would ask me frankly surreal questions like, "Hey Paperback writer!" and "It's getting better all the time?" which are difficult to answer unless you too resort to Beatle songs. If I tried Hungarian it was "Obladi Obladah" otherwise I'd stare at his facial hair and dread blurting out "I am the Walrus". Usually I settled for a compromise of "Let it Be" or "The Fool on the Hill" I also had this paranoid fear that he thought I was a complete cretin, for no reason other than I was a Westerner and had never struggled. He is very patriotic you see and is on record as saying passionately at the last election, "We must stop licking the arses of the British and the Americans!" which I agree with actually but it's difficult to explain that.

So yesterday we met again and the conversation started again on Beatles songs. We were getting quite good at this.

"Hey Jude," I said

"Rain?" he said.

"Here comes the Summer," I contradicted.

"Happiness is a warm gun?" he said.

"Savoy Truffle," I said. We were clearly in a 'White Album' mood.

Finally he said, "Why don't we do it in the road?" and I thought to myself, he really has no idea what he's saying! Actually in my dreams I hope that I can manipulate a conversation round to some fantasy scenario where Andrea breaks into a song he could respond, impressed, with the immortal, "And your bird will sing!"

So anyway we have some food, drink some fine dry Tokaj wine and clearly he's had enough of our Beatles game and has decided this English fool must have learnt some Hungarian by now surely. So he asks me 'What news with the school?' in Hungarian.

I exhale loudly, my brain racing and all my Hungarian words run to the furthest, darkest recesses of my brain. I try to explain that four students are leaving, but probably said the Hungarian for 'Why don't we do it in the road?' judging by his baffled face. Anyway a German word must have got in there somewhere because he suddenly switches to German and we have a conversation. How it never got communicated that we both spoke German remains a mystery but off we went. And blimey was it the most intense German conversation I've ever had! I had to secretly wolf down two glasses of Tokaj to fortify the brain. So he asks about the school and what the problems are and I let it slip how much the American International School charges ($15,000) and was speechless.

"Funfzehn tausend dollar," he kept repeating, genuinely outraged and calling in various other people to tell them this news.

"I work a whole year part-time at the architect academy," he said, "and do you know how much I get paid for the whole year?"

I didn't.

"200 dollars," he said, "for a whole year!" Hungarians talk about salaries like the British talk about the weather.

I looked suitably sad and shrugged the shrug I have learned from Tibor the one armed physicist.

The rest of the conversation involved me praising the family values and strength of people here and how I actually liked living here, which surprised him. After an hour of solving the world's problems in an alien tongue I went for a lie down, exhausted.

"Blimey," I said to an impressed Andrea, "I didn't know he spoke German."

"Neither did he I think," said Andrea laughing, "but he was impressed by your answers and the way your mind works."

So I got away with that. I think I will try and revert back to Beatles songs, it's less stressful. Maybe Stones songs if he fancies a change, but then you get "Let's spend the night together" or "Turd on the Run," so maybe not.

Monday 18th January

Gerry is at the School and not saying why he is here. I have concluded that it is something to do with the Government, or the embassy refusing to ratify us a school and give us a seal of approval. As Jessica said, "I am not surprised," but it is clearly bugging Gerry because he spent most of lunch (bean soup with a boiled egg in) whispering *sotto voce* to The Headmaster about the bastards this and the bastards that. I have been unable to look him in the eye at all because I have had enough and want out and he is the person who is going to be most 'let down' as it were. He keeps patting me on the back and saying "O.K mate?"

There is also a Headmasterial mood change too. He seems to be on a "show the staff how much we're spending on stuff" trip at the moment. He showed me the plans for the gas taps in the lab ($900) and told Jessica that £3,000 had been spent on books.

"What are they special invisible books?" said an unusually sardonic Jessica this morning.

I also read a fax that came through as I was calling the exam board showing that the school pays a lot every six months to advertise the school in the Budapest Sun. So they are spending money but I bet word of mouth is a better advert and we will never do that without equipment.

Larry had a crazy weekend. He was doing one of his shows at the Jewish society on Saturday and invited some of his Iranian friends to see the show. According to Larry they were let in no problem, but suddenly, once they were in all hell broke loose. Mossad agents and heavies wanted to search the Iranians, take their photographs and see some I.D. The Iranians didn't want to give their names because their embassy might find out they were frequenting with Israelis and that would be end of them. So the scene was getting nasty and Larry, who is an Israeli citizen finally solved the problem by going completely insane and screaming at everybody that if they wanted to do this they should have done it at the door, not let them in and then give them hassle. Finally Larry dropped his trousers and was allegedly yelling "Look down here man! I'm Jewish too remember! Do you think I'd bring your enemies in here?"

So everything was O.K. "And the stupidest thing was," said Larry, "there was an unclaimed hold-all just sitting in the middle of the room AND a tobacco tin on the floor. Now tobacco tins is the Afghanistani way of bombing and these muscle-bound jerk offs aren't even looking!"

I love Larry, he is a typical loose cannon. Give him a syllabus or a scheme of work and he will ignore it. But he is a genius with kids. He walked into the year 8 classroom today yelling, "I am the barber of Seville" in his reedy tenor, then bellowing four "Figaros". I can guarantee the kids talked about opera for an hour and then wrote something brilliant after and he was supposed to be teaching Animal Farm or something. I walked past again later and Larry and the whole class were staring at the sky from the window.

He likes to find what gets to people. Jessica, the very devout Christian gets a lot of attention and she cannot argue with Larry because he has been doing this for years and she just has her faith. Larry would yell things like "And I bet she wasn't a virgin!" to try and get her to come at him. Jessica is too focussed though.

"That's outrageous," she would say quietly.

"Hey leftie," he would then say to me as he remembered I was working on the computer (I'm left handed). "I'll find out what makes you tick as well so don't you sit there quietly!"

He hasn't found it yet, we usually agree with where humanity is going and it is not a good vision. Besides he can only work on you if you tell him anything and I tell no-one anything!

Larry and I fight every day to get older kids in the prep classes promoted to their proper age group. Usually they are held back because they can't use the present perfect tense or something but they are so much happier in the right class. We were rewarded with Minoru, a Japanese boy who we begged to be promoted reading out his own story of a stroke victim in assembly today. It was brilliant and, yes an irregular verb was wrong sometimes but the work was fantastic.

Larry and I are chalk and cheese. He plays the NYC Jew too hard. Sometimes I tell him and sometimes he tells me I should quit pretending I'm a "tight assed Limey". But I think we are the only two teachers here who genuinely like children and that probably explains why we were recently voted the school's favourite teachers by the kids…I think we were the only two who even got a vote.

Sasha the Russian boy gave me some cherry liqueurs today form y birthday, bless him.

Tuesday 19th January

At the language course things are very pleasant, apart from the Americans answering their phones during the class. I have also found out what Christina, the half Swedish half somethingorother's other half is.

"I'm half Hungarian," she said blowing out Lucky Strike light cigarette smoke into the air as we sat in the "For Sale"[28] bar after class yesterday. She looked at me with pride through confident blue eyes.

Wow, I thought. If you were going to choose the nations with genetically the most attractive women in the world and merged them you are going to get a pretty dangerous woman. Of course I didn't say that. She did look predictably Swedish if you know what I mean.

"And what brings you here?" I asked in a stereotyped way.

"I teach Swedish in a school," She said.

"Really?" I said, trying to think of a way of saying, "why the hell does anyone want to learn Swedish?" without making it sound rude, but she saved me.

"I think it's because of Ingmar Bergmann," she said. "He's very popular here you know."

"And nothing at all to do with the wonders of Swedish Social Security," said Nenet, the Croatian, ever the realist.

Amy and Susan the American girls were also there. They explained why they kept their mobile phones on all the time.

"It's not because we're like rude," they said, "We just can't turn them off."

They have no phone in their flat and their school has given them these phones but all the instructions are in Hungarian.

"I would kill to turn it off," said Amy.

"I was at the movies watching 'Lolita' the other week," said Susan, "and this guy Mike calls right in the middle of a love scene. It was so-o embarrassing. 'Who's that crying in the background?' he asked. 'It's Lolita and she's not crying' I said and the whole movie house was like staring at me!"

So we had a good time. I have mellowed to the Americans, and Christina is cool by default I think. I spent most of the time telling anecdotes and they were so fascinated they had 'big ears' on. You know when they are listening so intensely they are almost sucking you and the world into their head. Bill Clinton and other politicians fake the 'big ear' syndrome but they were genuine. I took the Metro home a few stops with Christina and avoided making any reference to the fact that I live near IKEA or that I was swaying a bit after two pints.

"Didn't you learn Hungarian as a child," I asked.

"No, my father, the Hungarian, always translated for us so I never learned. I'm kind of catching up now though."

"Don't tell my fiancée this," I said. "I have convinced her our children will be bi-lingual."

"I'll keep it quiet," she said.

---

[28] Vamhaz Korut,2 – easier to walk to the freedom bridge end of Vaci Útca and look for Burger King. It's next door

The Hungarian Girl Trap

Wednesday 20th January

Some things never change. One is the Lithium, Sodium and Potassium lesson. It will fascinate kids the world over and the kids will always yell, "Oh please put a big bit in!" and the spoilsport teacher always refuses[29]. I had the metals (industrial amounts of them) the problem was what to do the experiment in. You need a glass water bath really and we have no such thing (we don't have such basics as spatulas). So I used a glass test tube container eventually and cut the sodium and potassium with a knife I stole from the dining room. The kids loved it and I must admit I loved it too.

Brittany's international cooking club begins today. It was wildly popular when first announced, mainly with the ruffian boys. I suspect their interest is more in the consumption than the preparation.

Thursday 21st January

Today was very interesting. We had another Chinese rebellion. It started on Monday with my plan to stop the swimming lesson skivers of period seven by giving them another class at school. My plan though was for the Headmaster to timetable in an *extra* ESL lesson here with a paid teacher. This never happened so we teachers were roped in to sit with the non-swimmers while they didn't go swimming on a six week rota. So, as I predicted, all the usual skivers opted for swimming. Larry, who does swimming took a note of who went and saw that two Chinese girls got on the public bus with him but didn't go swimming and went home. As Dean of Students I pointed out that this was an unexcused absence from school and they should serve a detention. Naima issued the detention yesterday and the two Chinese students left the school today because 'we are too strict.' After I'd stopped laughing and calmed down a hysterical Naima I pointed out that we could not be held to ransom by Chinese girls who have no idea what strictness is. The problem is that these kids are sent over to Hungary by their families to live alone and receive an education. They are literally fending for themselves and living off the parent's money. Therefore a normal adolescent strop, which would normally be stopped by the parents is not stopped and the kid, who no-one is responsible for, takes her own decision.

This decision led to Wendy, the Chinese teacher receiving her weekly complaints session from the Chinese but with much higher stakes. I sat with Wendy later and sympathised with both sides. Firstly the Chinese kids think the people teaching them English are no good. This is because none of the ESL teachers are native speakers. The teachers (Pakistani and Hungarian) really force the Chinese to say the "L" and the "R" sounds they cannot manage. They make them roll their R's even though we do not in English. In the other English schools they see their peers being taught by native speakers and conclude it is better. They think the school is not academically rigorous but their English cannot cope with the essays they have to

---

[29] And quite rightly, it is impossibly dangerous

write. They want a school bus and a school uniform (!) one of them has even designed a school uniform and they want internet all of which they swear was promised to them by the Headmaster when they came to the school. None ever materialised, but then neither have books! Finally they are leaving for the American School because 'it is much cheaper and you get everything there which this school hasn't got'.

This last point is particularly interesting as the American school's fees are $15,500 per year and the Churchill's fees are $8,500 per year which means they will get a shock when they see their bill and feel the discipline in the American School. On the other hand they are absolutely right. This school is a Mickey Mouse school scrimping and saving and conning the customers. I find it very difficult to get up in the morning and justify being associated with the school. In a way it could be a huge millstone around my neck. The reputation of the school is enough to seal my Hungarian fate and how do I get back for interviews in England? On the other hand, I love the chaos.

At break time, the Chinese six decided they wanted to speak to the teachers but then decided to give a letter of demands to the Headmaster instead. Then I went in and taught them some biology, we had a great laugh and I could not see where all the simmering resentment was. I guess I am not associated with the evil school, I am not what they are complaining about.

In the end it is all about communication. Larry wants to call all the parents in to talk about things and that's a good idea. We are down to thirty-five students now and the numbers won't go up. I think the whole school idea was a bad one. If you are going to build a school you build from the bottom and the kids work through the school and so the numbers increase. To be like us and take any non-speaker and try to integrate them (and go about it the wrong way) is crazy. The prep classes are farcical with age ranges of eight to eighteen. The school should offer term-long English courses to beginners where the English is brought up to standard then they go into normal lessons for their age group.

I won't suggest it though because my heart is not in it. I have no interest at all. Gerry and the Headmaster stay locked in the office discussing things. Ági, talks to Gerry about the fact that the kids aren't ready for GCSE and a 95% failure rate is on the cards. Gerry gets worried when Ági says "the school's reputation is doomed" and he then says "I don't want to undermine the Headmaster on the management of the school" and Ági says "Well the reason I came to you is because nothing gets done otherwise."

We need a timetable change desperately but it won't happen because we would need more teachers for no extra kids. They have hired another teacher to teach English and he is English and I almost wanted to tell him to run for the hills.

Add to this Bea the art teacher is still not in her flat because Gerry has stayed longer – did he tell her? No he didn't. He pays only £10 a night to take over her whole flat and Bea has had enough. £10 a night is not worth uprooting her life for.

And finally, Andrea rang the priest of the church we want to get married in in Miskolc and he wants Andrea to sign a declaration promising that any children we have will be brought up Roman Catholic. I actually don't have any objections but I think the way they went about it is a little brusque.

Friday 22nd January

I introduced sexual reproduction in plants with the Year nine today by pointing out that plants cannot mate like animals because they cannot move. Year nine, who have been goading me into discussing sex education all term, asked yet again how humans did it, so I decided to tell them how the English did it. I drew an English man on the board (he had a bowler hat on) and an English woman (skirt) and said "Well what happens that lots of men and women go down to the local disco. The women dance around their handbags and the man stand at the bar drinking beer and watching. Once the men have drunk enough beer they stare at the women and act cool. Three years later babies are made."

There was uproar.

"What about the bit in between?" asked Yevgenia, the Ukrainian girl.

"Between where and where?" I said.

"Between the disco and the baby?"

"Courtship," I said to confused looks. "For three years the man can take the woman out once a week to the movies and kiss her on the hand upon returning her home. After the first year he may kiss both hands. Then they get married then babies come."

More hysterical uproar.

"But what happens after marriage?" asks Lu Yi, a Chinese girl.

"How should I know, I'm not married yet!" I said.

"I don't believe you," said Kata, Hungarian.

"It works," I said. "How many Hungarians are there?"

"12 million," she said.

"Well there are 50 million English so it must work…and the point is plants have to have stigma and stamen and use insects because they can't go down to the disco!"

I think I should be fired.

Sunday 24th January

I had another strange weekend. Andrea and I went to the National Art gallery to admire the Monets and Manets and Cézannes and things that no-one remembers they have there, then we had to rush to go a 'relative's' graduation from school. I am not sure if she is a relative of Andrea's actually but she is called Eszter and has been taken under the wing of Andrea's father's fiancée. I was quite interested because we don't have school graduations in England.

The Hungarian Girl Trap

In Hungary things are very different. We drove to the Népstadion (Budapest's Wembley) and joined the parents of the school's children in the volleyball hall. There in the centre stood the children in neat lines according to their class. And old duffer read out some words of wisdom and nobody paid any attention at all. I mean *nobody*. Everybody just chatted to each other.

The first thing that struck me, and I am happy to challenge the argument that it was my Y chromosome that noticed this, was that there were five classes of about thirty-five children in each. Of these thirty-five or so, at least twenty-seven were unfeasibly attractive girls and the rest were rather scraggy looking boys. The girls, who all looked the way air hostesses look in adverts, were dressed in matching mini dress suits, colour dependent on which class they were in. The gentlemen were in suits.

"Is this what all schools are like in Hungary?" I said to Andrea, amazed. "I mean where are all the boys?"

Andrea had no idea and I had to conclude that these blokes were the luckiest teenagers on Earth and probably very exhausted. A more reasonable and less interesting answer is that it shows how many boys actually bother to graduate out of school here, or that the boys go off to technical Gymnasiums and this is some of school geared for non-academic female subjects (like languages)?

Andrea was most perturbed by something else.

"When I was at school during the Communist era," she said. "We were fit and strong because of all the sport we had to do. But now look at all these girls. They are fat!"

"Excuse me," I said, wondering if we were looking at the same women. "There are over a hundred women down there and two are what I'd say mildly chubby. The rest are ridiculously attractive."

Andrea gave me a strange look. "Are you serious?"

I then explained that at my school, girls fitted into two categories: ones who spat in public and ones who had spots, spectacles and did their homework.

So I was quite impressed, and was assigned to Camcorder duty, as everyone else had a reason to be there or in the video. After the presentations there was dancing. Now never has the phrase from the sublime to the ridiculous been used in a more appropriate way. First up we had the two star ballroom dancers, who danced to a medley of songs. These songs, and I swear I am not making this up, were the themes from the TV programmes "The Addams Family", "Neighbours", and, most bizarrely, "The Muppet Show."

After that we had thirty girls in wedding dresses and chaps in tuxedos waltzing to the Blue Danube (magnificent), then we had a dance by another boy deficient class. This was supposed to be like a boy band routine I guess but with 20 boys and 20 girls but there were only five boys. The girls wore deely boppers and short shorts, I can't remember what the guys wore (that y chromosome again). To a well known pop tune they pranced around and at one highly weird stage simulated sex on stage (remember there were not enough boys to do this properly as it were).

Next was Bavarian beer dancing in lederhosen, again not enough boys so fake boys had to chase girls and try to molest them in a typically Teutonic way. At this point I concluded that they could have invited various pervy Japanese businessmen to pay $80 to see this and they would have gone away happy. After this was another disco dance to 'Hot Stuff' which was quite fun and finally the wedding dresses returned. All in all it was highly surreal and you may not believe me but I have the film.

Later I stood with Andrea's father who had enjoyed it enormously and we both tried to avoid looking at all the passing women. I swear this was a supermodel convention, it was madness. Eszter, the girl we had gone to see, was very happy and I had to kiss her on the cheek and speak English to her. Her friends didn't believe I was really English you see.

We needed a drink after that so Andrea's father took us to his favourite restaurant, *The golden fish*. It is a nice restaurant. I like going with Andrea's father because he goes in and shakes the waiter's hand in a show of mutual respect. Then he orders obscene amounts of *Vilmoskurte*, a strong Pear Schnapps and everything goes a little blurry and Andrea scolds us and says "Why can't you get drunk at home[30]?"

Monday 25th January

One of the Chinese girls has returned but only to do her exams. I am dreading this week. Will my exam timetable hold up? I feel there are a few minefields I haven't noticed. Still today went smoothly enough.

Tuesday 26th January

Today was a bad day but for no tangible reason. It was everything. As I trudged through the snow to school on the thirtieth consecutive day of sub-zero temperatures I had no life in my brain at all. I had given up. It was a culmination of various foolish things. Tibor, the one armed physicist had taken all the science past papers home with him and that meant I could not prepare the science paper for GCSE. I called him and he said he hadn't got them. Then as I was about to search the rubbish skip for them he phoned back and apologised that he had forgotten he had them. He drove them round to me from the university. I had nine exams to prepare and the 'new' replacement for our photocopier that jammed on every leaf of paper was jamming on every leaf of paper. Brittany had not read her exam timetable (published by me ten days in advance) and expressed surprise at the fact there were three History papers for GCSE. She had prepared one, a paper that in no way resembled the GCSE our kids are supposed to take. My swimming pool idea of not allowing the kids to skive is greeted with such indifference by the Headmaster that I told everyone that the kids

---

[30] Which highlights a huge difference between English and Hungarian drinking. The English alcoholic goes out to drink, the Hungarian alcoholic stays in.

could do what they liked because if they didn't care if they went, Larry the swimming teacher didn't care and the Headmaster didn't care why should we care either?

Tibor, the one armed physicist drove me home and sensed my mood after I declared my pessimism for everything in the universe.

"There are two types of people in this world," he said. "The optimists and the realists."

It took a few minutes for me to realise this was a very witty remark indeed. I laughed at his wise words. He took my misery well and I am sure he was thinking, stop moaning, you have two hands.

So I went for a comisirational Big Mac and went to meet Father Gábor with Andrea. He was his usual brilliant self. We even talked about suffering for a while and he enthused about the Pope's latest book.

Wednesday 27th January

Despite my pessimistic (realistic) assumption that the Headmaster would not change the timetable, it appears that he is going to. However I now wish he wasn't because I had forgotten the Headmaster's first rule of anything: don't spend any money. The claims for a new year ten to split up the non-GCSE students from the GCSE students must happen but for it to happen either I work every period on the timetable or he pays for another science teacher. I know what will happen. So the other option is to cut down to one prep class of English speakers but that doesn't help the real beginners. We need two prep classes and a year ten and it can't work without more people. Also he wants this to come into place at 9 a.m sharp next Monday. Remember he hasn't started work on it yet.

To give you an idea of the weakness of some kids in year 11 English, here is an example of an answer from an IGCSE ESL paper. Q: Which three countries on the map have a shortage of water. A: The United Nations and a water pump.

Judit, my Hungarian language teacher really likes the new group I am in. "You are the best group I have ever had," she said seriously today.

Nenet and I were very pleased because it meant we had been in her best AND worst classes: a great record. She has invited us all out for a meal and beer on Saturday but I cannot go because I have to be in Miskolc to go to church and meet the priest who runs the church, the one who wants Andrea to sign that our children WILL be Catholic. Even Andrea felt sorry for me.

Thursday 28th January

I am very pleased to say that my exam timetable is working splendidly, despite two full time members of staff equating the words 'exam timetable' with the other words 'well Ray'll sort that out I'm off to New York, or maybe skiing'. I am actually rather pleased with myself because it is so smooth that no-one has noticed it is going on. And considering how much chaos usually surrounds anything here I am very happy.

The Hungarian Girl Trap

News on the Headmaster's new timetable is worse than I thought. I warned Andrea last night that it was going to be bad and although I have not seen the Headmaster today, rumours via Ági, his stooge are terrible. He is planning to move practically every kid out of the prep classes except the three beginners. This means Brigitte, a ten year old beginner will end up with thirteen year olds, as will other kids who are beginners. This will slow down the only classes where academic progress is made. The other alternative is to keep two prep classes and not have a year ten, but promote another couple of kids into the 10/11 class, further lowering the English ability and ruining completely the chance of GCSE. The haunting word DIFFERENTIATION would then be used to explain how to teach this class. Parents do not pay $8 000 for differentiation by laziness. What is the point of changing the timetable to favour two students when the rest of the school will be adversely affected?

The other nightmare is that Réka cannot come in on Mondays anymore and Árpád is rumoured to have decided to use me as the German teacher. So the school's ambition is such that they think it is fine to have a man whose German is barely comprehensible after two pints of beer, teaching the language. No wonder there's a waiting list to get into this school. He hasn't told me this and we are one working day away from this thing starting. I do like a brave man. I have decided to write a rather biting resignation letter and hand it over as soon as is reasonably possible after the timetable change.

Friday 29th January

I am fighting a losing battle with Láci Bácsi, the caretaker. For the last two days I have moved all the desks into position for exams. This meant moving two desks from another room, a large aspidistra and other large removal jobs. Every morning this man has moved everything back. I am secretly amazed at how far he will take his job in order to do this, as it is enormous work and surely he must notice that it is back to my way at 9 a.m. In revenge I brought the art room smoothly into exam room mode and promised faithfully in 'beyond broken' Hungarian to return the desks to their original places, then 'completely forgot'. Dexter 1: Communism 1

Sunday 31st January

This weekend Andrea and I went to church that we will marry in. It is the actual church that Andrea was baptised in so she was very pleased when the priest found her Christening entry in the huge book. Church was packed, we had to stand at the back. The congregation didn't take their hats or coats off, it was a bit nippy, and the priest gave a twenty minute sermon on the evils of money and how it does not bring happiness. Andrea kind of said that he suggested we unburden ourselves of our money and give it to the Catholic church but I cannot confirm this. He might as well have been talking about raccoons for all I understood.

February

Monday 1st February

Today was more fun than I expected. Even Naima our gloriously loyal Pakistani has had enough of the Headmaster and, as he has been absent for what seemed like days, the whole staff were in revolutionary mood, which is what happens if you don't have top-down communication.

Brittany, bleary eyed from Superbowl night in the 'Ball 'n'Bull',[31] wanted to kill him for not keeping his morning appointment on Friday. Everybody else just wanted to see what the new timetable would be like. In the end it didn't materialise at all, it is apparently postponed.

Most annoyed was Jessica, who still had not received her books, ordered in August. Today was her deadline for the books. She said if they were not here she was going home to Pittsburgh. The Headmaster promised them. Guess what…

"They are held up in customs," insisted the Headmaster who had been insisting this for two weeks.

"I don't care," snarled Jessica, "I am not coming tomorrow, I am on strike." Then, with the kind of inevitability that shows we cannot win and that the Headmaster lives a charmed life, the telephone rang. It was the Customs and Excise people. The books would be delivered straight away. Jessica changed into a happy bunny and said things like "I can teach for the first time in three months." I moaned and wondered how the Headmaster got away with it again.

But he had tried one trick too far. In his eternal quest for money saving he leapt on a Naima remark about the joy of the week, the Chinese food on Mondays.

"Oh we could do with a change sometimes," she allegedly said to him.

Right, thought the Headmaster and got rid of the Chinese food. Instead we got the grottiest slice of synthetic pizza we had ever seen. Nobody ate it.

"Where's the Chinese food gone?" was the cry from everyone.

"Naima!" yelled others.

Naima walked in.

"Why did you tell the Headmaster to change the food on Mondays?" yelled one teacher.

Apparently the Headmaster had subtly changed the story to the spin in the above quote. Naima, appalled as everybody else, took one look at the pizza and ate the ham fritter and spinach paste the other (supposedly inferior) Hungarian school we share the building with had. She had forgotten her Muslim world view she was so offended. The teachers of the other school looked incredibly smug as they saw our food.

---

[31] American sports bar. Rákóczi st 29, Pest

"How come we are a private school and they have no money, but their food is so good?" asked Naima. "Why does that man have to penny pinch everything?" she said to me. "I said to him, casually that a change would be nice, especially if it was pizza from the Pizza Hut, you know. I didn't expect him to do anything and this isn't Pizza Hut."

"Where's the democracy?" yelled someone else.

Wendy, the Chinese teacher, who organised all the Chinese food was put out because she had worked hard to get the food. The Chinese, who are all rebellious right now, are rattling the bars still further. Crazy times

Anyway the pizza was so foul, half of it was uneaten and the Headmaster ate alone in the dining room, impervious to the outrage and seemingly believing he was good at his people management. He offered passers-by a slice. Later ten slices of the orange horror appeared in the staff room for the afternoon. Ági flinched as she walked past it.

"Jesus, it's nuclear," said Larry.

I covered the German class indifferently and reluctantly because no-one has said it is permanent. I will wait for Naima to confirm the permanency when he talks to her, not me. Then I will resign. Nobody had noticed/cared that the French teacher didn't show up so, whilst I was covering the German class, I popped out into the corridor where the kids were hanging around and talked to them in very rusty French. It was quite funny actually but don't tell anyone I enjoyed it. That is tantamount to asking for the job permanently.

Tuesday 2nd February

We have a new student and he's English, he's seventeen and he's flunked his GCSEs. He dropped out of sixth-form college and has run away to live with his entrepreneur brother in Budapest. The Headmaster is slavering at the thought of a native speaker and impressed them by letting me do all the talking. The guy has little brain but I'll sort him out.

Wednesday 3rd February

What a crazy day! Now as you know staff dissatisfaction is running at an all time high. None of the staff have anything good to say about the Headmaster and we don't even get mad at the damn photocopier anymore. We shrug and give up. Naima, a most diligent woman was shocked with herself yesterday.

"Ray you will not believe this but the Communication Skills woman did not show up again and the class was sitting quietly waiting. There was no-one available to cover and the Headmaster will not pay for extra cover so I just looked at them and told them 'go home'."

She laughed out loud at this point. "I've never been so naughty!"

The main reason for today's tension was Larry. Larry, as I have said is the loosest of loose cannons. He's so loose he's often completely off the ship. He's emotional, dramatic and argumentative. Often he argues but he's not debating. He's not interested in the other's opinion, just expressing his. I love him of course but he can make people's life a misery.

The first problem was that Larry went away last week to New York and we had to cover his classes. Naima disliked this, as the Headmaster will not pay for cover teachers. Therefore the four salaried teachers have to make up 19 periods between them. The other problem is that Larry's other business (he acts as an agent for getting young Hungarian basketball players into US universities) is hitting a brick wall because of the closed ranks of Hungarian basketball's ruling body. Larry comes into school mad, as he had been fobbed off yet again and spends ten minutes berating the world, accusing only Israel of being a more corrupt country than Hungary. So he was in one of his moods. He sets off marking exam papers (he expressed surprise that he had to mark papers he set) and commented that a Russian girl had written a great story. Naima, a woman who loves to butt into other conversations, butted in at this point to contradict Larry.

"I am her ESL teacher Larry and her English is terrible," she said.

"Whaddaya talking about?" said Larry.

Naima explained that the girl wouldn't know her present perfect tense from her elbow (I am paraphrasing).

"So what," said Larry, "I'm from the Bronx, as long as you can be understood it's O.K."

He came over to look at the girl's ESL paper that Naima was marking and proceeded to criticise her marking.

"What's wrong with 'I booked a pizza'?" he said. "I understand it. 'I am waiting in the bus stop?' I understand it. What's wrong? You are stifling her creativity Naima. I know poets in New York who would kill you if you corrected this stuff. Leave her alone!"

He took apart the whole marking process. Naima was upset and silent.

At lunch time Naima came up to me and asked me to help her. She took me to a private room and sat me down.

"Now Ray, I am an old Pakistani woman and maybe I am not as 'with-it' as I was. Can I ask you…was Larry right? Is my English wrong? You are the only one who can help."

I sat with her and I pulled out all the things in the paper that was bad English and she was so happy because she agreed with every one.

"Naima," I said, "You teach E.S.L. It is your job to get them speaking correct English. Larry can't do grammar, he is in denial. He doesn't want people to find him out. What he does creatively with the kids is fantastic but you know your job and just do it. Kids have to learn the rules before they can break them."

Naima was so happy she said the words, "I am so glad our paths have crossed in this life!"

There was a staff meeting for the afternoon and with Larry 'out there' it promised to be a good one. I took up my usual position as secretary and wrote them live in to my lap top. It means that my minutes do reflect the emotions of the meeting and this meeting had one hell of a lot of emotion.

Within minutes of the start Larry was off. The Headmaster said the 'other school' had invited us to a party and it was reported that our kids do not want to go for racial reasons. Our Chinese girls get teased a little by the other school's kids. Larry took this as a starting point to berate Hungarian society for being intolerant and then went onto a monologue about the bastards in the Hungarian basketball ruling body. Then in mid-rant he remembered that in gym today one boy had choked another boy. It was a serious assault and the boy should be punished. I ventured that the school rule said that such an attack meant a suspension but the Headmaster demurred (which was the reason I suggested it). Ági agreed and said, "why is he telling this now", which was a good point. What did Larry do? Why didn't he send the boy to the Headmaster? (Answer he might as well have sent the boy to see the school cat) Larry launched into his old monologue about Slava, a Russian boy last year who blew up a classroom (!) and wasn't punished and who also beat a boy senseless and nothing happened.

"I just guessed the same would happen," he said, "nothing."

The Headmaster ignored this but Naima didn't. She was a bit behind

"Someone blew up a classroom? I thought he was playing basketball? If he blew up a class room he should be expelled I think."

Brittany got us back on track with a suggestion to talk to all the relevant people tomorrow and then suspend the boy.

"Good," said the Headmaster, " and you Brittany, as Dean of Students can sort it out. Unfortunately, I will not be available in the morning (surprise surprise)."

This took people by surprise as I am Dean of Students in the staff room but the Headmaster has simply transferred the old title onto the new person who had taken the old person's job. I said nothing and Brittany said, "Am I?"

Ági was still needling Larry about why he did nothing at the time the incident happened and Larry yelled "Well what would Miss. 'know it all perfect pants Ági' have done then? Let's hear her words of goddam wisdom…"

Silence.

"I'm waiting," said Larry. He knew he had messed up and was blustering.

The Headmaster saved him by going on for a while about the fact that books were on their way and look how good the primary books are! Jessica, who wasn't at the meeting said the Headmaster was convinced she would stay at the school now the books were here. He also promised internet (again), Bunsen burners (again) but no tripods (how many times have I tried to explain?)

Then Larry wanted to say something else.

"I get the feeling that there is some resentment about the fact that I was not here last week and people had to cover for me. I wanna say something. First of all I RESIGNED last year and only came back when the Headmaster and Gerry promised me I could have this week off. I didn't know that the school wasn't going to pay for another teacher. But remember last year I covered a hundred classes and now my other jobs mean that my timetable is too tight to cover any one else."

Naima was waiting for this. "The reason is that the Headmaster is not prepared to pay for other people to cover classes. Therefore it means there are four full time teachers, Ray, myself, Brittany and Ági who cover every class. We cannot do it."

Headmaster: Yes but you are of course paid if you do more than three extra a week.

Dexter: That's not true, you tend to apply a rather obscure mathematical equation to the figures (I hadn't forgotten how nine extra periods in 7 days became 3 a week for two weeks)

Headmaster   (trying to be clever) There is not a list of teachers I can call. People can't just wait at the phone in case someone is sick. (not really getting the idea of supply teaching).

Naima   I have a list of people who would happily come in and cover classes. I showed it to you.

Headmaster   But they are not qualified teachers. We cannot use unqualified people (with a smug look).

Brittany   I'm unqualified.

Dexter   Jackie, the woman who does communication skills is unqualified, Wendy, the Chinese teacher is unqualified, Steve the Dance teacher you hired to teach English was unqualified and incapable of teaching English, Oxana the personal assistant to Jackie who you had taking over from Jessica one day is unqualified. I am unqualified to teach maths, German, French, E.S.L and geography yet I have taught all of them this week!

Larry   I was supply teacher for twenty years. There are people out there.

Naima   All the people on the list are qualified teachers and are keen to work.

Headmaster   No, they are not qualified.

Naima   Oh yes they are. I know them.

Headmaster   (Perspiring) No…(said with weary but unfathomable finality).

Ági (pursuing her own agenda)
        But Larry don't you think it is unfair that you are paid as a full timer but cannot do covers?

Larry (yelling at Ági)
        Right that's it. I've had it with you! O.K folks I need to say this but one year ago after I HAD COVERED A MILLION CLASSES FOR THIS WOMAN…I ask her to cover one English class for me while I go to my chiropractor. Guess what she says (puts on a whiney voice), 'I'm not doing it, it's not my English class' So don't you come at me with that holier than though shit.

Ági (interrupting with her own shouting)
        Oh here we go…now you have brought this up I might as well tell everyone that after this you wrote me the rudest, foulest letter I have ever received.

She stormed out to compose herself.

I had heard this story before from Larry but he never mentioned that he had sent her an abusive letter.

Larry (In blackmail mood)
        I know that I have other jobs and I love the kids here but if the Headmaster and governors think that I am a hindrance here then I'll leave. I have a life and if it can't fit in then…O.K I'll go.

Silence from the staff. Much as I love the guy he causes as many problems as he solves.

Headmaster   I haven't said I wanted you to leave.

Next was an unminuted section. The school isn't keen to pay excessive tax and has avoided doing so in its short time in existence. I am paid by an overseas company, as are Brittany and Jessica. But the native Hungarians are just paid cash in hand. The tax man is snapping on the heels and it was now revealed that the Headmaster has spent most of his time recently coming up with a way of avoiding paying tax. The school is a charity and the staff will be doing research into education here. They will receive a 'grant' from the trustees of the School which, by staggering coincidence, is exactly the same as their normal salary. I found it all highly dubious.

The swimming pool was argued about. The kids hate it, the staff hate the hassle but the Headmaster insists they swim because "It is part of the curriculum. What next they give up maths too?"

"What curriculum is this?" I asked in my smart-alec way. "If it's the UK National Curriculum then we'd better add technology, R.S and PSHE pretty fast."

The Headmaster refused to be drawn on which curriculum we used: an imaginary one I think. I suggested we did swimming in a one term block like in England but the Headmaster said it was 'impossible' to book a swimming pool in such a way(!)

After two hours we still haven't discussed the relevant thing which is why the hell hasn't the new semester started yet? Answer, the Headmaster hasn't done the timetable yet. I will be on an extra four periods a week but I don't mind because it will be four good science lessons with a new 'year 10' being created. I will also double up another period where I am teaching one period and set work for the GCSE candidates. I want them to get their GCSEs more than I care about anything else. I doubt the rest of the staff will be so accommodating.

This new timetable caused even more furore because all the part-time teachers wanted to get more time for their GCSE subjects. Tibor, the one armed physicist and Bea, the art teacher were gamely trying to grab the Headmaster's attention. He was ignoring them. Both then grabbed me to do the business for them.

"You are better at it than us, we get emotional, you are concise," they said.

So I told the Headmaster that we needed extra periods in these subjects but he did his usual trick of hearing the phone ring or changing the subject because he does not want to pay the part-time staff extra.

"It's so important," said Tibor, "that I would sacrifice an IT period with prep class to have the time."

"No," said the Headmaster, "who would teach the one period of IT to the nine year olds?"

"Aaaaaah," said Tibor.

So the Headmaster changed the subject to the new English boy.

"Maybe he could be given more time and could take his GCSEs in November."

"And then what?" I said.

"Well we could unofficially start him on an A level course."

"Where will he do A levels?" I said.

"Here of course," said the Headmaster.

I shut my eyes and prepared to launch into my 'there is no way we are prepared for A level' speech again. I have said it a hundred times to his face already. He never listens.

"One," I said, " we have four students in year 11. Two, the only A levels we can offer are: maths, but they all got F's in their mock GCSE, and languages."

"There is no English as a Second Language A level?" said the Headman.

"No"

"But there is chemistry and physics"

"Look I've told you, to do it properly you need to employ a part time technician, you need the students to get A or B to even cope with A level and they are entered for the C to G GCSE paper. You need to spend £10,000 on equipment, you need access to the lab when I want it not when you have negotiated it. You need running water on every bench…"

"Oh we can get water, that is very simple."

"So was getting gas and we are six months down the line. You do that at A level and you stop the course."

"Water is no problem,"

"But is it economical to pay me my salary and teach A level eight periods a week to one student?"

"Eight periods a week for A level," said the Headmaster with a smile that suggested he knew better. "Do you really need 8 periods a week for A level?"

At this point it was time to go home before someone murdered him. Tibor gave me a lift and I promised to write on paper exactly why A level couldn't happen so the Headmaster had it in front of his eyes.

I was shattered and went to language class. There I was so wired I understood everything whilst fellow students begged for alcohol and flagged.

The problem is the school relies on me to tell the Headmaster everything. Every teacher whose job, whose livelihood is tied up here depends on me to get things done and I don't have the motivation.

Thursday 4th February

The big day dawned, the first ever decisive disciplinary action was going to take place.

"I'm twenty-three," said Brittany and I'm the Dean of Students. How is this possible? I look younger than they do."

I grinned. "You'll be fine," I said.

"Oh no you don't scumball, you're coming in with me," she said with a look of fire. "Just because the Headmaster thinks I'm the Dean of Students doesn't mean that the real one is going to get out of this."

However nothing actually happened. Larry, the witness, rang in sick having 'remembered' an important dental appointment; Ági, the boy's tutor 'overslept' and turned up at 9.40, and the boy himself didn't show either.

"Right that's it," I said, giving up. "The Headmaster can deal with it tomorrow."

The Hungarian Girl Trap

Friday 5th February

Larry arrived early with the receipt from the 24 hour dentist AND the still bloody tooth to prove he was there. He then wrote out his resignation letter, his fifth of the year, saying if he didn't quit he would never get his businesses going properly.

Shock of all shocks the timetable arrived and is the kind of sensible document we should have had six months ago. I have lost my prep. class maths (hooray) and now only teach science and somehow I finish at 1.15 on Mondays, Wednesdays and Fridays. Suddenly my life is very simple indeed. Brittany's probably annoyed though, what I gain she will lose and her four afternoons a week off are a distant memory.

Talking of Brittany, she has being doing a 'who is the most significant person of the 20th century and her suggestions on the blackboard have been almost unanimously American (Roosevelt, Eisenhower etc). The kids were more British orientated with The Beatles getting one essay and Churchill getting a few others. However I was most interested in two Chinese entries. The first from an 18 year old girl called Li Fan, fresh out of China, who nominated not Chairman Mao, but Deng Xiao Ping, the recent (but may be dead actually) leader of the People's Republic. Reasons? "He opened up China and people's lives improved" Fair enough but the British will like this one. "Deng Xiao Ping suggested to recover Hong Kong. Finally in 1997, 1st July, Hong Kong came part of China. He had the foresight to plan two systems in China (in Hong Kong we have a capitalist system in the other parts of China we have socialism). He has also trained up a successor."

I love it, I never realised that us giving back Hong Kong was part of Chairman Deng's great plan.

The other one is from a girl called Lu Yi, who nominated her parents because, "they always help me. When I wrote a bad examination I was sad because I could not go to the very good school. But my parents said no problem we will send you to the bad school, you can study hard and then you can go to the good school."

So she has a high opinion of us then.

Brittany knows I love these and is making a collection of them for me. I can see why she has trouble teaching modern European history to these kids. One couldn't find China on the map!

So somehow the timetable is how we want it, but the Headmaster still isn't sure about A levels.

"Look Ray," he said. "I know we are miles off International Baccalaureate but isn't there an International A level?"

"I've never heard of one," I said.

"Because in Hungary students don't do all these experiments. I'm sure it is not necessary. Isn't there a course where they don't have to do experiments?"

I said, "I don't think so." I thought, if there is I won't teach it. Our Headmaster still believed in the Prussian method of teaching, dictation and endless facts learnt and no practical work. It was gloriously outdated but prevalent still in

Hungary. It made him so unbelievably unsuited to run an international school though.

Naima told off the French teacher today for teaching her students in Hungarian. This is perfectly justified, the school is a British school, however it should be pointed out that the teacher is Hungarian and both students were Hungarian and therefore to speak to your own people in a foreign language when you are learning another foreign language could be seen as being a bit pointless. I am glad Naima loves those jobs because I am too practical to be bothered with daft rules like that.

We also suspended the violent boy today, a momentous day it was then, as this was the first time it had ever happened here. Brittany said to me, "Well everybody including the Headmaster is here, why don't we do it?"

"Good idea," so I grabbed Larry, Ági and the boy and marched them into the Headmaster's office. He was on the phone.

"We're all here, let's get on with it," I said. The Headmaster gave me a 'do I have to' look. Then I realised I had taken out all the staff from the school to do this so I went and covered four classes whilst they got on with it, I justified this because Brittany is the official Dean of Students and the Headmaster was there. I was called back in later when the two Americans and the two Hungarians couldn't agree on the length of the suspension. The Headmaster and Ági wanted one day, Brittany and Larry wanted two days. I said two and walked back out again. The boy cried as the Headmaster told him his fate, although it must be said that the Headman didn't want to deliver the blow, he wanted Brittany to do it.

Sunday 7th February

The Weekend can be summarised with two words: Homosexuals and nuns. Don't tell me I live a boring life! On Saturday me, Andrea, her sister, Endre went out and met Robbie, who owns the Pirx bar. Pirx was a bit dead, has the novelty worn off? Besides they've sacked the barmaid who can't calculate bills properly. So we sat there wondering where to go. Andrea claimed to have itchy soles (she wanted to dance) and Robbie said that Café Cappella[32], a gay bar was quite cool for dancing. Andrea's sister wasn't too keen and thought the 'tattoo evening' at the E-Klub was a better bet. I just shrugged my shoulders and let the evening happen. So we went to the gay club under the assumption that that's the place with the best tunes. I also asked Robbie what he was doing in the gay club in the first place.

"Oh it's not *that* gay," he said, "it's just full of tourists."

Not on Saturday night however. I've always been quite keen to go to a gay club – not for the clientele of course but for more scientific reasons. O.K I have in the past, usually in Germany, stumbled accidentally into gay pubs if you like and only realised about ten minutes in. Once a pal and I wandered into one in Frankfurt and realised only later why everyone was so nice to us. But a night club was different and

---

[32] Belgrád rakpart 23, by the Danube on the Pest side

I was interested. Why? Because this is the only place I am likely to get any impression of what being a woman in a night club is like. Now if you are a woman in a club you spent most of the time being stared at, letched at, touched up and generally hassled. Women aren't so predatory and to know what it must be like you've gotta have a man after you. Of course it is horrible to be errm pursued and now I know.

"If I was that way inclined," said Endre, "I'd have five boyfriends by now." We had been in there five minutes. I walked the thirty metres from the bar to the toilets. One gentleman thrust his groin hard into my hip as I went past, two stared me up and down, another gentleman blew a kiss but I stared steely eyed at my destination. The toilets were guarded by two sniggering guys who must have noticed my dark look as I went in because they stopped giggling. The experiment was over, the liberal Dexter was gone and he found himself thinking, the next person who makes a pass gets a good slap. Then, mortified that it had taken a gay bar to find my violent male side I reprimanded myself and sashayed back outside and grabbed the Sàri sisters in a show of heterosexuality. I hope my admirers didn't think they were drag queens!

The cabaret consisted of middle aged women singing Spanish songs, a 'woman' dancing to Madonna. I say 'woman' because Endre said she wasn't a woman but a cunningly disguised chap but she damned well curved like women do. There was a camp dance troupe and two Matadors in thongs. I wasn't sure which one was the bull. All good clean, camp fun but I always watch these bizarre things thinking, do you really do this for a job? Then the 'great' music turned out to be Erasure covers so we gave up and went home. Endre and Robbie stayed though.

What about the nuns. Well on Sunday we went to see a stage performance of "The Sound of Music" in Hungarian. It was perfectly pleasant and I recommend anyone see it. The nun was prettier than Julie Andrews, which, if unlikely, made the production more watchable.

Monday 8th February

Ah bless the Headmaster. He had told half the staff what the new timetable was but not the other staff. So which one do we use? I was all for getting the change done but it was undecided. 9 a.m arrived and finally the Headmaster turns up.

"There was a slight problem with the new timetable," he said. "Here is a new one. I only have today's. I will work on the rest now."

To various aaaaaahs, we set about changing the classes, as to my suggestion. Unfortunately we had to change classrooms too because of the different sizes of the new classes. Naima was so flummoxed by the whole thing that she refused to leave the staff room all day and left five periods untaught. She wrote her reports instead (due tomorrow). The photocopier was shedding bits of plastic and springs and so the man was called out again. He has been in every day for ten days. He fixed it, but the copier would then print half the page, the other half on the next page, nothing, another half, a side, then jam again. We are getting another photocopier tomorrow (another refurbished one).

"Doesn't he ever learn?" said Ági.

Larry is up to no good too. He has invited all the native speakers around to his flat tomorrow to talk about 'school stuff'. Brittany thinks he wants to form a union. Alternatively I expect he will want us to write a letter to the governors saying you will lose all your native speakers at the end of this year.

The new English boy Chris is turning out to be rather stupid. He did not know what 'exuberant' meant in class today and seemed to have never studied a language or a humanities subject. We have given up on literature after he'd only heard of one book on the reading list, Frankenstein.

"Oh I think I saw a film of that once," he said in his Bristolian accent. He mixes up basic things in science too, but he is pleasantly full of incredibly daft questions which brightens up the usually mute year 11 class.

Tuesday 9th February

Naima never ceases to amaze me. She admitted today to being a great fan of the almost taboo 1970s British comedy "Mind Your Language"; a show that poked fun at immigrant ethnic minorities as they learned the English language at night school.

"Oh I have every episode on video cassette," she giggled. "It is so funny!"

This I found rather strange. There is no way that this show could ever be shown on television now because it is (an I have no doubt about this) peopled entirely by African and Asian stereotypes and the lines uttered by the cast would never be used in a modern society. Yet Naima genuinely loves it and quotes her favourite lines to me as I quote 'Monty Python' or 'Little Britain' to my friends. I am not exactly sure what I make of it all and may go and watch some with her to see if it is my memory or her sensibilities that are failing.

Larry's grievance session at his house was fun. Jessica went tutoring instead so it was just Larry, Brittany and I. Larry was unable to keep our meeting secret and everybody knew where we were going. This surprised me. If a bunch of Yanks had come to an English school and were having meetings together to discuss school issues the English would be most put-out, maybe even angry. But here the Hungarians seemed to think it was a good idea and seemed to expect this summit meeting to solve all the problems. I think Larry's advertising was very shrewd.

At 7.49 we arrived at Larry's flat.

"You damn Anglo Saxons," he beamed. "You're ten minutes early! If you were Israeli you'd arrive at 11.30 and say 'Why didncha wait for me?' when you find I gave up and went out at 9.30."

So over hummus, pitta bread and listening to Herbie Hancock we just talked as six inches of snow fell outside. The grievances weren't new but the politics got tougher. The Headmaster was attacked.

"Some schools are pro parent," said Brittany, "Some are pro student…and we are pro money!"

"He's crazy," said Larry and claimed all of his 'sort' had a similar 'leave it alone it'll be fine' attitude. "I had relatives who were the same," he said.

Larry told stories about the early days of the school, one classroom in an office block and they were about to be evicted because the teachers couldn't control the kids and the were rioting. The Headmaster was simply the maths teacher at the time. One day, Larry, new to town, turns up looking for work. The Jewish network had pushed him in that direction.

"I walk in and Gerry (the English governor) and the Headmaster were in the corridor tearing their hair out because they did not know what to do with the kids in the class room. 'I need a job' I say. They say, 'Well go in there and sort that lot out.'

"So I walk in and just stand there for two minutes. I always do that with a new class and soon everyone is staring at me. A girl has sunglasses on, I put them over my eyes and say, 'these are too expensive for you, they suit me better.' Then Slava walks in…he's the guy who blew up the classroom a year later. He's a Russian Greek God, tall, blonde like some Russian super athlete. He walks in twenty minutes late, puts his feet on the desk and puts his walkman on. I go over and turn it up to the loudest volume. He pulls off the phones and I do some mime talking, pretending he can't hear me. The class is in hysterics and he's laughing too. They were fine after that."

So we put together an agenda for change and felt happier for doing so. I was happy just to talk with friends though. I stopped caring a long time ago.

Wednesday 10th February

Tibor the one armed physicist had forgotten he still had some of his university work in his pocket. It was a superconductor, Yttrium Barium Copper Oxide. It looked like a slither of carbon fibre.

"It's formula is $YBa_2Cu_3O_{6.5}$," he said with a grin. "The oxygen has to be between 6.5 and 6.9 or it doesn't work…oh and you have to be at about 93K" (that's about $-200^{\circ}C$).

It must be strange for such a brilliant man to have to teach IT to ten year olds to make ends meet. I can't see Hawking doing the same thing. He's very kind to me considering my beloved subject chemistry is only considered to be applied particle physics to him.

The staff room ears were flapping as Brittany and I continued our grievance discussion. The Headmaster's secretary kept coming in to make litres and litres of tea. Ági, was also pretending not to hear. I don't think Ági is in the Headmaster's pocket (although Larry suggested something so disgusting I cannot even begin to put it down here) but Brittany was convinced.

"The Headmaster knows everything now," she said.

"So what," I said.

The suspended boy was back with mother. She had decided to pull him out of the school, which was the correct decision. She had a business in America and left him in the trust of the father who never came home until late at night. He promised to work hard at school but it was taking its toll. A mother should be with her children. She will take him to Pennsylvania in March. Brittany, as Dean of Students and Naima agreed with the tearful woman and hugged her and told her she was doing the right thing. The Headmaster took her into his office for an hour and tried to convince her to change her mind. This neatly answered Brittany's question from last night: we are a pro money school.

Wouter my lazy Dutch boy brought in the greatest excuse letter ever to justify his week-long absence from school. His father, a writer, who signs his name in the shape of a mouse (his surname means mouse in Dutch) gave me this note.

"This is to notify you that Wouter was absent because of the unexpected death of our oldest, eighteen year old cat.

We had to grieve about this lifetime companion, and there were things to be arranged, so nobody felt like going to school, work or anywhere.

I guess you can understand this.

Michael Mass."

This set the entire staff room off in giggles. Firstly what was so unexpected about an eighteen year old cat dying and secondly what the hell were 'the things to be arranged'? Did it have a last will and testament?

At break time the Headmaster's secretary Éva sidled up to me and said.

"Ray what do you think of the school?"

"Errm, I think it has some great teachers," I said, "but then I would say that wouldn't I!"

She was on a mission though. "It's just that I want to see that all the books are ordered in advance so that they are here for you in September not six months late. Would you tell the teachers to put a list of everything they need and we can sort it out.

"O.K," I said.

She sensed my scepticism. "The Headmaster was very cross that the books were held up in customs," she insisted. "We want this school to be the best."

I sense three reasons for this conversation from a woman who hardly deigns to talk to me most of the time. 1) She overheard the American's moans (and I include myself as a Yank here for clarity) this morning and saw the writing on the wall. Her job goes if we all walk out. Therefore she will try her best to keep us here. 2) She is genuinely upset (all of a sudden) over our lack of resources and feels morally compelled to help us, despite refusing to lend me 'Blu-Tak' six months ago 3) The Headmaster put her up to it.

The Hungarian Girl Trap

Thursday 11th February

Jessica has a problem with one of the mums who helps her in the afternoons. She cannot control the four children in her care and Jessica said as much to her. It doesn't help that this woman has another baby child who she brings with her. She changes the nappies in the class, leaving them in the bin. I am sorry to say that this woman is British by the way. The reason the Headmaster hires her is because of some kind of *quid pro quo* arrangement where her autistic, but don't tell the school, kid gets reduced fees and she doesn't get paid. So Jessica said something along the lines of:

"Well if you can't cope don't come in anymore," and guess what, the woman hasn't come in today.

The notes Larry took at our native speakers meeting on Tuesday have disappeared. I am all for a conspiracy here but as they were in my possession and I can't find them. Anyone who knows me might suspect I have lost them under paperwork. However here are the facts. The notes were in my cupboard, I got them out to show Jessica who took them with her. She returned them to my part of the teacher's table in full view when I wasn't there. Then I come back and they are nowhere to be found. I prefer the conspiracy theory and suspect someone has stolen. Larry loves this idea too as you can imagine.

"What do these people think we're gonna have forgotten what we said or we won't go through with our plans?" said Larry.

Teacher morale hit an all time low this morning when the Headmaster's secretary told me that the new timetable, "was only for this week".

Groans from everywhere.

The secretary explains, "Oh the Headmaster forgot to take into consideration the use of the laboratory."

So draft number 7 is awaited with eagerness.

Tibor, the one armed physicist brought one of his students to the laboratory today. He is going to look at all the equipment and fix everything that is broken.

"But EVERYTHING is broken," I said. "They have demonstration voltmeters up there and not one has a working needle. There are 100 Newton metres all that have a maximum 'load' of ten Newtons and we have no spatulas."

"Maybe we should make a list of what we need," said Tibor.

I showed him the six page document I wrote 10 months ago. "We need all this," I said.

Friday 12th February

Well I feel a right Charlie after watching TV last night. Guess who was on? Yep the 'woman' (Diana) last seen cavorting to Madonna songs in the gay nightclub. Surprise surprise she is, or was a chap once. So the curves I saw were all in my heterosexual imagination or do men curve like that as well and I just imagine they don't? Shall I stop asking such strange questions?

Larry has now decided that the powers that be want to preserve the status quo and will marginalise the dissident native speakers. I thought this was nonsense.

"You're not thinking Jew again," said Larry at his most paranoid.

He may have a point. Upon being told that the school needs a bell to ring to announce the end of lessons he responded to Naima: "Don't the teachers have watches?"

Naima's psychology continues to baffle me. She hates taking responsibility. She loves being number two. She has personally organised an Easter Bazaar to raise money for the school but for some reason she does not want to be the person responsible. So she has roped in Brittany and keeps telling her it is HER bazaar. So Naima calls up all her contacts after twenty years in the city and then when she is asked for a contact name she gives Brittany's. It is very strange.

Sunday 14th February

The weekend was spent losing badly at some dice game in Pirx. Actually I spent all but five minutes playing dice but it is the clear memory I have of the night. I had gone there with Andrea, her incredibly tall friend Zsuzsa (6'4" tall in flat shoes) and György, who I had last seen at the party chasing Melanie in November. He had been unfeasibly busy with some architect dissertation but it was good to have him back. He is easy-going company and the kind of good-looking blond swine that gets barmaids over to our table far faster than is normal. I was delighted with the new barmaid actually. O.K she actually charges everybody at the time of the round instead of five hours later but she does remember me and what beer I drink. Fair enough I am the only 6'5" monolingual Englishman who goes to Pirx but still it makes me happy to be 'known'. Anyway György charmed her into being very attentive and we spent the rest of the evening discussing '6-3' a Hungarian film[33] I saw last night – in Hungarian. Then Attila and Orsi, who only speak German, arrived and so did the dice. I had the rules explained in about four languages and I still lost terribly. I admit I was slightly worse for wear and I am pretty sure the long haired bloke (who I'd never met before) threw far more double sixes than is possible in this universe. So I escaped eventually. I know as many German words as Attila, unfortunately all the words I know are the words he doesn't know. Eventually Orsi, his girlfriend translates for both of us in proper German. I have also realised now that each time we meet we have the same (drunken) conversation about where the best looking girls in the world live. Anyway it's quite a good conversation considering everything. Finally we danced to this Gloria Estefan covers band and got home some time on Sunday.

---

[33] The score in the famous football match between Hungary and England, Hungary became the non UK country to beat England at Wembley and the legend of the Golden Team was born. All eleven are still household names, Ferenc Puskás being the true great. Directed by Peter Timár (1999)

The Hungarian Girl Trap

Monday 15th February

Gerry was in from England with two teachers from the sister English school. The teachers do love coming here. They escape from their inner-London hell of thirty three yobboes in one prefabricated classroom in Hounslow and teach five attentive children in beautiful Budapest. You can see that Karen, a Head of English, is seriously considering quitting and moving out here. She keeps asking me questions like, "So what is it like to actually live here in Budapest?"

I took Gerry aside for ninety minutes to talk about the future of the school. This was the crux of the native speakers' recent council of war I knew that to let Larry make the headway would lead to arguments and one of my talents is that of diplomacy. Gerry has great ideas for the school and the only thing holding him back is the Headmaster, which is the weak link. I could not make myself say exactly that and without that point every other point looks like whingeing. It was clear that there would be no real investment in science because the school may move out of the building soon and so they would not waste money plumbing in water which they couldn't take with them. I said that I had to return to England then and Gerry was upset but understood my need for A level teaching.

In the evening I went to my language class and in the spirit of sociology I took Endre, a native speaker along as well. It was a particularly hard lesson, I could tell it would be because the teacher gave us some sparkling wine before we started. So Endre did the exercises that we did and came out shaking his head.

"Hungarian is such an impossible language to learn, so many exceptions," he said.

I felt a little happier at my tortoise progress.

Wednesday 17th February

Today was fun. Gerry was planning a meeting for the staff at 3.15 but the staff showed their indifference by not showing up. Well Naima, Ági and I showed up along with the Headmaster. Everyone else blamed the short notice given. Gerry was most annoyed and complained that the school did not have enough work up on the walls. He then told us that we were bloody lucky to work for the school. It is the easiest school to teach in in Hungary we were told. I agreed that it was the easiest school in the world to teach in but it is the hardest to work in. It's an important difference.

Naima complained again about the covering required by the staff and why was no provision made for it. In fact why were teachers allowed to bugger off during term time? The Headmaster defended the staff saying we all have things to do but then he doesn't have to cover. Gerry said that if a teacher couldn't combine a class once in a while then they were 'pathetic.'

Ági asked when the reports would be given out to kids. They were now three weeks late. All the staff had written them. What was the problem? The unofficial reason was that they wouldn't get them until their parents had paid, Gerry thought this was a good idea.

"Ah but some of my kids have paid," said Ági.

Silence.

So it was a good meeting! Gerry stopped the meeting at four, so we did not have time to discuss the problems. As Larry wasn't there anyway ("Let's just say I don't see the point. I know what's going on," being his remark.) I didn't venture forward but instead offered Jessica's list of gripes which were to be discussed. It was a mistake, as that was not Jessica wanted.

In the evening Andrea took me to a film that was in French, English and Italian with Hungarian sub-titles[34] which was confusing enough without being arty nonsense as well. Scene two for example involved John Malkovich behaving weirdly and staring at an Italian girl. He follows her around town then she turns and says "I stabbed my father twelve times. He's dead." Then they go to bed for about ten minutes. End of story!

The only antidote to this stupidity was to go to Old Man's Blues Bar where "Hobo", Deák Bill's ex-partner was putting on a show. He is not as good a singer as Bill but he is a better showman and his band are from the Rolling Stones school of blues: duelling guitars, slightly scruffy appearance. All this was free and I also had the largest schnitzel I have ever seen in my life. Endre was there too. He was having an interesting week too. He is currently dating his Boss, a forty-seven year old woman. This woman, who is loaded, has rented them a 'love nest', as the Sun would call it, with a swimming pool and a sauna. She loves her employee. Endre looked a little exhausted, to tell the truth and I soon found out why.

"My employment contract says that I must comply with any reasonable requests my manager deems appropriate. That involved going to bed all afternoon," he said with a grin.

I find the whole thing 'ciki' (Uncool, uncomfortable), especially when Andrea started asking astonishing personal questions to Endre about the specific nature of their sex lives. I couldn't be Hungarian! I know I try to tell Andrea to live and let live but in this case I can't help thinking that sleeping with one's boss is a highly dangerous pastime. It can only end in tears. However I must practise what I preach, I shall live and let live.

Thursday 18th February

Lots of problems today. I nearly saw the Headmaster shout. However considering I nearly killed the Headmaster it is irrelevant. I walked in to Jessica crying her eyes out in the corridor because Naima had told she was unprofessional for not being at the meeting and handing over a written list of problems. Now, as that was my fault, I went and had a sharp word with Naima, but Naima said "Don't defend her Ray."

---

[34] "Beyond the clouds" Wim Wenders and Michaelangelo Antonioni

Now as she thought Larry was going to speak at the meeting she had given me her things to add to the list. As that didn't happen I did the wrong thing. I apologised but she wasn't cross with me either. Why is nobody mad at me?

"I just wanna work in a school where I can teach," wailed Jessica as kids walked past.

Gerry bollocked all those who didn't go to the meeting, and I am glad I wasn't there when he spoke to Larry.

"I will come in, do my job and go home and not care about the school," said Larry finally. He had been forced by Naima to double up all his classes in the morning in revenge for his week off three weeks ago, although he was contractually obliged to have the time off. You could tell he was mad though because he randomly attacked Hungarian's for throwing paper in the bin and leaving the staffroom door open. He then made a point of moving all his stuff out of the room.

"You can have your stuff stolen but not me," he said.

Then the Headmaster sprung another classic. The whole school was to go to the theatre to see our English sister school's drama society perform "The Prince and the Pauper". That was news to us. So all the teachers, except me, who doesn't think fast enough, all remembered urgent appointments and left at one o'clock. So Dexter and Bea, the art teacher were left to take the school to the theatre. The Headmaster yelled at Bea to get the money and get the kids out of the school. I was so mad it was untrue.

I got the kids outside.

"How many children, do we have," asked the Headmaster.

"Twenty-eight," I said. I had counted them.

"No," said the Headmaster. "There cannot be that many. I counted this morning."

"There are twenty-eight," I said with menace in my voice.

"I think you should count them again."

With silence I let him count the twenty-eight children and then I stalked off with the kids to the tram stop. The play was O.K, the players poor. I left the kids to it, bought Bea a drink, and wrote a furious letter to the world and the Headmaster in the coffee bar. "I am a professional," I wrote, "and I cannot work in a place where my professionalism is not matched by my superiors or my colleagues."

Friday 19th February

Larry and I wrote a list of grievances and gave them to Gerry. Gerry saw me later and seemed to forget I wrote the list.

"Larry is full of shit," he blustered denying everything. "Americans always need books. I've spent $11,000 on books for Jessica and she's still moaning. (the point was the time delay). Oh and I have asked the Headmaster to speak to you to offer you more money in an attempt to make you stay."

I went back to my work. There was no way through to anybody. I don't care about the money!

The reports are still not dished out. Ági has reported that there is a catch 22 situation going on. The kids cannot get the reports until the parents have paid, but parents want to pay. The Headmaster hasn't decided how much to charge yet so they cannot pay. Also some have paid but no-one has a list of who they are, so no-one can be sure who has paid. So until all this is sorted out no-one can pay so no-one gets the reports. There is a ski trip next week so at the earliest last term's reports will reach the parents by 1st March!

The staff tried to hurry up the process by dumping the reports on the headmaster's desk but they were dumped back on ours because Naima had not calculated the sick days, late days etc for her classes.

"Oh I can't do that," she wailed. "I hate numbers," and walked out of the room, "I would rather resign than have to do that."

I laughed and laughed.

Monday 22nd February

I have decided to have a cultural week in Budapest despite the cold climate. It is half term but Andrea has not taken any time off, so I am entertaining myself. Today I visited the Széchenyi baths. Now I know that visiting the baths in Budapest is 'must-do' thing for tourists but I am not a tourist I live here. Besides I was quite happy with the cave baths in Miskolc, genuinely a modern wonder of the world. I could resist no longer however, so I took the yellow metro almost to the end of the line, got out and then entered a very confusing world. It's an imposing yellow building, built from 1909-1913 in a kind of Baroque style and circular. Finding the entrance was tricky enough. At the time it seemed to basically be the door you least expected the main entrance to be. Inside there were enormous chandeliers in the lobby and Baroque sculptures of Neptune and Venus surrounding several large courtyard pools. Like the Chain Bridge, Széchenyi was named for Count István Széchenyi (1791-1860) who vigorously promoted Budapest's development and was a champion of government reform. There were no signs at all in English, but an excessive amount of furious looking old ladies in that kind of polyester white coat you see all blue collar women wear here. I did my usual trick in these situations; I hung around the lobby watching what others did, translated the signs as best I could, then went up to the cashier woman and simply said "One", as I concluded that could not be misconstrued at all. It seemed to work and I was let through. I found a cubicle and various mildly camp male attendants chalked hieroglyphics on a locker so that I would have no way of finding my clothes again. I changed, then I walked through the doors entered a kind of paradise.

The Széchenyi indoor pools are damp, in need of refurbishment but the essential concept is magnificent. You have to do them in order. First pool is small and freezing. Now you have woken up get out fast and swim languidly in the pleasantly warm pool next to it. This is surrounded by ornate columns and is quite full of old men hogging the water jets, mildly amorous couples and more enthusiastic swimmers. Don't stay too long because on your right is a hot pool. Aaaah, wonderful. The temptation is to stay in this large bath forever but you must be disciplined. Get out, walk through the plastic door at the end, turn the corner and step into the mildly cold pool in the corner. Get out walk into the long thing pool and swim a little. Stay long enough to catch the new tidal wave thing. Get out, walk through the door and ease into another gloriously hot pool full of people sitting with their elbows holding them to the side, all with blissful smiles on their faces. Tempting to stay, but get out and go into the steam room. It's a right pea-souper in there, and the steam burns your slightly bemused skin. Stay as long as you dare, get out and go in the sauna. Ignore the obligatory Germans and then step out, and plunge into what seems like the world's coldest pool. Now reverse this and go back to the start. I guarantee you will feel so alive afterwards.

Outside is a lovely warm basking pool, steam billowing from it, lot's of old men were in there playing chess. There was also a proper swimming pool but as I needed to wear a swim hat I refused that and simply spent the afternoon plunging into different pools.

Tuesday 23rd February

One-hundred years ago Budapest had almost a thousand coffee houses. Sounds like paradise to me, even though 'Starbucks' is attempting similar blanket coverage in London right now and I pretend to hate it. There are far fewer coffee houses here these days. I'd suggest there were way over a thousand alcohol bars in modern Budapest. Shame, as I have always felt that wiling away an afternoon in a coffee house is far more civilised than wiling it away in a pub getting horribly drunk. At home in England I had always looked across the English channel to European café culture and frankly been very jealous. You could sit there with a book and there would no pressure to move on, no pressure to keep ordering more coffee. It seemed perfect to me. I had had little chance to sample the Budapest coffee house scene up until now, Andrea was not a big coffee drinker. Coffee culture was undergoing a bit of a renaissance. I couldn't tell whether it was tourist trap driven, or a genuine desire to reclaim something that had been lost. Thankfully none of the new coffee houses had a Starbuck sign anywhere near them.

Although the choice is now quite widespread I guess you don't really need to look any further than the Gerbeaud on Vörösmarty square at the end of Váci Utca. It's not the oldest coffee house in Budapest, it's only been here since 1870 but it has an opulence that means the tourists flock towards it. It's all chandeliers inside, but does one really go there for the coffee? No, it's for the pastries. Try the plum pastry things[35]. Way too busy though, even in February, so I nipped off to Centrál instead. On Ferenciek square it was originally popular with writers for purely practical reasons: it offered a warm refuge from cold rented rooms that they could scarcely afford - and paper and ink were free. So, for form's sake I wrote some words in my journal but then began to appreciate what Sàndor Márai said about coffee culture: [36]"In espresso bars one can only chat. One cannot write a great work as there is no space at the table." So I gave up and watched the world go by instead.

Wednesday 24th

Andrea and I went to see her father in the evening for a meal. We ate a kind of solid soup called kocsonya, which Anglo Hungarian cookbooks will translate as 'jellied pig's feet'. Andrea's father loved it, citing it as a Miskolc speciality, and as a Miskolci man one must taste it. Then he told a possibly apocryphal story about a woman who made kocsonya once and put it down in the cellar to solidify and a frog got stuck. When the woman took it up to her husband for him to eat, the frog's eyes still stuck out of the top of the gel. Whether Andrea's father was putting me through another bizarre initiation ceremony to see if I was indeed worthy of marrying his daughter is up for debate. Andrea, loyal, proud Hungarian that she is was having nothing to do with the kocsonya and ate salad instead. I ate a portion which tasted exactly like a pork-pie made entirely of the jelly.

Satisfied that I had passed the test Andrea's father showed me some of his latest architectural plans. He loved entering competitions for the great new Hungarian buildings going up right now. His idea for the national opera house was simply striking. I looked through the competition book, which had all the designs submitted and, yes I had had a pàlinka or two, but all the other submissions were classic modern box-like buildings with lots of glass, or Frank Gehry-style curved metallic plates. Andrea's father's design was essentially a building that exactly looked like the famous Hungarian crown.

"How did this not win?" I asked sincerely.

Andrea's father was pleased at his admiring audience and showed me his design for a tower on the end of Margaret Island, which lies in the middle of the Danube between Buda and Pest. Again it had that air of brilliance I have come to expect. The 200 metre tall tower was shaped like the shape of the city since Buda,

---

[35] szilvás lepény

[36] Sàndor Màrai was born in Hungary in 1900 and by 1930 was one of Hungary's leading novelists. Driven into exile in 1948 when the Communists came to power and banned his books, he lived first in Italy and then in America. He committed suicide in 1989. The recent rediscovery of "Embers", a masterpiece of Central European literature originally published in Budapest in 1942 and unknown to modern readers until recently had brought him posthumous international acclaim

Pest and Óbuda came together in 1811. So the top of the tower was shaped like 1811 city, the middle (wider) was like the 1900 city and the bottom was the shape of the city in the present day. Down the side was the Danube with all the islands and all the bends. It was gorgeous. Of course he didn't seem to win these competitions, in many ways I guess that he allowed his own patriotic pride get in the way of his judgement. His designs were almost too bold, too in-your-face. How quickly would they date? I'm no architect, so what do I know, but they would stand out, believe me.

After that he got the guitar out, a guitar that looked like it had been bashed against a few walls in its time and he belted out old British pop songs from the sixties.

March

Monday 1st March

The weather has turned for the better. I seem to have spent the last four months struggling to work through massive snow, cold winds cutting my exposed skin. The digital thermometer on top of the building near the tram stop at Astoria has stubbornly read -9 degrees for as long as I can remember. Some days I'd be so bent double against the bitter weather that I was sure I resembled a Lowry matchstick figure in his "Coming from the Mill" painting and that would set me off laughing. But today it is a very pleasant twelve degrees here and all the snow has disappeared. The school is pretty much the same, but I am re-energised. The Headmaster talked to me about my leaving and tried to convince me to stay but offered no more money or any A level incentive. I said, I don't think so. The reports are out, except for mine. The Headmaster has blamed the staff for the delay when parents asked him. This was so stupid I couldn't believe it until he re-iterated his argument in the staff room.

There is a new American teacher called Tony. He's here to teach English and German. Tony seems very serious and almost unfriendly. But he was probably cheap so who cares. Also, the English teacher from the sister school is, as reported before, almost certain to be joining the school from September. She has been seduced by the small class sizes and the holiday paradise she sees. As Brittany says, "She hasn't seen all the crap administration involving the Headmaster."

The kids looked brown from their ski trip. One very studious Chinese girl fell in love with a blue eyed English boy at the resort and has been crying ever since. I am pleased because the Chinese insular mentality has been broken. There are other places in the world apart from China.

Also Brittany reports that hormones have broken out in Year Eight. The Russian girls have started flirting and giggling and are, "allowing the boys from the other school to buy them ice cream".

Thursday 4th March

Picture the scene, it's after school, all the children, the Headmaster, the secretary and all bar two of the staff have gone home. The two people left are a tall, mild-mannered science teacher from England and a female teacher. The teachers are together stapling school art work onto various available notice boards. The work is simple, rewarding and involving lots of teamwork. The tall, mild-mannered science teacher from England is stretching to staple paintings into high corners, the female teacher is watching his every move and the Englishman knows it. The female teacher reaches up to replace staples occasionally.

"You know," says the female teacher finally, stopping the man from working with a hand on his shoulder, "you really are a very good-looking, man. Very, VERY handsome."

Dexter, for it is I, thinks about how terrifying those words and this situation would be if this was any other woman on the Earth than the one who had actually done it. Instead I try to work out what Naima was getting at.

I grin as I think I have read her mind. "That's why I prefer to teach in boys schools," I said.

I looked at her and saw her face beam with pleasure. "I got two stories from the Russian girls in class today, both are about you. I have been sitting here watching you trying to think like a thirteen year old girl," and she burst into more laughter.

Today was Naima's day entirely. She was on top form. I must admit to finding the woman fascinating. She's fifty-two and undoubtedly the woman I can least imagine ever going on a hot date. She was born into a country still dominated by British culture, was educated in a British school in Lahore but has set foot in England only once. This is the thing I find most strange because she speaks perfect 'English' English. She will use phrases like 'White Elephant sale', which rarely used these days, and she understands imperial measurements better than metric. She is incredibly perceptive and intelligent one moment and one minute later claiming to be incapable of adding four numbers together. I always feel she knows far more about me because my people oppressed hers for years and she knows that all I really know about her culture is Islam and Jalfrezi chicken. Once again I feel unworthy.

There are so many Naima incidents today I can't tell them all. Firstly the Headmaster has hired a 'marketing expert' to help promote the school. This caused some mirth in the staff room when it was announced because, as Brittany pointed out, the best marketing is by word of mouth. However the marketing whiz arrived and his name was Tibor. Now this is not Tibor the one armed physicist (who is in Tel Aviv at a conference for jolly clever physics chaps) but Tibor the two armed marketeer, I will try to distinguish between the two.

Tibor the marketeer was set to task to type a Hungarian letter advertising Naima's bazaar. This took him quite a while and suddenly, Naima, who was there watching him said to me.

"Ray, can I have your attention a moment."

I gave it to her. She wrote something on a post-it note and handed it to me. It said, "How can I work with this idiot? He is so slow. He has taken four hours to write one letter!"

Just to make sure I knew who she was talking about she then pointed in a highly theatrical manner at the two armed Tibor in the corner, ruining all the subterfuge.

"It is a curious situation," I said cryptically.

"Curious," she said. "I'd say hopeless. What shall we do with him? He's slower than the Headmaster!"

"Well what do you expect," I said, "the Headmaster hired him!" and at that Naima collapsed into a heap of hysterical cackling that lasted a full five minutes, causing both the Headmaster and Tibor to stare at her.

Jessica's mother is in town for two weeks. She is very like Jessica, all teeth and curls. She has been going around admiring all the art work.

"Look at this," she would say holding up a particularly awful piece, "Did one of your primary class do this Winnie?"

"Err, no," said Bea, the Art teacher, "that's GCSE course work."

Jessica had warned us that she asked direct questions but even we weren't expecting her to ask Naima where she had bought 'those beautiful pajamas" she was wearing.

Then Jessica introduced me and Brittany as "the two people who I sit with and bitch and moan with."

"But you must talk about the good points too," said Mrs. Robinson.

"Yes but that takes only a nano-second," I said as I headed off for class.

Larry was in a reasonable mood today although he lost it slightly when the Budapest Sun arrived. The Sun remains a very shoddy paper but we staff grab it with the excitement of a new Shakespeare play, read it for two minutes and put it down. Larry who writes for the paper occasionally has filled me in with all the personalities on the journalism team so I now have great fun checking out the articles to see their personalities. For example the film reviewer is a feminist, (which explains why action films get short shrift). The classical music guy has deliberately unfashionably long hair and is the only foreign guy Larry knows in the city who came here for a reason other than meeting a very good looking local girl. Anyway Larry had noticed that the headline screamed that neo Nazis had been given suspended sentences. He immediately composed a letter of protest to the editor of the paper then screwed it up.

"They could trace this," he said, "I'm not writing it."

Then he revealed that he had translated his contract and had discovered that we staff are not getting paid through the summer. This surprised Naima and him but it didn't surprise me.

"This must be the only school in the world that does this," barked Larry. "I'm going to sort this out."

"Don't worry," said Naima, "the Headmaster will not get away with this one."

Actually I think he will.

Summer weather has arrived. Andrea says this is normal but to me, a Brit used to complete unpredictability, this is incredible. Spring lasts for a month and then, WHAM, we hit the real summer temperatures for about two to three months. It's such an exciting thought I almost feel like hanging around outside in skateboard clothing and just sitting on the grass playing summer tunes and watching girls go by on roller blades…

Here is a letter to Brittany from the students she used to teach in the Czech Republic. It is in English, we think.

The Hungarian Girl Trap

"Sweetheart Brittany

Power you thank for o'clock English language which you are with us for – sufferance. We're sad, that already you will not have on the English language a power with us will hundredth - twisting

Yours class 6A"

"Did you teach them on acid?" I asked semi-seriously.

Monday 8th March

I am currently in a slight quandary over my Hungarian classes. I had gone to England for a few days and returned having used precisely no words of Hungarian. I find that the next class I attended was the final test for this course. Nenet saw me walk in and simply grinned evilly.

"I suggest you turn around and walk right back out the door," he said.

It was predictably bad, mainly because I didn't have any clue it was coming and had not revised or even looked at any Hungarian. However I seemed to still be doing better than Nenet who, if he had any hair left would have torn it out. As is the way with this course Judit our teacher had already written out the diplomas but hadn't written me one. I explained I was in England and didn't know and she said well if I have failed I will have to redo the course.

"But hang on," she continued, "there isn't a second course next term…I'll call you."

That was five days ago and she hasn't called me. I have no idea if I passed or whether I can continue. I am working on the assumption that no business is going to reject my 13000 forints and if I turn up with an apple for Judit she will let me carry on. If not I am in trouble.

Tuesday 9th March

Today everybody was in a furiously good mood. It is woman's day, which helps I guess. This is a day when every man has to buy women flowers to show how much we appreciate them…Aaaah.

"Is there a man's day?" I asked Andrea rather unwisely with hindsight. "You know, a day when the women allow us to go to the pub and drink beer and talk about sport?"

"All the other 364 days are men's days I think, if that is the definition," said Andrea with great wisdom for one so young.

So I bought her some snowdrops for 30p from an old crone outside the station. I noted that my fellow gentlemen were doing pretty much the same. This is not stingy by the way I probably paid over the odds.

Wednesday 10th March

Language class proved to be a pain. I met Christina, the Swede at the tram stop and we caught up with the news. I explained that I had been unable to prepare for the test. She sympathised but doubted it would be a problem. However it was. I arrived and Judit the teacher would not let me into the classroom, saying I was not ready for this class.

"But I just missed the exam," I said. Nenet, who was delighted to see me, nodded in agreement. I am better than him at Hungarian.

But Judit wasn't having any of it. "Go and see the secretary to organise taking the second course again."

"But if I could just have time to prepare. I am being penalised for having to work! I have 15000 forints here. Just let me sit in the class," I said.

No.

I went to the secretary, who told me there was only one second level course and that was an intensive course at midday every day for a fortnight.

"I can't do that, I work," I said.

"Sorry then," said the secretary.

So I left and went home and doubt I shall ever go back to this school. Here I am, a keen and vaguely intelligent student, who can pay and will do all the work that my time allows and because I was away I am effectively excluded from all classes! It's crazy. They are turning away money. I cannot understand it. They have so few students of their language anyway one would think they would welcome students!

I got the books out, got out the white wine and started studying on my own. They had made me mad and so I will learn it on my own and I shall save myself 15000 forints. I shall also write a very long letter to the director asking exactly why he his turning away good students.

School was fun today. I was interviewed for the school magazine. Now the school will know that my favourite colour is black and my favourite label is Calvin Klein. Yes the level of journalism is very high.

I have a new private student: Chris the British boy, although he is not keen.

"Look, my brother has got me spending every second studying, can't you turn him down."

"It's for you own good," I said, ignoring the fact that his brother will pay 3000 forints an hour.

What happened to my old student, Petra the arms dealer daughter? She did not approve of me not visiting her and celebrating my birthday instead and we decided to terminate our agreement. Much as I don't necessarily mind taking money off millionaires I *do* mind being paid to simply do someone's homework and then get blamed if she does badly in tests when she finally has to work alone.

Thursday 11th March

An old computer was put into Jessica's room today. Foolishly I assumed she would be delighted. I wasn't thinking. When I mentioned it to her she gave me a dark look.

"It's just furniture," she said. "I might as well use it as a chair! There is no software on it, we have no cd ROMS of course and even if I did have some software I couldn't print anything out because there is no printer attached."

"Ah, but think what the parents will say when they look round." I said.

Prospective parents are currently something I don't wish to talk about. Naima has covered all the walls of the classrooms with paper and each class is covering their walls with relevant work – except year eleven, whom I have decided are far too busy with GCSE to worry about posters. However they have produced their own from home and we have a wall consisting of dead American rap artists, alive American basketball players and attractive females. Naima is giving me the most withering of withering looks. It doesn't help that Brittany (one of the finest administrative teachers I have ever met – in fact some of the staff here are extraordinarily talented and considering the job satisfaction our Headmaster should thank the Lord every day they are here) has covered her classroom with a frieze of "Great figures of the Twentieth century, with photographs and biographies nicked from Time Magazine. It is superb, even if does have Margaret Thatcher and far too many American presidents (and even their wives) on it for my liking. In response I have decided to do year 11's classroom but how I am not yet sure. I was hoping New Scientist would come to my rescue with an equivalent "great 20th century scientists" but instead all they seem to care about is genetically modified food. I may have to surf the internet and make some 'element of the year' posters.

I am still receiving post one month late. This is not a criticism of the Magyar postal service but a criticism of the secretary. Today she gave me a letter, stamped by her as having arrived at the school on the 16th February inviting me to a conference in Budapest on February 25th. And then I get blamed when I miss exam entry deadlines for Key Stage 3 tests (it's a bit difficult to return a form if you have never seen it).

Tony the new American is better than I thought. He is a little darker in personality than we are used to and doesn't crack jokes all the time but he is O.K. He has been in Hungary for six years, another caught by the Hungarian girl trap. He speaks excellent Hungarian (swine) and German (bless him) which solves the "Ooh Réka's away, get Ray to take the German class problem". He also watches soccer which makes him very strange indeed. I am not 100% sure about him yet but I am giving him the benefit of the doubt.

The Hungarian Girl Trap

Evening

I dragged Andrea along to the Merlin Theatre[37] to watch a local English language theatre company perform some self-written plays about life in Budapest. We met Brittany and her boyfriend (Michael) there and Andrea was amazed at how many ex-patriot Americans there are.

"I feel like a foreigner in my own country," she wailed after she warned someone her drink was being spilt and the person didn't understand her.

To compound her misery Michael's American accent fooled her too. He used the word "Dog" but pronounced it the American way ("Dug") meaning Andrea thought he was talking about the past tense of 'to dig' and confusing her completely.

"Oh I see," she said, "You mean DOG!" pronouncing it the English way. I have never been so proud of her in my life but hid my admiration of this Hungarian telling a native speaker how to pronounce his own language by subtly miming someone digging behind her. Andrea was mortified by what she had done and spent the rest of the evening practising American pronunciation as a penance. The problem is there are no accents in Hungarian really so to come across someone pronouncing vowels wrongly is confusing.

The theatre was tiny and precarious, with loose seats hanging close to a very high drop. Brittany was very worried indeed and I must admit I sat rigidly knowing there was a two metre drop directly behind me.

The plays and players were a varied mixture. There were four plays entitled 'short plays' and all consisted entirely of the lines "So, what is this play about?" "Well it's short," followed by the curtain.

There were two rather nice observations of foreign life here in Budapest. The first "Tie" (by Ray N Drop) was about a rather dumb ass American (there are a lot of them over here) called Jeremy Cakes who flunked university and drifted to Budapest. They like it here because they can drink and smoke and their money goes a long way. These guys then drift into ESL teaching and have very little knowledge of grammar and don't do well. They then yell and say "We don't need grammar, grammar is for you studious Europeans" etc (see Larry for this too). Cakes was horrible and was trying it on with the gorgeous blonde secretary who organised the lessons in the school. She gave all the lessons to other people and Cakes was furious but he was willing to forget his fury because her aesthetic appeal over-ruled. Enter even more obnoxious English man, Ernest Britain (played hammily by a tall Englishman) who was the secretary's ex-boyfriend and the two find that instead of being rivals they have a lot in common, they are wasters. I am not sure if the writer was meaning to make the Anglo Americans so horrible but he succeeded. They were selfish and arrogant and believed that merely being native speakers meant they should be superior. They also tried to apply western morality to a culture that won't have it. *They* could make generalisations about Hungary, but feel a Hungarian could

---

[37] International theatre, Gerlóczy st 4, Pest

not do the same about their land. Cakes, for example, is outraged at the secretary's comment that New York is the only good city in America and the rest is nothing.

The next good play was "Tartózkodási Engedély" which means Residence Permit, that Holy Grail all we ex-pats desire. I have long given up trying to get one because I haven't even got a work permit yet. The process involves about a million visits to a red-tape nightmare with a million Chinese and Romanians, waiting, fighting, shoving, and pushing. All to get seen and then, in Larry's words, "They bring out your file and IT'S GOT THE SAME DAMN DUST ON IT AS LAST TIME YOU CAME and the guy studies it for five minutes, closes it and says 'Come back tomorrow' – and the process continues."

The play was a monologue in which a speed crazed American loser talks to the audience as he waits at the office. It is funny and you sympathise with the guy although you are not surprised the authorities are reluctant to grant him residence rights. He talks about getting stopped by the police.

"They ask for I.D and I give them my passport. They look at it for five minutes. 'Why do you leave the country every ninety days?' they ask, even though they know the answer. 'Do you have any more I.D?' they ask. What's wrong with a passport for chrissakes? 'What about a drivers licence?' they say. 'I don't drive,' I say. 'All Americans drive,' they say. And remember this is Hungarian so I'm getting 5% of this conversation. So I give them 5000 forints (the standard amount a foreigner pays to stop the police hassling you) and they leave."

It was a very good play and we all enjoyed it, even Andrea who is aware of the immigration authorities behaviour.

There was also a four part play set in a charity clothes shop where a romantic American tells stories to the attractive female owner based on the clothes found in the shop. It was very good indeed .

So all in all it was a fine evening out, if only to hear two hundred foreigners speaking bad Hungarian in the bar afterwards.

Thursday 11th March

School was fun today. The bazaar, scheduled for Saturday week is occupying everyone's thoughts. The hired Marketing Man, (Tibor two arms) is proving himself to be remarkably incompetent. He has sent a flyer to all the embassies citing that our school is the only registered British school in Budapest. Unfortunately, as the Australian ambassador pointed out with a sharp phone call, not only are there other registered British schools but we are not registered! There were some serious guffaws from the staff room over that one.

I was having a busy day with an experiment, a demonstration and the construction of spaghetti bridges with the year 8 students (forces you know). It is much more fun to teach this way.

The Hungarian Girl Trap

Friday 12th March

Tony is getting better and better. He used to work at "Little Darlings", a private kindergarten owned and run by a woman of similar attitude to our Headmaster.

"What's Superkids like?" asked Brittany over lunch.

"Why do you think I'm here?" said Tony.

"Blimey," I said.

Then we discussed our theory that Yevjaniia a 15 year old Ukrainian girl with a huge crush on me is not from Kiev as she says but from far closer to Chernobyl than she is prepared to admit. She is pale, has a heart condition and looks sickly. She has been off school for at least 30 days or so in total this year. How does one even go about asking such a question. I have postponed the topic 'radiation' for a few months just in case.

Actually we have had a good week because the Headmaster has been busy and uninterfering. I received a good Science revision cd ROM through the post and I have the entire 'BBC bite size' series on video courtesy of a parental donation. Some more books arrived too for the English department. I expect the good mood in the school does have something to do with the weather.

Brittany and I took the school to see "Shakespeare in Love" at the Pushkin[38] cinema in the afternoon. Ironically the Russian population refused to come because it was not in the cinema they wanted to go to (they can only tolerate the multiplex with McDonalds and Coca Cola) so they stayed behind with Tony. The Pushkin is marvellous, a refurbished little palace. I got Kata, a Hungarian student to buy the tickets and get the official receipt because I didn't want to make a mistake but of course the foolish girl asked for the wrong amount of tickets anyway. Bea the art teacher arrived as well and we settled down to watch the film.

The kids loved it, as did Brittany and I, even though we'd seen it already. Bea was crying after ten minutes.

"It's the gorgeous colours of the costumes," she wailed. "When I see beauty I have to cry."

"Does that include Joseph Fiennes?" asked Brittany.

"Yes," said Bea, until she saw Rupert Everett and wept again.

So we all loved it because the film is like a Shakespeare play. It had rude comedy, fights, romance, sex and sadness, something for everyone. As Brittany wiped another tear from her eye she tried to distract me by pointing out that hard man Esko our Estonian was also looking a bit tearful. Bea was very emotional indeed and spent the next few minutes telling me how lucky I was that I could "understand Shakespeare as it was supposed to be written, in rhyme and in context, not in translation."

So that was a success and it makes me wonder if Larry's fanciful idea of an "Experience School" would be possible. Larry thinks there should be school

---

[38] Near Astoria Metro stop

somewhere where the kids are always on excursions living life. If they are studying the Second World War they go to concentration camps and battlefields, if they study the Renaissance they go to Italy. In a way we are trying it. We are going to a refugee camp soon to give refugees clothes donated by our kids, Brittany wants to take Year 8 to Florence and Venice to feel the Renaissance and heck I suppose I'll take 'em to the zoo again.

It's our mid-term break. I have until Monday off. Monday is Hungary's national day, celebrating the 1848 revolution over the Austrians, and everyone wears a flag and has a good time. Last year Andrea took me to London to join a Hungarian evening at the Hungarian Cultural Centre. This consisted of lots of flags, dancing, Liszt, the National anthem (difficult to sing owing to it moving up an octave or two), a speech by a famous woman for an hour in Hungarian (much foot shuffling from a standing Dexter) and lots of alcohol.

I remembered this evening well, as it posed a few questions. Firstly how did modern Hungary's founding fathers think that anyone would be able to *sing* the National Anthem, as it goes through at least three octaves? I have to remember to start singing[39] it in my lowest voice possible to have any hope of hitting the high notes later. Secondly I remember being very bemused (bored) by the long speech the famous Hungarian woman made because of the rapt attention the audience gave her. At the time I thought it was because she was particularly important and famous, but now I realise that all Hungarian speeches are received in the same way, and not only that but the speech is considered all the more special if it contains obscure allusions, complicated words and long sentences. Therefore Hungarian intellectualism is defined not in terms of how clear you can make something but how much you baffle the audience. As if knowledge must not be shared with the masses: a closed shop as it were. Hungarian language truly is a mirror image of English. Thirdly I remember getting into a conversation with a middle aged guy in the bar. He was a rather typical Hungarian male I realise now, cynical, proud, beaten by the world and trying to stay youthful. He was drunk and ready for confrontation. He asked me to translate what he was about to say in German into English to test my linguistic ability. I did as I was told and he triumphantly told me that was *not* what he had said and told me what he *had* said (which definitely *wasn't* what he said in German). He then told me he spoke five other languages equally well (which amused me for all the wrong reasons – and probably didn't help matters) and he then launched into a tirade about how the English can't do anything properly and had no soul. Andrea told me to let him talk, as it was his pride talking.

---

[39] And I mean humming here of course. I have no idea what the words are.

The Hungarian Girl Trap

Tuesday 15th March

Miskolc

National holiday the red white and green of Hungary flies from a thousand lamp posts, tenement buildings and trams, trains, buses and cars. On this day in 1848 there was a fairly bloodless revolution in Pest against the Habsburgs of Austria. A chap called Sándor Petőfi, was a leading figure. He was a poet and it was his national song and the publication of his twelve points outlining the wishes of the Hungarian people that caused the free press to be born. The revolution was however followed by a less successful 'war for freedom'. Hungarians like to remember the sentiment of those who wanted a free Hungary. See October 23rd for another celebration of a failed revolution. I am not entirely sure what is expected to do on such a day but Andrea took me, her mum and her sister to the local baths. Now in Hungary this is not just a swimming pool but more a way of life (or a torture chamber depending on your disposition). The Hungarians get their aquatic obsession from the conquering Turks five hundred years ago. There are two astonishing pools here in Miskolc, one set inside a mountain and the one we went to which is more like an holiday resort.

We got in for free of course, Andrea's uncle is the director of public amenities or something in Miskolc and so our name opened doors. Remember business is done by who you know not what you know. Andrea is always worried about what will happen to me when I go to the gentleman's changing rooms and gave me explicit instructions as to what to do in there.

"Now go in, take your clothes off, keep your towel and then do what all the other men do."

"It sounds like I'll get arrested," I said with a grin.

I did see her point, there is a ritual involving the right coat hangers and handing your clothes to an old crone hiding round a corner. I waited for some other guys to follow them trying to look as innocent as possible but they took so long that Andrea, waiting outside, sent up a another man try and find me.

"Raymond! Raymond?" yelled this rather bemused looking man and sheepishly I followed him down.

"*There* you are," said Andrea with folded arms. "What took you?"

First up was the 'cold bath'.

"I think I'll pass on that," I said.

"Oh no you won't," said Andrea.

"The words Cold and Bath do not go together well," I said, protesting.

The cold bath was inside under a huge tent construction which they remove in the summer months.

"Put this on," said Andrea. She was holding a blue swimming cap.

"No," I said finally. "I have spent thirty years building up a reputation as a cool, stylish member of society. I am not going to ruin all that work now by putting that piece of nylon on my head."

A scuffle followed which resulted in the cap sitting firmly on my head. I have not ascertained why we had to wear the headgear.

"Now we must shower," said Andrea, which were pleasingly warm.

"Now the cold pool," she said and leapt in. Clearly she had lost her senses but I dipped a tentative foot in the water and found it warmer than a typical English swimming pool.

"This isn't cold," I said. "You should try Hastings beach in August," and dived in.

"No you don't understand," said Andrea, "it is cold compared to the hot pool."

"The hot pool?" I said suddenly nervous again. How hot was the hot pool?

I soon found out – bath like. It was fantastic, you could play chess in there and you didn't have to wear the cap. Steam billowed from the pool skyward making seeing anything difficult.

"Right, I'll stay here," I said with a blissful voice.

"No, we need to go to the massage sprays?" said Andrea.

"?" I said.

We crawled to the shallow end where various people sat in front of powerful jets of boiling water being physically pushed forward by the power. Their facial expression was interesting to say the least.

"Now you are not telling me this is healthy," I wailed.

"Of course it is," said Andrea and we sat in the water cannon for a few minutes. O.K it was rather good especially if you have an itch on your back.

"Now what," I said.

"Sauna," said Andrea.

"I see," I said. "It's getting hotter each time I notice."

There was a slight delay when I walked into the ladies changing rooms by mistake (well the signs were in Hungarian!) so it was quite a relief to hide in the sauna for a while. What a ridiculous pastime! You sit in this outrageously hot room staring at the wooden walls, or the egg timer in the corner. There is always a German man in the corner, eyes shut in ecstasy, who gets up every so often to pour some kind of scented water onto hot coals and the room heats up enormously as a consequence. Your nostrils and mouth burn as they dry out and you smell the smell of hot pine needles. Then you sweat like mad (scrape it off YUK with a toothless comb) then leg it outside to a ludicrously cold shower. Then you go and sit in an ante-room with other slightly shell-shocked looking people until you can cope with doing the same thing all over again.

Andrea, her sister and mum then went off to have a massage. The masseur was a rather burly looking stud-type gentleman and I was pretty sure the ladies would get far more out of this than I would. So I turned down the offer and nipped back to the cold pool. I returned to find the ladies grinning far wider than I have seen them grin for a while. Apparently the buttocks were massaged and they didn't expect it(!)

Andrea, turning into Jane Austen's Emma again decided she was going to get the guy to marry her sister and so was most disappointed to find he was married.

Finally, I retired to the bar and drank a refreshing diet coke. The ladies had an opportunity for a stint on the sun bed but I know when to stop the healthy stuff.

Then we had lunch. Gábor, Andrea's cousin turned up with beard and I hardly recognised him. I hadn't seen him since his unconscious exploits at the New Year's party. Andrea's grandmother was there too. Lunch was traditional, meat soup, meat main course and cakes. Fantastic. Then we all sat down to watch that family viewing treat "The Big Lebowski" dubbed into Hungarian. Well I fell asleep within four minutes of the opening and I only woke up when Andrea's grandmother asked repeatedly why people have to swear in films these days (echoing my own Grandmother.)

"Grandmother, we are not Communists anymore," said Andrea's sister. "People can say what they want."

Hooray for capitalism, I thought and returned to my slumbers. Next time I woke up the film had changed to a swashbuckling film about events post the 1848 revolution, the reason for the National holiday in the first place. Great, I thought, I know very little about my adopted country's most famous historical event, I shall watch this and learn. Unfortunately the plot seem to have disappeared somewhere and instead we had lots of shots of lone men on horses repelling the white coated 'bastard' Austrians. There was also a bloke with a big nose who I am sure died early on but kept returning. I blame the excess of good food and the sauna, my brain was addled. I drifted off again. Next time Andrea's sister was complaining about the number of homosexuals around and how there had been none around in the time of the Communists. She used the word "buzi". Andrea's grandmother, mishearing the word slightly, thought she said "bugyi". To which she replied indignantly, "of course we had bugyis in Communist time!" and everyone laughed because bugyi means knickers.

We returned to Budapest at 9 o'clock and the police were out in force, checking everyone's I.D card. This is it, I thought, I've had it now. I don't have an I.D card and I don't carry my passport out of principal. I am in trouble. Fortunately they let Andrea and I through without even stopping us. They were after the slightly swarthy types who frequent terminus train buildings.

Wednesday 16th March

"Bazaar," said Réka, the German teacher this morning as she came through the door, "what bazaar's that then?"

This rates pretty high on the all-time *faux pas* top ten in my book. Up there with Prince Philip's finest foreign gaffes. Naima gave her the sort of withering look only Naima can give people. I solved the problem by making a rude remark about Réka's new hairstyle, which diffused the situation.

Tony, who is now highly cool, has started to do some mathematics, the same mathematics I did when I came to the school. The 'how can we be in debt? I know what the fees are' kind of maths. However he has more experience of Hungarian schools (he's worked in them all) and said simply "they all say that, they just never wanna spend money."

There are also rumours that Gerry, our governor is in town, which put the wind up everyone. If he arrives unannounced then there are usually problems.

Brittany is threatening to quit over a point of principal. The Headmaster needs her teaching certificate for a work permit (ha!) but Brittany refuses to have the original sent over citing the inevitable fact that it will get lost in the post. She therefore asked for her local US post office to copy it and stamp that it is an official copy. However the guy just said 'there's no need for that, of course it's official." and wrote "this is an official copy of the certificate signed". However the Headmaster will not accept that because "Anybody could have written that". Hungary is a stamp culture. If you don't have 'em nothing gets done. Or it could be a simple ploy to delay work permits still further. Anyway it's stalemate.

Thursday 17th March

Naima was tearing her hair out over the bazaar.

"Why does our Headmaster have to have things explained to him so slowly," she fumed. "And why does everything here have to be so chaotic?"

She was referring to Hungary specifically here. "I have worked with the British and the Americans," she fumed, "but here the smallest details become so important."

The Headmaster had decided that the rules of the games "Pin the tail on the donkey" and "Throw the ring over the bottle and win a prize" needed to be written down or preferably typed. Brittany gave Naima a hug. However she was homesick too after an altercation at the market. She handled tomatoes by mistake so the market stall person yelled and gesticulated at a sign for a while, grabbed her two tomatoes and jumped up and down on them.

"That sort of thing never happens in America," she wailed. However you don't get sold things in obscene manner on TV every five minutes in Hungary I thought, but didn't point that out.

The water stopped running in the laboratory at a crucial point today. The gas supply is in however but we have no beakers, Bunsens, tripods or thermometers, and the test-tubes crack on applying the slightest heat.

Friday 18th March

The bazaar preparations took over the school today. On paper it looks really good. Naima has rallied round the Budapest Women's Institute and there are Pakistani food, craft, white elephant, book and furniture stalls in the gymnasium. There is also pin the tail on the donkey, rudimentary ten pin bowling, play stations, face painting, clay modelling etc. It's passing me all by. I walked in to a meeting at 8.40 about concerning the running of the fete I had forgotten about. I got away with it because I will only be there in the morning to supply muscle and with that in mind I got all the boys to move chairs and tables into the gym that afternoon. The Headmaster was finally getting involved with the fete but with negative effect. He had decided that there should be only one payment point (read, he doesn't trust anyone with the money) therefore if you see something you want to do you have to return to the entrance to get a ticket. Besides Brittany was annoyed because she felt charging 100 forints to pin the tail on the donkey was a bit pricey considering they have paid to get in already.

"This fete is all about advertising," she said slowly and precisely. "Money is not important."

The Headmaster gave her a strange look.

Saturday 19th March

All the stallholders were there, so were some kids and Brittany and Naima. I helped a little and usually offered a non-stressed shoulder to cry on. I found Brittany hiding in the staffroom at one point.

"I don't know Ray," she said head in her hands in that way Americans do in TV shows, "why can't people just do things simply?"

I offered no reason at all.

I left at 11 o'clock. The fete opened at 10 and there were no customers except the occasional loyal parent. I am worried about how disastrous this fete will be and who will get the blame. The fact that they held it at a school two miles from the city centre and the only publicity provided by our marketing wizard Tibor was a one-inch paragraph in the Budapest Sun, which didn't actually say where the fete was being held.

April

Monday April 4th

Miskolc

Easter in Hungary is full of traditions which we don't have in England. Easter is associated with spring and that also applies to the food. There is also the Catholic significance of the end of Lent, where meat is given up for forty days, in fact the Hungarian word for Easter is *Húsvét*, the *hús* bit meaning meat. So the main meal consists of ham, boiled eggs and horseradish sauce. The ham will come from a pig killing festival, but (for fortunate squeamish reasons) I haven't had the chance to go to one of these yet.[40]

Easter Monday is cool too. It is traditional for Hungarian men to sprinkle perfume on the heads of females in some ritual involving the reviving of wilting flowers. Chaps wander the towns in suits knocking on doors reciting a poem along the lines of "I was walking in the green forest, where I saw a blue violet, It wanted to wither away, can I water it?" and sprinkle the perfume over the lady's hair. The girl then rewards the man with an egg. I took a long look at this tradition before getting involved and then, with my words written in front of me I too became Hungarian.

The weather over the weekend was indeed fabulous. The family went for a walk in the mountains and the Wartburg broke down. Dexter managed to bump start the thing back into life so I was very popular. The forests by the mountains were startling in their beauty.

In the evening Andrea and her friends took me to "Black Tracey's" a night club so full of beautiful people that in London voyeurs would pay £20 just to go and watch the people. It was staggering.

At about midnight the mafia turned up and the atmosphere became a bit icier. There were two Al Pacino-like characters who stood in the centre in sharp suits and strange moustaches. They weren't chewing on toothpicks but I felt they should have been. They were surrounded by eleven, yes eleven 'gentlemen' with heads shaved to their skulls. These guys were huge, ugly and mean. I was pretty sure these guys do nothing all day except go to the gym to make their biceps bigger, shave their heads and hit people over the head with the Hungarian equivalent of a pool cue (probably a swimming hat!). I was fascinated and watched from behind a pillar (note

---

[40] Pig Killings are pretty much a definitive Hungarian tourist experience now. I doubt many villages now go in for a ceremonial slaughter of a pig followed by the entire village helping to cut it up, make sausages, save the offal and drain the blood for other foods. Most Hungarians I knew went to Tescos just like the English, although the Hungarians wouldn't dream of buying pre-packed meat. Hungarian supermarkets still employ butchers to prepare the meat in front of you.

the bravery of this Englishman). The eleven monsters (if Hungary ever takes up rugby union, here are their forwards) stood almost to attention watching the dance floor intently. The nightclub bouncers, who were also huge and bald (were they also mafia?) came and stood with them (either because they were part of them, or this was where trouble would be, or because they admired these guys and wanted to be part of them) making thirteen nut-cases all standing, casing the joint. The monsters stood and eyed the girls and seemed to be wishing for some trouble, but none came. Apparently Coppolla's 'Godfather' films are seen here as almost the definitive way for men to be. Allegedly the local mafia base themselves on this rather than any real mafiosi.

Andrea was hiding even further away because she was well aware of the fact that she would be a top 'pull' for one of these guys and had no faith in my ability to deal with that scenario. As I hadn't brought any English sporting equipment with me in case of trouble and I didn't believe my previous claim that they were armed only with swimming caps Andrea was correct to hide.

In fact only I seemed to be paying them any attention. Miskolc people have got used to them I guess. Finally, about half an hour later they decided to leave and filed out towards me. It was at this moment that I nearly got far better acquainted with them than I planned. A particularly good tune came on and I, having had a few drinkies, started flailing my arms around in a vague parody of that leisure activity known as 'dancing'. One of these arms managed to end up in one of these guys' faces, nearly poking his eye out. Clearly I was about to die but I did my usual trick in these situations, which is to diffuse the anger by apologising as rapidly as possible and looking suitably harmless. It worked although I hyperventilated for about twenty minutes afterwards. Andrea gave me a withering look.

"I cannot leave you alone for five minutes can I?" she said.

In case any of you ever get into a situation where you have just poked out a Hungarian Mafioso's eye with a fingernail, the Hungarian for 'sorry Sir' is 'bocsánat uram'. You'll thank me one day.

Tuesday April 5th

I returned to school to a surprise from Brittany.

"Guess what," she said. "We're not getting Internet."

Now if I'd been Jessica I would have been outraged.

"For a second I was surprised," I said.

"Apparently the Headmaster can't get the deal he wants and he is convinced it will be unbelievably expensive," said Brittany.

"What it means is that we are probably the only international school in Western Europe without the access to the world wide web," I said. "And think how much business we lose with no e-mail address?"

Ironically I have no home access to the WWW either at the moment. My access number is down and no-one seems to know why and the only way I can find out is to call Eire for about an hour, only to be told it is to do with maintenance. My question is why does Poland have ten lines, Slovenia, a tiny speck on the map has two and Hungary, a reasonably big country has only one? I got desperate after a while and accessed my mail via the slowest modem in the world in Slovakia and it probably cost me more than my honeymoon. I will simply have to be off-line for a while.

Naima got wind of the no e-mail and has made it her term's job to get the internet in the school. The worse thing is that many students came to the school on the promise of Internet and we have let them down. Are we now going to advertise ourselves as the only school in Western Europe without it? A return to traditional education, none of these modern new fangled methods, just plain, simple blackboard work..

Wednesday 6th April

"I don't fancy teaching Shakespeare to Year 9 today," said Brittany. "I am going to talk about Kosovo instead."

Kosovo, Kosovo. Hungary is the only country in NATO with a direct border to Serbia. The war is happening less than two-hundred miles away from where I write this. Hungarians are worried, not for any association with the Serbs, who they dislike, but for the simple reason that they are far too close. Secondly there is the fact that this time it is ethnic Albanians being cleansed. In the north of Serbia there are ethnic Hungarians and you can guarantee that they will be clobbered next if Milosevic can get away with it.

Jessica is traumatised by the whole thing. She knows a Kosovan girl who was a refugee out of Kosovo last year and lives here. Yesterday she learnt that her whole family had had their throats cut in the last week or so. Jessica has asked for funds from her American church in Pittsburgh and plans to "go to Albania or something at the weekend and help in some way."

I pointed out that 'popping' down to Albania might be slightly difficult. However she is determined. Larry says he has been asked to go to refugee camps somewhere and do some mime and clown work. Americans are going for this in a big way. Most wars have been a long way from home for them. Now they are very close to one indeed. Of course we are safe here but it is making them think. There is also their firm belief that 'we' are right and we must sort this guy out. There is no question of not doing anything.

In the classroom Dima the Russian boy is said to be 'cross', Yifan, a Chinese girl is said to be 'worried' but about what I don't know, Wouter's father a journalist for a Dutch newspaper is in the Balkans somewhere reporting. Brittany is very gung-ho and showed me Greek outrage in the Herald and Tribune with disbelief.

Thursday 7th April

Jessica was in class today forgot about British English.

"Today children we are going to talk about colors," she said. "Now Thomas (English boy aged 4) what color are your pants?"

Thomas stared at the wall next to Jessica.

"Come on Thomas," coaxed Jessica. "What colour are your pants?"

Finally Thomas, with the shy, cuteness of a four year old, undid his trousers, looks down at his underwear and said slowly, "White"

Jessica finally realised what was happening grabbed him and screamed "No trousers! No trousers!"

Being from a litigious society she immediately called the mother to explain what had happened.

"I'm not getting sued over such a little thing," she said.

I gave her a look.

"NO NOT that little thing!" she wailed. "Oh nooooooo."

Americans – they're so easy to tease.

The Headmaster is still absolutely hopeless. Naima sat him down to address the serious question of what was happening with recruitment next year. As all but two of his staff are leaving it might be worth doing something - anything. However the Headmaster's eye was caught by the newspaper and proceeded to flick through it absent-mindedly.

"So what are you going to do?" asked Naima.

"This advert is too small," said the Headmaster. "It should be much bigger."

He was more worried about his advertisement in the paper.

In the evening Andrea and I took Endre and Éva to the Chinese restaurant. Endre has not heeded my sensible advice to not date his forty-seven year old boss and seems to be completely in love. So I am paying no further attention to the matter.

Friday 8th April

Today was a typical day at the office. Brittany was sick, Naima was at the doctors, Tony is in America because of a bereavement, the French teacher (a woman whose strangeness never ceases to amaze me) told the kids on Wednesday that she wouldn't be in today but neglected to inform any members of staff. So it was basically Ági and I running the show with our own classes to cover. It was video time for the morning.

The photocopier was dead and had been dead for two days and the exam board were still neglecting to act on their own mistakes. I was attempting to call them again to discuss something in the spare five minutes I had when the Headmaster looked over my shoulder.

"Ah the invoices," he said taking them from me. And proceeded to ask questions and suggest that I call the exam board immediately to sort it out, not letting me explain that his chatting was stopping me doing just that. By the time he had said this I had to go and teach again.

Jessica has had a complete change of heart and wants to stay in Hungary, "but I can't afford to," she wailed.

"If you're serious, why don't you write down what salary you want and hand it to the Headmaster. He wants you to stay and can only say no," I said. I said this with the knowledge that she is paid half of what I am, and if I am not here they could certainly find the money.

In the evening Andrea took me to one of The American Company's parties at the 'Blue Tomato' club[41]. This was great. The American Company are clearly ready to enter the world attractive female formation dancing team as I found myself on the dance floor and noticing I was the only chap with fifteen women all dancing in a circle around me. Being brave I decided to go the bar instead. Andrea was pleasantly drunk and introduced me to an Australian boss of hers. Nice chap. I like talking to Australians because you can re-run Eddie Izzard routines to them and claim them as yours as they are unlikely to have heard of him. So as we talked about the war I managed to sound extremely witty as I described the Italian contribution to the NATO effort as a bunch of guys with slick hair zipping around on scooters going 'Ciao' a lot.

Monday 11th April

Right I've had it with Tescos. Call me a sad ex-patriot but I liked the fact that I could go to the local Tesco on Pillangó Utca and, amongst all the typical Hungarian fare (obscene amounts of dairy products, every type of cheese in the world except Cheddar, live fish swimming around in crowded tank for immediate purchase, bottled vegetables and no frozen ready meals at all (hooray)), one could find the British section shelves. On there you could find such eclectic necessities as Heinz baked beans, brown sauce, Newcastle Brown ale, marmite. But it has suddenly disappeared. I could accept this loss of the British section but further inspection showed that they have completely removed brown sauce and baked beans from the shelves. It is unpatriotic. And never ever make the mistake of buying Hungarian baked beans. Awful.

Tony was back from his bereavement.

"California's still there," he beamed. "I ate a lot of fast food too. But the world is changing. I saw the Manchester United vs Juventus match live over there. Soccer on TV, what is happening to America?"

Brittany is suffering from slow news access.

"If they send ground troops in that's it," she said hysterically today. "I told Michael (her boyfriend) yesterday, 'how fast can you pack?'"

I just gave her a strange look. This was my stress last Friday afternoon. Where had she been? Then I remembered I have Sky news. The Russian president had been warning about WW3 on Friday and then she had read the new Newsweek which is a little old. I was also going to point out that running away from WW3 would be very pointless because America would be nuked just as fast as Europe. My

---

[41] Pannónia st 5-7, Pest

theory is that Hungary's actually pretty safe. However the Russians and the Serbs are Slav brothers and snubbing the Russians over this is not clever.

As you can tell by the above we take this Balkan thing pretty seriously.

There is slapstick too. Brittany had me laughing today when we were having a serious Balkan discussion. Suddenly she broke off to say, "I'm sorry Ray we have to stop here because your hair is completely out of control."

Tuesday 12th April

The Russians are furious still. Andrea met one in the bank the other day. He was most annoyed with the Hungarians joining NATO and reiterated the Slavic brother line. I think we in the West thought the Russians secretly wanted to be like the West when we were in the Cold War times. From my current viewpoint there is nothing an average Russian wants less than to be like an American, but hypocritically they still want their consumerist lifestyle.

At school the Internet mystery cleared a little bit. Tibor the one armed physicist cracked under severe Naima interrogation and admitted that the Headmaster had cancelled two appointments for a company to come and install the ISDN line necessary. However as he wanted the cheaper option, a company that never answered the phone nor ever responded to messages, he kept blowing the useful company out. Under pain of death Naima forced the whimpering Tibor to call the good company and get them down here as fast as possible.

In the evening Andrea and I went to see Father Gábor, our priest. He is still a lovely guy. Andrea was slightly uncomfortable because she had 'accidentally' worn her shortest skirt to work that day and was therefore taking great pains to cover her legs as she sat down. I must accept that if I were a Catholic priest subjected to the sight of Andrea in a short skirt I too would question my vows of celibacy too.

She first draped her long brown coat over the offending limbs but Gábor immediately stood up and insisted that he hang her coat up for her.

"How rude of me not to take your coat on arrival," he cursed to himself.

Andrea reluctantly handed over the coat. She then took two pieces of paper from her bag and rested them over her legs.

"What's that?" said Gábor.

"Um, um," said Andrea having no idea what the papers were. Fortunately they turned out to be early print runs of the wedding invitations so she could waffle on about this for a while to the fascinated Gábor. However this did not solve the leg problem so she spent the next ten minutes trying to shrink back under the hem of the skirt and failing miserably. I was little help as I was aware of the huge embarrassment in the room and the blissful ignorance of Gábor to the embarrassment and found it all rather amusing. However Andrea gave me a fierce look and I managed to stop sniggering and ask Gábor a very pertinent question about the nature of body, spirit and soul to molecular systems (he had a good answer and I was very pleased).

The Hungarian Girl Trap

Wednesday 13th April

"Are Russia in NATO?" asked a gloriously sleepy Jessica this morning.

"I think the whole point is that Russia is NOT a member," deadpanned Brittany.

"Oh yeah how stupid of me," giggled Jessica.

I accept her vacuousness today because she is dithering about her life. She did as I suggested and told the Headmaster she wanted $1000 to stay. The Headmaster of course offered $900 and Jessica then got even more stressed.

"Oh no Ray, this means I can stay, I'm not sure I want to now," she wailed.

"Do you really want to put up with all this Headmaster crap for another twelve months?" asked Brittany.

"Well no," said Jessica. "But I like it in Hungary."

I think she will stay but I hope she goes just to wipe the smug grin off the Headmaster's face.

Karen, the keen English teacher from our sister school in London has accepted the job and is coming to Hungary. This is a massive boost for this school and I hope they do her justice. I hope they get her a bloody work permit. I have of course not completely burnt my bridges. The 'life' is great here but the school is not viable right now. In five years time it might be…

There has been further dissent from the staff room today, led unfortunately by Ray 'Scargill' Dexter. The problem, as usual was the slight lateness problem associated with everyone with the school. The reason for this is that the Headmaster will not get us a bell because 'it interferes with the other school'. Therefore which clock is the clock which correctly tells the time? The staff run off the staff room clock but is that synchronised to the class clocks? The Headmaster wandered in to the staff room at break today to tell us that it was lesson time as we sat having tea.

"Come on you are late," he said.

"We'll get to class on time when you get to school on time," said Brittany a little louder than was necessary.

This is of course referring to the Headmaster's habit of arriving religiously at 9.23 a.m every morning wearing a daft beret: parents, phone calls, etc waiting impatiently in the corridor. Five minutes later the secretary turns up.

Then Naima who has a moral duty to uphold the Headmaster's decisions then nagged the teachers at every break between classes.

"But who says we're late?" I said, enjoying this. "This clock says we're fine. Brittany's watch says we're five minutes late, yours says one minute late, Tony's says we go now and Wendy the Chinese teacher doesn't wear a watch at all. We need a bell."

"But we can't have a bell," said Naima.

"Then how can we get to class on time?" I said. I admit I was being annoying but there was a valid point here.

In the evening Andrea and I took Andrea's boss, an American called Angela Mancini to the brilliantly named 'Crazy Club' and 'dzsungel restaurant'[42]. The restaurant was remarkable: a cellar done up like a rainforest. This sounds crazy but this *is* the Crazy Club. You are surrounded by tree branches and creepers and eerie jungle noises. Every five minutes or so an elephant trumpeted, the lights went out (there were candles) and a crack of thunder sounded out. The food was also themed and you could order such gems as 'Baloo's foot' and 'Elephant soup'. It was great. Angela was cool too. She's kind of my age but has got lost somewhere in the career chaos and seemed remarkably jealous of my teaching lifestyle. The point is I guess I'm doing what I want to do and she's doing what she has to do. She happened to keep up the 100% score for Americans I know who are writing the 'Great American novel.'

"I see the point of leaving to write it," I said, "How can you see something properly when you're inside it?" Angela thought this very profound but then she works for The American Firm, talks business all day and has no time for profound thoughts. I spend my day with Larry and Brittany, they keep me alive. Mancini also snuck into Metallica concerts when she was a teenager and showed her country folk's ability with languages: six months here and can't say "Thank you" yet.

She also gave me my first outright huge belly laugh for a long time. After discussing the Priest problems yesterday Angela said,

"Is Gábor good-looking?"

"Of course," said Andrea.

"Don't you kind of find that frustrating?" said Angela.

"Well I personally don't," I said.

"Yeah but even as a guy don't you look at him and say, 'Hey man you could get some'?"

It was this that set me off roaring with laughter. I can't even say why. I think it was because it had no bitterness about it.

Friday 14th April

The school has its own Balkan parody. Karim, our tiny Egyptian boy plays the Kosovo Albanians. Within the school it is almost an unwritten rule that you do not make any bad comments in the boy's diary because the boy has a kind of fit and is guaranteed a beating by his father (playing Slobodan Milosovic). On Tuesday things reached a head when Karim arrived at school having been severely beaten because his mobile phone hadn't been working when his father wanted to reach him. The boy arrived with two huge red welts on both his cheekbones. Naima (playing the Macedonians) was very upset about it and suggested that we do not write anything at all in the boy's diary again just in case it provokes more violence. Brittany (playing Gung ho America), Jessica (playing bible belt America) Larry (playing paranoid

---

[42] 30 Jókai st, Pest.

conspiracy theorist take the bastards out now America) and Dexter (playing Great Britain) decide that this father has to be nailed and nailed now by the relevant authorities. We tell the Headmaster (playing the United Nations or somebody else who is pretty toothless) who informs us that nothing can be done as it is an internal matter, the man is Egyptian and their culture is utterly different from ours.

Fast forward today. I arrive late just as Larry and Brittany are talking with raised voices about the problem.

"It's been three fuckin' days," bellowed Larry, "and nothing's been done. These Hungarians are all the same. Turn a blind eye and hope it goes away."

"We need a camera in this school to record this beating," said Brittany. "Can we set up a meeting with this guy."

"We should get a doctor, a psychiatrist, and a policeman round there straightaway before he kills the kid," yelled Larry.

Ági slipped out the door. (I can't think of a role for Ági.) "There she goes," muttered Larry, "she's supposed to be in charge of personal issues and she's skulking out the door. I tell you I am so pissed off about this I don't even wanna teach classes now."

Dexter manages to stop the Americans going to lynch somebody. I suggest that we get the guy in on the pretext of discussing the boy's lack of work and then broach the subject as sensitively as possible. Further constructive work continues but by then it is ten past nine and all three of us have missed the start of our lessons (no bell). Naima comes storming in.

"What is wrong with you?" she screams. "You do realise that if you are late for class then you are docked a day's pay."

This was the wrong thing to say.

"Listen," snarled Brittany, "I happen to think that this kid's well-being is more important than anything right now so dock me a day's pay, screw the school and I'm outta here."

She storms out of the school building and only some tiny part of her brings her back fuming to take her class.

At the next class turnover Naima informs us that the Headmaster will not be in until lunchtime.

"Well dock him a fuckin' days pay as well then," growls Brittany.

Jessica then arrives with her huge smile.

"I still don't know whether to stay on here or go home." she said.

"Jessica," we said. "Go home and get away from Headmaster crap."

"Dexter you and I are going to see him this afternoon and if he gives me one ounce of crap he's gonna need a new history teacher," said Brittany

So Brittany and I got to see the Headmaster at 3.15. He was quite sympathetic and said he did not want to broach the subject with the father for fear of making the violence worse and I believed him. However we pointed out that as this was a Western School we had a moral right to tell him how to treat his son. If he chose to educate his son in the British way then he should at least know what we feel.

So a meeting will be arranged. The Headmaster will make the call (although he wanted to send a letter with the boy) and no women will be involved with the meeting (the wife (playing Bosnia) also gets whacked).

They are diplomatically immune that is the problem. That is why we must act so carefully. I hope we can get the instant camera in though.

"You do realise if we weren't making this fuss," I said, "he would do nothing."

"Of course," said Brittany.

It has been decided that Larry is to be nowhere near any meetings. He is a little too emotional. Every class he taught today was about child abuse.

In the afternoon it was just Larry and I left in the school. Larry voiced the feelings I had been feeling. My vision of myself is of a 'Flashman' style coward/charlatan who by some means manages to convince the world he is very brave and very efficient when he is actually the opposite. Therefore the thought of me personally being the one to speak to this violent Egyptian father was, for me, laughable. However as the day progressed and I thought about who else could do it I realised we had few options. Brittany is a woman and therefore unlikely to be listened to, ditto Naima, Larry is likely to kill the guy and on another level would an Egyptian appreciate an Israeli telling him what to do? Ági is another woman and the Headmaster is unlikely to be the right person either. This left the odd-job man Laci Bácsi (a professional alcoholic) or me. Now obviously Laci's the man for the job in my eyes but Larry turned to me and said, "Ray, you know you're the guy who's going to have to do this."

Some stupid part of me said, "I know, and I will do it gladly."

It was inevitable really.

Saturday 15th April

Miskolc

I was in the Black Crow with the local lads. My Hungarian wasn't so bad now with a skinful of beer inside me so I played a few games of pool and even won a game or two. The lads even taught me profoundly useful words, like spots and stripes - in the context of pool balls.

"Slowly you are learning Hungarian ways," said the Doctor, rattled by my new found talent.

"I will be a Hungarian soon," I said in a gesture of solidarity.

The Doctor stopped puffing on a cigarette for the first time that evening.

"Impossible," he said. "You can't be a Hungarian because you aren't a Hungarian."

"That's crazy," I said. "Supposing I learnt the language perfectly?"

"Even your wife-to-be can't speak it perfectly. She has lived outside Hungary too long, she can't do the official language[43]. You would always have the accent."

"But if I lived here the rest of my life, changed my name to László Kovács, went somewhere new."

"Impossible, you don't look Hungarian, you can never fully understand us. You would always be the Englishman. Look at Yenki over there."

He pointed out a very Hungarian looking guy chatting to a girl at the bar.

"Yenki is Hungarian born but he spent his teenage years in America and now he is known as Yenki[44]."

"But in England we don't care about such things," I said quite astonished.

"We are different, we know who we are. We say our names backwards[45], light switches go up rather than down. We are different. And now I feel it is time to play darts," and the conversation was over.

Monday 17th April

The staff were all fired up this morning because we were expecting Gerry and the Headmaster of our English school. So we had great assemblies lined up and Dexter planned to go on nature trails. However nobody turned up at all. There are hassles somewhere in the bureaucracy.

Larry, Brittany and I shared a giggle today. In deference to the current Kosovo refugee situation Brittany had organised for our students to bring in any old clothes and toys they do not want. The Chinese students had brought in some rather eccentric clothing. Inside one of the bin liners was an outfit that Michael Jackson would look right at home in. It was like a fake military outfit with tassels and lots of gold. The thought of some poor Kosovar wearing this in the mud of Macedonia made us laugh far louder than was probably appropriate.

As my e-mail has been a little erratic I have had to brave the Hungarian postal service – something I have to brace myself to do. Now don't get me wrong, the British post office I'm sure was pretty similar twenty years ago, but I can't cope with the pointless bureaucracy of it anymore. You enter and there are maybe one million queues that go back at least five miles (hey I don't exaggerate). There are various counters where you can pay bills, send parcels, do obscure Hungarian things which no other country does, or even send letters, but it is often not particularly clear which queue I am supposed to be in. I usually just join the one with other people holding

---

[43] Hungarian has three forms of address, the informal, the formal and the official. The official is usually only learnt in adulthood, when one tends to meet officials. So if you spent time out of Hungary in your late teens you could miss out.

[44] "Yankee"

[45] Hungarian are big on introductions and all Hungarian's introduce themselves surname first, followed by Christian name.

letters, or find myself accidentally in the queue for doing obscure Hungarian things and get sent away when I reach the front of the queue.

Now the first problem is that Hungarian banks are a little bit backwards. This means there are no cheque books, direct debits, standing orders, or credit cheques. So when you owe a company money, you receive a 'cheque' stating how much you owe. Then you take this 'cheque' to the post office and pay with cash. So *all* bills are paid at the post office. The second problem is that there are no visible stamp machines so you have to queue for *all* stamps. Even if you do have the stamps you cannot send them airmail without the relevant stamp (as in ink stamp). So you have to queue for everything and everyone has to visit the post office a few times a week. Then, when you have queued for 120 years the lady behind the counter puts the stamps on for you. Yes the Hungarian post office do not trust people to lick stamps. So the whole process takes forever.

Tuesday 18th April

The Headmaster surprised us all today by speaking to the violent Egyptian father. Gerry's here too and happy and has promised to pay me through August. I don't believe it and am cursing myself for not getting it in writing.

"In that case I promise to leave the exam files in some order then," I joked.

Wednesday 19th April

The Headmaster said that the violent Egyptian father had been waiting three hours for his son to turn up and at 9 p.m finally found him at a friend's house. His way of expressing relief was to beat the son senseless. The Headmaster accepted that man was profoundly sorry and that it wouldn't happen again. Gerry echoed these sentiments, saying "I think the man genuinely loves the boy." My blackest humour was awoken.

"I'll have to give the boy back all his bad comments to see if the man is telling the truth," I said.

Thursday 20th April

I have a confession to make and it is about the television I watched last night. My choice of TV is severely limited: if I want it in English. O.K there are nine Hungarian channels that show dubbed films and other foreign shows but I refuse to watch them. Andrea cannot understand this at all but my argument is that you lose half the acting performance if the thing is dubbed and besides I wouldn't watch "Beverley Hills Cop II" in English let alone Hungarian. Maybe it's just me being snobbish, I don't know. The best is when Andrea gets very excited and says, "Ooh '*För att inte tala om alla dessa kvinnor'* [46], Ingmar Bergmann's magnificent treatise on blah blah blah is on tonight! Have you seen it?"

"Um I missed that one," I'd say.

Andrea gives me a withering look that says, "What did you do with your life before you met me?" and then insists I watch it despite my protests that a Swedish language film dubbed into Hungarian is slightly inaccessible to me. I last five minutes and then I fall fast asleep.

So Hungarian TV is out, although there was an excellent show on Christie Moore (subtitled) last week; the German channels are similar, save for a rather good music channel (VIVA) and Eurosport which is also in German. So I am left with Cartoon Network, notable for the excellent "Dexter's Laboratory" *naturellement* and that's it, oh and Sky news which repeats itself every half an hour. I hope you understand therefore why I resorted to watching the world female aerobics championships on Eurosport last night. I am sure you would have assumed I would have preferred to watch a programme on the impact *Fauvism* has made on modern Hungarian painting in the original Hungarian but watching various young ladies in the peak of physical position jumping up and down in clothing designed to show off muscle tone and smiling from under bleached blonde hair is about the level of entertainment I need when it's 11.30 at night, Andrea is asleep and I can't turn the light on to read for fear of waking her up.

Not surprisingly a Hungarian woman is the world aerobics champion and Andrea goes to her gym every week to do aerobics. The Hungarian female is an amazing creature. Tony and I were talking about it at lunch today. Out of the blue Brittany suddenly said, "You know I think Hungarian women are the most beautiful women in the world."

She sort of sighed as she said it. Brittany is lovely in her own right of course (he says chivalrously). Tony and I swapped smug grins. His wife is also an Andrea from Hungary.

"Why do you think we're sitting here right now?" said Tony.

"It's the Hungarian girl trap," I said.

"Obviously this doesn't affect me," said Brittany, "but comparatively the women here just all look like thin fashion women. In fact it's like L.A but here there's no silicone or plastic.[47]"

I then went on about the fact that sometimes I simply cannot believe the women I see in this town. At the tram stop every day is a quite astonishing woman who just gets on with her life. In England she would be swamped or on TV or something.

"Why d'you start talking about Hungarian girls?" said Tony to Brittany.

---

[46] "Now, about these women"

[47] This is of course hogwash, another example of the traveller's wrong generalisation. Hungarian women spend *all* their money on beauty treatments!

"Well look at them," said Brittany pointing to the girls in the dining room. They just want to be women I guess, you know femininity rather than feminism is what gets them through the day."

"And you know what the best thing is," said Tony, his grin getting even smugger, "Hungarian men are such shits they throw themselves at nice foreign guys like me."

"It is indeed a hard life," I said as I ate my thin soup, salty fish and potato salad.

Tony and I took the whole school to the art exhibition put on by all the International schools in the city. Churchill's stand was remarkable and stood out from the others. Bea the art teacher had surpassed herself with her Matisse theme for the year. I had written the entire art blurb to accompany the exhibition and Bea was very happy with the result. She had also become best pals with all the other art teachers. Tony and I quit early to go for a beer. A Californian by birth Tony revealed he was a leading light in the LA punk scene of the early eighties. He knows the members of Black Flag and Bad Religion ("Who?" – the world) . He was a DJ, photographer, promoter, writer in the city at the time and had his photograph taken by Andy Warhol. He named dropped obscure British punk bands too and I was very impressed.

Friday 21st April

I am worried that my limited media is giving me a corrupted view of the English speaking world. Here are the media that inform my world: The Daily Telegraph, NME, Sky news, a paranoid NYC Jew, a Bible belt American, a gung ho American and Tony an old punk Californian. As a result the tension is tangible. I am starting to see conspiracies everywhere, in NME we have pages dedicated to loser drug taking types who think their retro music is good and are saying anything relevant, Sky news blanket coverage the world with hype and in-depth panic. I have decided that the Russians aren't coming now, but as far as my media informs me, the rest of the English speaking world is going to hell.

Of course I don't believe all the above but I am serious when I tell you that this madness is what reaches me. The only thing to do is continue watching the world aerobics championships…

Monday 24 April

Assembly. This is a rather pointless exercise in that the whole school sits in the big room and the Headmaster witters on in his flaky way (sorry my language is a little American) and then Larry tells stories well into period one. Today was ridiculous and highlighted for me the problems with the Headmaster. He spent five minutes telling the kids to tell their parents that they should pay their tuition fees for next year very soon, spending a good five minutes detailing what discounts and deals are available.

Now the average kid will not even listen to this let alone remember the details. Why not send a note home? What a good question! One would think that over such important issues as fees one could spend money on a stamp to send them directly. The other ridiculous thing was that Larry decided to organise a basketball match staff vs students. The Headmaster, in an act of lunacy, asks the kids when they want the match to be held. They all choose Wednesday afternoon, art day. So the democratic choice is Wednesday but no-one thinks of course to phone Bea the art teacher to warn her. There will be problems.

Tuesday 25th April

There was a staff trip to the Szent Jupat[48] restaurant, recommended by Tony because the food is greasy, the portions are huge and it's really cheap. Present were Brittany (and boyfriend), Tony (and wife), Ági, Peter, a maths teacher, Larry, me and Jennifer, a friend of Tony's. The restaurant was great. The place was so greasy you slipped on the stairs, every surface was covered in a thin film of oil. I ate a whole mountain of liver and beef and, of course the 'soup for the just married man', and was as witty as I could manage. I think I overdid the old wit on Jennifer, an Italian American from New Mexico, who was there for no tangible reason except Tony knows her, because she kissed me as she left. Silly girl, don't believe the Dexter hype, he's not cool at all. Tony did his usual trick of asking the waiter exactly who gets the tip money, and received his usual non-committal reply from our excellent waiter.

"Because, you see I want you to get the money, not your boss," said Tony.

The waiter didn't want to enter a discussion about it, and Tony got quite upset about the unfairness of the system and as we left he tried to force the tip into the back pocket of the waiter, to the waiter's huge embarrassment. He looked around quickly to see if his boss was looking.

Wednesday 26th April

Success, Réka and I managed to complete the German orals without any major cock ups. I am so happy.

Today was the day of the staff vs students basketball game. The staff team of Larry, me, Ági and Peter were looking a little light. Tony was teaching at another school. The student team consisted of four very sharp players, who played every week and were fit. They also had substitutes.

I had to play at top form and scored about fifty points to stay in the game. The whole school was there screaming. Bea, the art teacher was screaming too at the blatant disregard for art in the school and blaming Larry for no art class. Larry was keeping out of the way. Somehow we were leading at half time: 32 – 24 to the staff, Dexter having scored 24 points. Larry, an ex-pro, eased off in the second half

---

[48] Just off Moszkva Ter, dodge past McDonalds on Retek st

clowning around and substituting some less talented kids onto our team. The school team double teamed (a basketball thing) me too, but the staff still won by four points. The kids were furious; on the one hand they couldn't believe such a bad staff team could win and on the other hand they complained that I was too good. You can't have it both ways.

I met Tony at five o'clock to go to the football game between England and Hungary. I had been looking forward to going for months and planned exactly what I was wearing (my mock Hungarian shirt). I wanted to sit with the Hungarians. The only problem was how was an Englishman going to get into the Hungarian area? I mean the English hardly have a reputation for being polite in the vicinity of football grounds. Tony concocted a plan whereby he bought the tickets and I would hang around looking suspicious. If anyone questioned my nationality I was prepared with a variety of accents to prove I was anything but English. I could be Scottish, American (but Tony couldn't keep a straight face when I tried his native accent), South African, Pakistani (although I was trying for Welsh!) and New Zealand. In the end it wasn't a problem. Tony's Hungarian is so good it was a very simple procedure. Tony is not your typical American. He speaks four languages fluently and will happily admit that most of his fellow countrymen are the dumbest, most ill-informed people on the Earth.

"I went to UCLA man," he said to me in bar later over beer and plum palinka. "That's one of the top universities in America and the students were all completely dumb. You had the genuinely dumb, the sporty dumb, the surfer 'hey dude' play dumb, and the plain and simple ill-informed dumb." So he loves living in Budapest.

There was a huge bouncer with a moustache on the gate (it was a garden bar) who told us we could only come in for half an hour as they would be closing at six. They were scared of nutty Hungarian fans and nutty English fans. However we were meticulously polite and bought lots of beer and two hours later we were still there. There were some English and Hungarians there and it was quite nice.

At seven we picked up István and Tony had a profound effect on the man. Normally István, a guy who would list "watching Italian splatter core movies dubbed into English alone" as one of his hobbies in "Who's Who", is rather shy and usually takes six months to say 'Hi' to you. If he needs to say something in ten words he will use one and say it in his native tongue if possible. Tony is the opposite, if one word is needed he'll use ten and in whatever the hell language you want. This meant that he forced István to smile and converse.

The game was good, surrounded by Hungarian fans, eating sunflower seeds[49] and swearing in unison at the German referee. Tony spent the game cheering on the Hungarians (so did I, I was surrounded and you didn't see the football violence between two Hungarian teams last week). I sang the Hungarian national anthem and

---

[49] The only sustenance, along with pumpkin seeds dipped in paprika available in Hungarian football grounds

Tony spent most of the game admiring Rio Ferdinand and espousing his theories on how soccer could be improved. "Man you need ad-breaks!"

Afterwards in the mutual satisfaction of a 1-1 draw we repaired to a local *Söröző* for a few more beers. Sörözős are the lowest of the low as far as drinking establishments are concerned. Tony believes that why should he pay $1 for a beer in a fancy bar when he can by the same pint of beer for 37 cents in a Söröző? Because then you hang out with gypsies, prostitutes, bag men, dirty men, men with beards or huge handlebar moustaches and other alcoholic types and sit on Formica tables - would be my response. I would always hang out in a place where the people are better looking than me you see and preferably these better looking people are Hungarian women in silver mini dresses. So anyway predictably a fight breaks out between two men who carry all their possessions with them in polythene bags and have a film of dirt on them, and on their beards. The language got rather fruity. The Hungarian's are the worst swearers in the world and István translated the insults for me.

"The fat guy just told the other guy that he is a homosexual who operates rather brutishly in a prison," said István.

"You have one word that can say all that?" I said.

István nodded proudly.

Thursday 27th April

I should have shut up about the smooth progression of the German oral. The cassette with all the results on has disappeared. I am very stressed and have turned the staff room up and down. The Headmaster said why didn't I put it in the safe and I was so cross that I had no answer, except that neither he nor the secretary were actually at school yesterday to do it for me. I still should have hidden it. I am envisaging plots where the kids have stolen the tape to re-do it, but know deep-down neither Dima nor Wouter have the wit for such a thing. So where is it?

Friday 28th April

I have decided the only way to save the German oral is to swallow ones pride and do them all again. I haven't told Réka yet, she was away today, she will be mad, as will the kids but we have no choice.

Today was a little chaotic. The school really seemed to be lurching, Titanic-like towards the bottom of the Atlantic. Another Chinese girl is leaving next year, seduced by the cheapness of the Christian School and its better facilities. They can do this because they don't pay the teachers anything, the teacher's local church raise funds for the teacher's salary. This meant that the Headmaster does not need Wendy, the slightly dotty Chinese teacher next year and so he fired her today, which is a little short-sighted if more Chinese arrive. Later Larry arrived saying he was going to demand x amount of dollars to stay on and if he didn't get it he was resigning. How many times now?

"Sometimes you've got to stand on the edge of a cliff and hope you can fly and this is one of those times," he said.

So he had a word with the Headmaster about the pay rise and the Headmaster must have said no because Larry immediately announced in a loud voice.

"O.K sorry to interrupt but I just want my colleagues and you Headmaster to know that I will not be here at this School next year," and walked off.

"Is he joking?" asked the Headmaster, looking shell-shocked.

The reality is that every year this school starts with a new set of staff and new students and over the course of the year they all leave, all to be replaced by a new set of staff and teachers. The only constants are the Headmaster and his secretary. Surely somebody must be able to put two and two together?

It was 'world math day' and we contributed by doing some of the natural world parts. It involved getting the kids into teams and getting them to make volcanoes, and hurricane models and asking mathematical questions about what they were doing. The team work was excellent because we teachers chose the teams. The kids enjoyed themselves far more than they expected and it was an all-round success.

In the evening we went back home to Miskolc. Now normally we take the Inter City home but for a reason I have forgotten we took the earlier 'normal' train home. This was a mistake. The train is from a different planet. It is much cheaper of course but you cannot reserve seats and even if you could you can guarantee that some swarthy type with the type of tan you aren't sure isn't grime or sun originated is sitting there eating a salami sandwich and his fifteen children are fighting in the corridor. It also takes forever winding round forgotten towns, and is packed to the rafters. It's not quite as packed as pictures of trains you see in India with people on the roof but it's still a bit tight. What made this particular journey worse was that the train was filled with national service soldiers on a weekend furlough.

They were pretty drunk and noisy as we got on. They occupied a compartment two away from us and they sang and bashed on the windows in rhythm all the way. Every time one of them left the train they hung out the windows chanting "Szervusz Zoli" in the case of Zoltan or "Szervusz Sanyi" if the guy happened to be a Sandor. Once they chanted "Goodbye Christine" to a fat American who had made the mistake of eyeing them up.

"You are a veree beauteefool wooman," slurred one, to the American's delight. Then they smashed beer bottles on the tracks.

Next was the charming cry of "Shit on NATO, shit on NATO" as they forgot whose side they were on for a minute (interesting fact language fans – I saw more NATO graffiti this week – "Halál NATO" – death to NATO. What is interesting is the Hungarian word for death. Seen it before somewhere? The Hungarian's middle Eastern origins sometimes show their roots)

As they got more drunk they got noisier. Andrea, with her more European temperament was getting a little annoyed. I was being typically British and ignoring the noise and studiously trying to complete the Daily Telegraph's crossword. Finally Andrea had enough. She was sick of the bashing on the compartment from the next compartment and went to confront them. She bollocked them in no uncertain fashion and to my amusement I heard the soldiers mumble "sorry" very quietly after she had finished. The rest of the journey was only accompanied by song not violence. I'm not sure what this all says about the backbone of the country!

"Obviously I was about to go through there and give them a piece of my mind," I said as Andrea returned triumphant.

May

Monday 1st May

I was late today owing to a bridge closure. Beautiful though the Freedom and the Széchenyi bridges are, they were built in more innocent times. The bridge's main suspension 'cables' go up to the two towers at a very climbable angle. If you are drunk enough or have sudden suicidal tendencies you can be on top of the bridge without much effort at all. Once your up there sobriety hits pretty quickly and you either jump (rare), or wait to get rescued. Whilst this is happening the bridge is closed. Happens quite often. I didn't care because I was supposed to be doing assembly and hadn't planned it. I missed out on daft Naima getting the kids to give me a round of applause for organising the maths day when all I'd done was wander around helping them with the answers. Ági, the real organiser was a little peeved.

Larry is worried about our Russian girls who have progressed from letting the dodgy Hungarian boys from the school we share a building with buy them ice cream and are now engaged in games of 'I'll show you mine if you show me yours'. Ekaterina, aged thirteen is coming to school in the kind of outfits you normally see strippers arrive on stage in. Because our school is so small there is no real experience of sex with any of the kids. There are no other peers to check their behaviour. There is no PSHE in the school and Larry is convinced a rape or a pregnancy will happen soon, which will finally put the nail in the school's coffin. He is proposing that he takes the whole school and lecture them about 'decency'. Brittany wants to introduce a skirt length rule and a no midriff rule and the Headmaster wants to do nothing.

I found the German tape! It was stuck in Tony's drawer, the one place I didn't look because I 'knew' he didn't take it!

Tuesday 2nd May

Jessica is in one of her moods again. She was ripped off by $100 at a money exchange place last month. She gave them $200 and they changed $100. She was furious, called the police but of course couldn't prove that she gave them $200 in the first place. So she spent this afternoon picketing outside the place telling anyone who would listen not to change their money there because they would rip you off. She was pleased with her success but, of course the owner came out and gave her grief, denying any wrong doing. So she spent the morning questioning the Headmaster about Hungarian law. The Headmaster predictably said she had no proof she had been ripped off.

Also Jessica is going to Albania to help refugees from the war. She has booked flights, got funds from her church in Pennsylvania. She is so keen and determined to do good. Unfortunately she is being a little naïve, and add the fact that her keenness is rather easy to tease and we in the staffroom are having a good time at her expense. Brittany, Tony, Larry and I just cannot resist and when Jessica said today in all seriousness that, "what they're really short of out there are sink plungers and I'm going to take as many as I can with me," a few sniggers were heard. Now I know what she is doing is admirable and we shouldn't make light of this and, in fact Jessica has got annoyed at us for not doing something. However Brittany summed up why we were right.

"She is going into an unknown, dangerous situation literally on a prayer. She is a beautiful American girl on her own. She just should think this through more. We are right to question her motivation."

The staff are slightly annoyed with the Headmaster because he has been seen driving a new car recently. So he's being paid well then.

The lack of PSHE within the school is becoming a real problem. The kids genuinely have no knowledge of real issues. Brittany asked me what British schools did and I told her. She had asked the Headmaster why this school had no PSHE classes and the Headmaster apparently replied, "well Hungarian schools don't have it all." This is classic goalpost moving and further proof that nobody in authority has any real idea what this school is all about. Whenever you read the leaflets we are a British school running the National Curriculum but the National Curriculum is forgotten when it suits, and we are informed that we are independent and don't have to follow it (but we sit the exams!). When they are really in trouble the Headmaster simply claims that we are a Hungarian school and therefore don't need to do anything. The PSHE is one example, the other is the bizarre placement of students in classes. Essentially it depends on what they have done in the Hungarian system and we are dictated by that. I suspect this is because they are juggling between both systems, for tax purposes we also have a different Hungarian name so we are fairly tied to Hungarian ideas too. It's a bloody mess basically.

In the evening we went to an American Firm soiree in an aeronautically themed bar near Nyugati Station. Somebody or other was leaving the firm and at my end of the table the conversation was entirely in Hungarian so, predictably my gaze drifted towards the television at the bar where they were showing more highlights from the ice hockey world championships (sponsored by Skoda). Andrea decided I was being very unsociable watching the television so she sent me away to the monolinguists corner, a newly formed area consisting of only me and Angela Mancini, her American boss.

I like Mancini, she's funny, pretty, wears Levi's well and has been screwed up by this guy who she followed to Budapest (he probably started sleeping with another one of these darned attractive Hungarian women). She's a little bit down at the moment, so the last thing she needed probably was me chatting to her, but she took it well, especially as half the conversation was drowned out by the Latino band playing right by my left ear. Latino bands it seems, by the way, are contractually obliged to play that Spanish song that seems to go 'there's only one can of Mayo, one can of MA-yo' for ever and that one by the Gypsy Kings that goes…oh you know it it's the only bloody Gypsy Kings song you've heard. So we talked about Hungarian language, Mancini has four words , hello, goodbye, thank you and 'on the right'[50] but she has taken the urban myth of Hungarian difficulty to new levels. She claims to have read somewhere (that mythical book no-one ever remembers) that Hungarian is phonetically more difficult than Japanese, which gave me an excuse to tell my jegg, jégy story. Next I tried to ease her broken heart by telling her my all encompassing 'big bang' (not the best term actually) theory about male-female relationships, and she was so keen I forgot it was a little graphic so I took a rain check and told her I'd e-mail it to her.

So she may move to London too as there's no reason to stay in Budapest any more. At ten o'clock she couldn't decide whether to go or not so I suggested flipping a coin. So she got a 20 forint coin out.

"Flowers I go, numbers I stay," she said, referring to the design of the coin.

"O.K," I said holding the coin, "so call one out while it's in mid-air."

"No I don't need to because if it lands flower side I go and number side I stay," she said, really slowly.

"Oh yeah," I said for some reason still not understanding. "So call then."

"No, listen Dexter I'm not sending any future children I have to your school if this is the level of science thinking you have," and collapsed with laughter.

Finally I got it, "Oh I see but you can still call because it's fun."

I flipped, it was flowers. "You gotta go," I said.

"Best of three?" said Mancini.

I flipped again: flowers.

"Best of five?"

"You gotta go," I said. "You can't fight probability."

Wednesday 3rd May

Larry has a problem with the summer pay. Some of us are getting paid through the summer and some aren't. The Headmaster has a new excuse to avoid payment to Larry.

"In Hungarian schools it is normal to only pay for two weeks in August and the new school to take up the next two."

"You gotta decide if we're British or Hungarian brother," said Larry, "you change your mind every week."

Thursday 4th May

A kifli flew through the window today as I taught Year 11 the fundamentals of thermal transfer. There are two points to be made here. Firstly Tibor, the one armed physicist has already taught them thermal transfer but I realised repeating it may be necessary after I accidentally walked into one of his classes the other day and my

---

[50] She says it to the taxi driver as he nears her apartment

mind boggled at the obscure calculations he was doing on the board to explain something for GCSE level physics. There were differentials, integrals and a million other things and Chris, our English student had sheepishly said to me that morning:

"We uh sort of didn't quite follow Tibor's explanation; it's our fault of course."

So I gave them a Dexter summary which took fifteen minutes.

Secondly what is a kifli? It is a hard Hungarian morning roll shaped like a boomerang. In the dictionary you will find it translated as croissant but it bares no culinary similarity to that masterpiece of French *petit dejeuner*. In fact it does indeed taste more like a boomerang than a croissant. This kifli flew through the window bounced twice and landed in the lap of Yifan, our Chinese girl who screamed. I investigated the incident and saw that Hungarian children from the other school were responsible. They were also throwing doughy comestibles at other windows of our part of the building. I was going to yell at them but realised I didn't know enough Hungarian so I stared at them for a long time then said simply "igazgató", which I think means director/Headmaster but could mean crocodile. Either way I saw they looked slightly nervous.

This marked a sharp escalation in the other school's behaviour to us. Admittedly we did ignore their party, and Larry has a one man crusade to stop our Russian girls going near the boys and Naima is known to grab the occasional urchin from this school to accuse him of stealing things from our classrooms and here I too must confess that, for a nano-second, I thought the missing German oral tape had been stolen by sabotage obsessed Hungarians. The worst previous incident happened last week when we were doing the maths challenge and the kids had to make scale models of tornadoes in the playground. As they worked outside various pieces of chalk, books and other classroom detritus rained down on us from above. Of course we complained but their Headmistress knows her school is dying (not because we are in the building too) and doesn't care if we move away.

Later I had to go to the British embassy to start the marriage paperwork. I am slightly nervous about dipping my foot in the quicksand of official bureaucracy but it has to be done. As I walked along the main street in Budapest towards the embassy three men in sheets walked past. One said as he saw me "Meg van Elvis" or words to that effect, which I roughly translated as "I've found Elvis!" I hoped he was referring to my sideburns and not to a beer belly I hadn't noticed.

The British embassy was rather fun. There was a very, very attractive Serbian girl in there getting very very upset/angry because she had not been granted a visa to visit New Zealand. The authorities did not believe that this lady, who had no visible means of support (financially or brassierely!) simply wanted to go to New Zealand for six months because 'she liked it there' and really *did* plan to come back. I hate to be stereotyped but I have a fairly good idea how this girl was planning to get by in NZ and it involved wearing very little clothing.

"There is a war on in my country you know," she said haughtily to our man in Budapest, safely behind bullet proof glass.

"Is there really?" said our man in a beautifully deadpan voice.

I had to pay a large amount of money to get the embassy to write me a form starting the process to confirm I am eligible for marriage. That means I had to swear in front of some high-up person that I was single blah blah blah and knew of no lawful impediment to getting married. And do you know how they are going to check this? They are going to put a note up in the embassy, so if anyone passes by who might know that I am a bigamist they can call in and stop the wedding! How likely is that.

Friday 5th May

Brittany is in Spain for the weekend. She is being very cosmopolitan at the moment. Two weeks ago it was Amsterdam, next week it is Istanbul. She is 'doing' Europe while she can. She has also resorted to counting down the working days until she leaves the school. On the one hand I can understand this, on the other I think she is a little silly. Soon she has to be in Houston to start her US teacher training. The first few weeks involve bonding with your colleagues and then you are in and teaching classes in inner city schools where the metal detectors are used to frisk the kids every morning. Suddenly a class of five slightly silly former communists and an eccentric Headmaster will seem like paradise.

Larry is in hospital having a colonoscopy. He described the exact procedure to me yesterday and it sounds like a torture technique rather than a medical one.

The kids are still sore about losing the basketball game. They are demanding a re-match because Dimitri scored many three point baskets in the game but they didn't count.

"That's because there isn't a three point line drawn on the court," I said practically, "so who says they were three pointers?"

Dima scowled in a teenage way. I know; I would have thought that was crap too if I were him.

"Next time draw the lines in before the game," I suggested. Not that there will be a next time. I use the gamblers maxim – always quit while you're ahead.

Saturday 6th may

Andrea and I went shopping to buy honeymoon clothes and shoes and came back with rhubarb (Andrea had never seen it in Hungary before), carrots and a yellow T-shirt for me. We are so focussed on the job in hand. In the afternoon we went to a park in Budapest on a beautiful afternoon to hang out at a European Council celebration of fifty years of the European Council. I am not exactly sure what the European Council is, but the only countries in Europe who are not in it are Serbia-Montenegro, Bosnia and Belarus. The event consisted of various soundstages playing music from all countries and obscene amounts of beer tents. Tony and his wife were already there and Tony, in his inquisitive way had already had a few samples of the beer. This was the first time Andrea had met Tony and she wasn't quite sure what to make of a hyperactive thirty-five year old American who spoke perfect Hungarian.

We went to the food street where ten of the countries had provided tents and cuisine from their countries. There were mile long queues for the magnificent Czech pörkölt[51] (I use the Hungarian word because Andrea claimed it was really Hungarian), the French provençale chicken, the Turkish kebabs, the Bavarian sausage and Sauer kraut. I want you to guess which country's tent had no queue: yep Great Britain. AND DO YOU KNOW WHY? Because British cuisine was represented by steak, jacket potatoes and tinned sweet corn. I am not making this up and I swear I have never been so ashamed of being British. Tinned sweet corn indeed. I could almost feel the rest of Europe sniggering away as they queued up for Italian pasta next door. It was hopeless and if I ever find out who was responsible for this I shall have a few choice words to say.

So we sat in the sun for a few hours listening to Irish bands, French bands, Romanian bands. It was all very nice and I recommend you move to Budapest.

Sunday 7th May

Andrea and I were invited out by Angela Mancini, Andrea's American boss to help her entertain her best friend (and mother) recently arrived from Chicago. We were going to a fine Hungarian restaurant and our role was to be witty and European. I was looking forward to it because Americans are so easy to tease.

There is something wonderful about the American setting foot into Europe for the first time. They are simply amazed by everything. Like, uh, everyone speaks a different language, which they know of course but the reality is astonishing. Every building is really old, there is public transport, they turn on the TV and their favourite actors are speaking foreign words. They were having a great time and Jennifer and her mom seemed to have bought all the porcelain in Szentendre[52].

We went to Karpathia[53], that had the air of a colonial gentlemen's club, with a high ceilinged dining room, arches, a gypsy band fiddling away furiously in the corner, various moustachioed waiters elegantly attired in bow ties - marvellous. Unfortunately the service was truly appalling. I don't necessarily think that all the service in the Karpathia is that bad, just this guy, who resembled Manuel from Fawlty Towers gone to seed. He came to take our order after a long time, we got two soups into the order when he said, "excuse me," and went off to take the order of the British quartet next to us. Mancini and Andrea were very annoyed indeed and I just managed

---

[51] A kind of stew made with the ubiquitous paprika
[52] Must see town up the Danube from Budapest, famous for looking gorgeous and typically Hungarian, and its pottery

[53] Kárpátia Étterem Ferenciek square 7-8

to stop them killing him because I feared the spittle factor in our future meals. He returned about twenty minutes later and decided he didn't recommend that we ate any of the selected courses, especially the wine. So we chose other courses but stuck with the wine. He returned again ten minutes later to say there was no more of that wine anyway, brandishing the wine list at Mancini again. Then he ignored her when she chose again. Mancini then threw the wine list at him to get his attention (Italian tempers, what can you do?). Finally he wouldn't serve our main course until Mancini's friend ate the innards of the fish in her soup because "That was the best bit"

He returned with the wine later and proceeded to open it in the required manner and let Mancini taste the wine. Mancini approved it but was ignored because Manuel was standing next to her lost in thoughts smelling the cork with beatific smile on his face. This was too much for me and I am afraid to say that I started giggling uncontrollably.

Finally our food arrived. Three waiters brought it in under stainless steel covers and simultaneously removed all of them with a cry of whatever the Hungarian for "Ta-ra!"

The food was tolerable but we could have saved £60 and gone to the Italian around the corner. Service was of course included in the bill. I have dined out most weeks in Hungary and this is the first time I have been disappointed.

On the plus side the gypsy violinist was excellent.

I wish I could remember the conversation, but it was very good. The Americans were quite impressed with my Hungarian and I wittered on in an intellectual way using my accent to cover up for intelligence. Actually Andrea praised me later for being a good dinner guest, I guess this is because I wasn't clumsy, didn't make embarrassing noises whilst eating soup and told stories that were passably funny. Andrea told anecdotes about life under Communism, how her school was. The Americans were fascinated by it and you could see they were thinking how lucky they were to live in America. And of course they are right. However Andrea's school anecdotes could really have been transferred to any British school (being sent home for wearing the wrong school uniform/ swimming kit, being told off for staring out of a window) And as for swearing allegiance to the cause, don't Americans have the Stars and Stripes in the classroom? I am not saying Communism was a bed of roses but nobody starved and everybody was safe. And there is a certain (tiny) part of me that says that who needs an expensive car, just one that gets from A to B and yes, a Trabant would just about do that. You can justify a Trabant culture in the same way an English school justifies a school uniform. My school's argument was that there would be no ostentatious clothes bragging, or trends so no-one would feel out of place in the school.

The Hungarian Girl Trap

Monday 8th May

I, being blissfully unaware of world events (Sky news is malfunctioning again), didn't know about NATO's latest cock up over the Chinese embassy before arriving at school today. I was therefore quite surprised to find Mimi, one of my Chinese girl students writing 'America is the second Hitler' in large chalk letters all over the front of the school. She spotted me, turned away with a look of fury in her eyes and stalked off.

"What the hell is going on?" I asked. Brittany quickly informed me.

Larry spotted the graffiti too and had an incredulous smile on his face.

"Isn't it amazing," he said. "They are upset about this but they know nothing about Tiananmen Square. They know nothing about Tibet. What should we do?"

That was a good question, one that couldn't be addressed there and then, as it was time for assembly, which over-ran as usual. Year 10, my class, containing three Chinese girls, one Japanese boy and two Hungarian girls had produced a magazine called 'BLEMM', named from their initials and it was due to be presented to the school. Naima asked Lin, one of the Chinese girls to present it and she simply snapped "No". Naima, even less well informed than me thought she, Naima had done something wrong.

So in we go to period one. Brittany has been doing some reconnaissance and has worked out that, of the eight Chinese students in the school the three girls (Mimi, Lin and Lifang) all recently arrived from China were really, really mad. Two are in Year 10, one in Year 9. Larry takes year 10 first lesson, the last person you want in there. It doesn't go well – I don't know why, I was with year 8. I gather that Brittany quit her prep class to go in there as well, meaning both Americans were in there.

At the end of period 1 Brittany told me that all lessons for the Chinese students were cancelled for the morning and they were going to sit in the year 10 room and have tea and cookies and talk if they wanted to. Brittany invited all the Chinese students in. The boys weren't interested, the furious ones were and the three other Chinese girls (very westernised) went along because it was better than classes.

The belief from the Chinese is that this was a deliberate act of war by America. They want to start World War three. U.S politicians were portrayed as arrogant interfering madmen who want the whole world to be like America and, isn't that they said about Hitler? They also mentioned the Chinese medicine men who have been predicting a great war for many years. To my uninformed ears I was very scared indeed. What was going to happen to the world?

By break time things seemed worse. The three westernised Chinese had apparently been talking and giggling and were furiously attacked by the three militants who accused them of not being proper Chinese and traitors. The Western Chinese were very upset and sat in the corridor in floods of tears, then used the tears to try and get the day off. Brittany and I referred that one to the Headmaster, who was of course unavailable and in a meeting. Naima was saying that if they were furious why did they come to school? And was the American school operating at all if the Chinese felt like that?

The three militant Chinese girls started to write a letter to the International Herald and Tribune and the Budapest Sun. They wrote about the victims and their shock. "When we knew the news we cried because we are Chinese. We don't know NATO wanted to kill how many people. But we think they should stop the bombing because we can see there is no reason for the bombing. Accident or on purpose we don't want it to happen again. It is a terrible example for NATO. It is enough it is time to stop." They refused help with the English although they accepted help from Brittany over e-mailing it.

I decided it was time to do something crazy. I still don't know if I was inspired, brave, stupid, naïve but I thought I want to teach my classes. I had year 10 next. I want to teach them cells. I am an Englishman in Hungary, teaching biology. What has this to do with me? So I went and said, "it is time for science class now. I am going to the big room at the end. You are in Year 10. I expect to see you there," and I walked away.

They didn't even look up, but I took the rest of the class up to the big room and began. Ten minutes later the Chinese girls arrived and silently sat at their desks. It was the quietest most sober lesson I have ever taught, but they worked and things were nearly normal.

It was Monday so lunch ironically was Chinese food. As I went home the Chinese girls smiled at me and said goodbye. Was there a thaw?

Elsewhere Larry was unshaven and restless. He claimed he and his wife broke up over the weekend. Twelve months after they married. Larry is so difficult to live with. He was not doing well.

Tuesday 9th May

There was a note from the three militant Chinese girls today.

> Dear Mr. Larry and Miss. Brittany
>
> We are very sorry about yesterday. Maybe our reaction was too acute because we are so sad. Accident or on purpose we do not want to see Chinese people die. We know American people are friendly, we just hate politicians and people who decided to start the war. Please don't misunderstand us, we are always good friends.
>
> Li Fang, Lin, Mimi
>
> P.S. Could you please tell the other Chinese girls that maybe we were too angry this morning. We can't control what they want to do although they are Chinese.

I spoke to Brittany and told her we should cancel our proposed Chinese meal for at least a week, owing to her nationality. She agreed. This Chinese meal has reached farcical proportions. It was organised in January and keeps getting cancelled at the last minute. Literally every week we plan it but cancel it.

All the chaos has distracted me from what I really wanted to talk about which was the BLEMM magazine and the School's new brochure. This is what BLEMM has to say about the staff at Churchill.

Miss. Naima is our English teacher. She is quite strict, she is a Pakistani. She likes teaching us grammar. When she is unhappy all the students are afraid of her, but when she is in a good mood we can talk to her like a friend. She cares about the students and school life very much.

Mr. Dexter is the tallest teacher in our school. He is never angry with students, everybody likes him. He is our class teacher, he is patient with pupils. He can play basketball well because he is tall.

Mr. Larry is the funniest teacher. He always makes us laugh. He is not a young person but he can do everything what the young can do e.g. playing basketball, running and talking for a LONG time.

Miss Ági is our maths teacher. In her lessons we have to work hard. She likes wearing short skirts.

This one is my second favourite…

Miss Brittany is our history teacher, she likes drinking something in the lessons (!). When she has a lesson she is always disturbed by outsiders.

This one is my favourite…

The Headmaster is quite kind to everybody. He usually doesn't come to school everyday but when he is in school he just stands in the corridor talking to students. I think he likes chicken, he always orders chicken for Monday's food, and he eats a lot.

It's a work of genius.

Tony and Jessica have noted that they rub each other up the wall. Tony loves it and Jessica won't back down. Whatever Tony says irritates Jessica and she goes all haughty on him. For example…

"I don't like our President. He's a horrible man," said Jessica.

"Yeah but he's done a good job."

"I didn't say he hadn't done a good job. I said he's a horrible man."

"But do you respect him?" said Tony. "I mean what would you say about Kennedy for example?"

"I wasn't saying anything about Kennedy."

"Yeah I guess but then who does ever respect bosses. They're all assholes really aren't they," said Tony.

"Actually some of my bosses I really love and respected," said Jessica.

"O.K I think it's time for class," said Brittany, ever the expert at removing problems. How is she only twenty-three?

Wednesday 10th May

Tony and I spent most of our spare minutes discussing a particularly crucial point to the English soccer season. Brittany was most unimpressed and Tony, as is his way began to deliberately change other conversations around to soccer. When it happened again at lunch time she said.

"All you two ever talk about these days is soccer, punk rock and how gorgeous Hungarian women are."

"I'm sorry," said Tony sweetly, "I didn't know there was anything else to discuss in life."

"Well World War three is looming for a start. I mean, why don't you just bring in the beer cans and be done with it?" she said. I think she was joking.

I cleared out my drawer today and behind it I was most embarrassed to find the notes of Larry, Brittany and my meeting last term, the very minutes I was sure had been stolen as part of a wider conspiracy to stop the truth getting out. Whoops.

The Headmaster was wearing a tie today because all the Headmasters from the other international schools were coming to our school to have a meeting. It was the first time I had ever seen him on edge.

I also provisionally accepted Wendy, the Chinese teacher's proposal that I earn £15 for an hour's work teaching absolute beginner Chinese people how to speak English. I was slightly worried that this was a trap to get to those damn Zionist Brits and Americans but I think I'll risk it for the money.

In the evening Andrea and I met Endre and Éva. Éva is Endre's boss and she is twenty years older than him. I have completely removed all concerns over this relationship. They are very happy and are planning to go into business together. She is also very rich, which has no bearing on their relationship at all. We were to have dinner at Levin's[54], a restaurant whose menu I helped translate into English. It was a

---

[54] Nagy Levin Étterem. Széchenyi st 92/b. I know it sounds fabulous and you will want to go there but it is on an island called Csepel in the Danube almost exclusively given over to heavy industry. Take a green suburban train MAV from Petőfi bridge to Csepel and ask.

rather complicated too because it has the theme of the wonderful Levin as the chef, from a Hungarian novel by P. Howard, or Rejtő Jenő as he is known in Hungary. Rejtő wrote stories about mobsters, gangs, thugs, and adventures in the times of the foreign legion. He had a nice, comical style that briefly had international appeal fifty years ago.

So dishes are called "as prepared for the Queen of Sheba", "having been served to xxx when visiting Tehran". Endre did the main work and I proof read his English. However he didn't put it through a spellchecker and the kind of mistakes that I hate in translated menus are still in it. For instance I am afraid that chicken bits just don't sound appetising (!) and 'occasional' is not spelt with two Ns. Still we were given a free meal for it and it was superb.

Afterwards we went to my beloved 'Old Man's Pub' for Robbie's (he who owns Pirx bar) birthday. We booked a table but Robbie himself didn't make it owing to over indulgence the night before, making a rather surreal event. I was under slight pressure because Andrea's colleagues from The American Firm included a Hungarian woman Andrea has decided is her nemesis. I had never met this woman before but Andrea had described to everyone in Hungary how much she despises her. Her crimes are that she has risen very quickly through the company and enjoys the company of the male partners. The two may be linked. Her second crime is to have 'penge' lips, roughly translated as blade lips, and, I quote, 'enormous false breasts which look ridiculous with her skinny body'. Andrea also made the mistake of asking male colleagues who was more fanciable her or her nemesis, leaving poor guys on the spot. Anyway being 100% supporting of my fiancée I was also quite intrigued as to what 'penge' lips exactly were and how ridiculous these breasts looked. So when she arrived I skirted a fine line between observing the girl and ignoring her. Put it this way I could see exactly why the girl had got where she'd got to and concluded that her personality was indeed as false as her chest. So I did what I always do and drank lots of beer and enjoyed the blues and forgot about it all.

I love Old Man's Pub. Live, free blues every night, my stag night is to be there. The waitresses are lovely, the beer is cheap, great food (although the desserts are a bit too healthy for my liking). Tonight the band had a brass section, looked like escaped convicts and started worryingly with a Blues Brothers song but soon got into a more interesting area and the singer (white) did a very passable James Brown impression. Afterwards there is always dancing 'til dawn with a DJ who looks like one of those nerds who were bullied at school. He just sits there playing funky stuff. Indeed he does have the funkiest record collection this side of New York. Andrea led the dancing and even guys in their sixties were up and grooving to the music.

Thursday 11th May

Irony of the day. The Chinese girls had to ask Brittany, an American, (in their usual courteous way) if they could leave early in the afternoon so they could go to the American embassy to join the crowds protesting outside and calling for blood. I lent them safety pins so they could pin Chinese flags to their shirts. All the Chinese girls went to the protest but the three Western ones left at lunchtime and the three militants left forty-five minutes after lunch. Conclusion the Western ones didn't go near the embassy and went home.

Larry and the Headmaster had a yelling match this morning. Larry is back to his 'are we being paid over the summer?' argument and the Headmaster was still citing the two weeks in August line although Larry remembers having a 12 month one. Then Larry asked why I was being paid through the summer. This is fine and the Headmaster can cope with money arguments so Larry took his glasses off.

"Oh and I can't see,"

"Larry," said the Headmaster in a pleading voice.

"You said when I helped the kid out of the tree and my glasses got broke you said I'd get them fixed. That was four weeks ago."

"I told you I have to wait for insurance…"

"Don't give any of your crap," said Larry

"I got the papers through yesterday."

"It's always yesterday with you. Whenever we get on your back the thing arrived just in time to save your ass."

This continued for a while until Larry got bored with it and said, "So Headmaster, by the way can you think of some topics for debates with Year 10."

I can't get Larry. Does he just argue for fun, or when he is on the ropes, does he simply change the subject?

Later Larry interrupted my class to ask me if I was with him to negotiate the same contract for all teachers over the summer. I said yes.

Then Larry showed his absolute ignorance of the English GCSE system.

"We could tell them if they don't meet our demands we won't administer those GSEC things you English have."

If Larry thinks I am going to ruin four kids futures for a few dollars you can think again.

Sunday 13th May

Miskolc

The Miskolc university festival is basically a booze-up of huge proportions with a few bands playing to justify the whole thing. Miskolc University students are like all other university students in the world, enjoying their freedom and alternative lifestyle. I have never seen so many similar leather jackets to my old one anywhere. In typical student fashion they were all drinking themselves senseless.

The university was large and sprawling, on what would be a leafy and attractive campus were it not for the fact that the architects had only one shape in their repertoire, the rectangle. In fact the whole scene started to remind me of exactly what annoyed me most about student life in the first place. I suppose there is nothing wrong with student life per se. The average student's fanatical devotion to soap operas, being into ironically crap cultural icons, having a 'great' social life and leaving the libraries - buildings containing our species' combined learning – empty, save for when a deadline is near. I guess I just find the waste of knowledge at university rather sad. I was a saddo (you see I'm doing it to myself) and lived in the library (admittedly because if I worked at home daytime TV seduced me.)

So I was rather in a bad mood and people noticed. The Doctor, one of the craziest men in the world and seemingly half way through an experiment to see if chain smoking and chain palinka drinking induces death, said to me, "don't you like drinking?"

"Of course," I said, sober but on my fifth pint of beer.

"But I have never seen you drunk," he said.

"That's because by the time I catch up with you you're unconscious," I joked, but I knew I was on bad form. This festival had nothing to do with music, just to drink with friends and I had no history or common language to allow me to enter their world.

Then it got worse, in the bar they started karaoke until dawn. Endre and Andrea were very excited but I refused point blank to have anything to do with karaoke. I find the whole thing utterly humiliating to watch and participate in (my I am a sulker!). So Andrea, thinking I was joking said, "well you can't marry me then," until she saw that it may not be a good idea to try this threat out at this time. So they sang "Twist and Shout," "Never gonna give you up" and some other song and had a great time.

We went home about five a.m.

Monday 14th May

In a typical manner the GCSE written examinations started in chaos. I had negotiated with the cleaner (in Hungarian) to NOT move the desks around and to give me the key. I thought I had covered every base but no. I went to the Headmaster at 8.45 a.m. to get him to open the safe to get the papers. He went to the safe but was missing a key. He then painfully slowly searched every pocket five times looking for the thing. He found tissues, paper clips but no key. The secretary who possessed the other set of keys was at the doctor in the morning. As you can imagine this morning's exam got off to a late start.

Then Larry attacked the Headmaster at lunchtime again over this holiday pay. He roped Jessica and I to sit on the table with the Headmaster while he made racist remarks about Hungarians, he told the Headmaster he would badmouth the school around the city and once again claimed the school owed him a lot. When he was gone, the Headmaster was clearly upset.

"You know I wouldn't willingly be unfair to someone. The systems here are difficult but Larry is impossible. Why should I pay him for twelve months when he is in breach of his contract anyway, which says eleven months anyway?

"When he arrived in Hungary he came to me and said he couldn't find work and he needed a job. So I gave him a contract. This was in May. This was for a full time post. I didn't see him again until September when on the first day of school he tells me he has two other jobs as well and can only work on these three days. He goes away for weeks without telling anyone then remembers covers from years ago when he is asked to do something."

As the Headmaster sat there pouring his heart out, looking like a dormouse in a man's jacket I felt very sorry for him. Jessica was almost crying. Of course he should have removed Larry when he had the chance but Larry is so useful as well and if you play with fire you get burnt

Tuesday 15th May

Naima told Tony off today for arriving late (three minutes) to class even though he was pretty ill. Tony was mad and let off steam in the staff room when she had gone. Various four letter words were uttered and Brittany and I managed to calm him down.

"Naima's problem is that she does not pick her battles well," said Brittany, a very apposite remark.

Little did we know that Naima was listening to the conversation through the key hole.

Earlier she had talked to Brittany and me about the Headmaster. She went as far as to say 'we don't actually have a HEADMASTER we have him!'

"He's scruffy," she continued, "I am going to buy him another jacket and tie because he only has one. It's embarrassing frankly. I brought some Serbian parents in yesterday. They didn't want the American school, they wanted a nice small English school, so I think we're perfect you see. They walk into his office and he's scruffy and he's picking his nose or if not picking PLAYING with his nose in an unprofessional manner. I knew we'd lost the parents after one minute, they were rich upper class people you know."

Brittany and I were amused but there was more.

"So he is halfway through his welcome to the parents when the phone rang. Now a professional would have told his secretary to hold all calls but not him. He speaks on the phone for twenty minutes ignoring the family. Remember I speak Hungarian. Do you know who he was talking to? His mother!"

I laughed again.

"So," said Naima, "the parents walked out. We lost them because of him. We need someone with dynamism, someone who actually has a vision. He gives them an education as and when something comes up not with a vision of the future. What we need is the Headmaster of the International College."

Naima was impressed with him because he didn't dither on the telephone.

Naima implored me to speak to Gerry, the English governor to get him to fire the Headmaster and make him the bursar or something. I said Gerry wouldn't listen. So our numbers stay low and the school dies.

Then Naima dropped another bombshell. "Do you know what I heard," she said. "I heard that our Headmaster was in charge of the Jewish school here and he was removed by a vote of no confidence. Now I wonder why that is?"

Brittany is planning one last try to do something. She is planning an open house for parents to see the new things for next year (as yet unclear) and to advertise this elsewhere for prospective parents. There will be fine food, a chance to talk to teachers and see the school. It is a good idea and she has the full support of the teachers but I wonder how much her idea will be diluted.

Andrea and I went to see Father Gábor the priest in the evening. I have missed him. He reminds me how easy it is to drift into an unthinking atheistic mind-set. It would be impossible for me to be an atheist by absolute conviction because I would feel that to justify my absolute belief in there being nothing out there I would have to be pretty confident in my academic argument to reject the entire culmination of four-thousand years of Western philosophical intelligence and conclusion. And, as I can't even fold a shirt properly I am not the man for that. Lazy bastard atheism isn't for me but is Catholicism? People can believe what they want of course, which is where Gábor helps me because our conversations are rarely about 'God' but about what it is to be alive – a subject that is of enormous interest to me. Most philosophy, even profound stuff like Platonism and Sophism is based on a fundamental assumption of God and if you accept those arguments you have to at least have some kind of belief in 'something else'.

Wednesday 16th May

Another charged day at the office. As reported, there was a Chinese girl problem last week and thankfully it all blew over until today. The political Chinese girls felt a little guilty of their 'acute' reaction. However what we didn't know was that, apart from their letter to the Herald and Tribune and the Budapest Sun, they also sent one to the Chinese newspaper here in Budapest. The letters for the English papers were about their sadness (as written) but the Chinese letter was a completely different matter. In it they said that there were three Chinese girls at their school who had betrayed their country and were traitors. The Western Chinese girls were furious.

"They can write what they like but they can't make it personal. How I deal with stuff like that is my business," snarled Yifan.

Wendy, the Chinese teacher sorted it out. The political girls had sent the letter, cooled down and regretted it, wrote another letter to the Chinese paper to say 'don't print it' and forgot about it. Unfortunately the paper didn't and loved the controversy.

Later Naima was putting red paper on the poster boards for decorative effect. Bea, the art teacher walked in and exploded, saying she should have been consulted over the boards and called poor Naima 'thick in the head' whilst in the corridor. This was strange for Bea who always complains when she is asked to do the extra work and has slammed the phone down on Naima when she has called her on such matters. As I sat eating my lunch alone Bea and the Headmaster sat eating. Naima walks over and says to the Headmaster.

"I am sorry but there is no Headmaster in this school. I have had enough. What just happened was the rudest thing I have ever heard. I am leaving the school."

Then she stalked out. I watched as the Headmaster continued to eat his food slowly then I went to see Naima. She was furious and brought in the Tony incident yesterday. She had been overhearing Tony's insults which she shouldn't have done but she has done so much for this school and Bea's comments were the final thing. She was not appreciated.

The Headmaster wandered in ten minutes later and in a wavering voice told Naima to not worry, but Naima insisted she was going. Then burst into hysterical tears which continued for ten minutes, the sobs punctuating a list of things she had had enough of. The Headmaster tried to calm her down and did rather a poor job.

I hope Naima is brave enough to stick to her decision then the Headmaster's record will be there for all to see: six foreign teachers at the start of the year, six left at the end of the year.

Thursday 17th May

Naima seemed mollified I'm afraid, and was toeing the party line again.

Dinner with Brittany was fantastic. Finally getting to the Chinese restaurant after six months of trying. We went to the Chinese near me and I showed her the sights of Örs Vezér Tér, or tower block city. I showed her how fascinating my walk to school is..

Larry bought the Headmaster a present today. It was a pair of those eye cover things airlines give you so you can sleep on planes.

"Here," said Larry, "this sums up your leadership."

Friday 18th May

The Headmaster is bowing to parental pressure again but in a good way. Three of our misplaced year nine kids aged 15, 16 and 18 respectively will move to year 11 for GCSE next year. The three political Chinese students are also to take A level next year.

The opposition school I thought had saved me a job today. They advertised in the English language paper that they were offering Hungarian and Russian at GCSE using the London board. This pleased me as it saved me job working out if an Exam board did Hungarian. So I rang up the London exam board and asked for a syllabus for Hungarian and found that they didn't do it at all. So are the opposition lying or assuming that it can be done? According to our Headmaster they are saying all this in adverts but actually have no students at all for GCSE!

Saturday 19th May

We went to a wedding today in a town called Szekesfehérvár[55], a rather gorgeous town about forty minutes from Budapest. The happy couple were Erik, a Dutchman and Zsuzsa, a former work colleague of Andrea's

We travelled with another couple of loose acquaintance: Marianne (another ex Andrea colleague) and Dries, her South African husband. Looking at the two girls as they readied themselves for the wedding I noted that the Hungarian female was on display today. Andrea was her usual glamorous self and Marianne was wearing what seemed to be an outfit from the latest Star Wars movie. It was a metallic green mini skirt suit with a lightning like flash across the front.

The wedding was in the Basilica in the old town. Father Gábor, our priest, was doing the wedding, which was nice. Andrea recommended him because he is probably the best young bi-lingual priest in Hungary. Gábor however was a little nervous. I doubt he does many weddings in basilicas, not that I am entirely clear what a basilica is. To my slightly uneducated eye they look like a church built rectangular instead of crossed and without a spire. Gábor eventually got into his stride, performing the psalms himself and being wise beyond his years. Then just as I was praising him to the skies he realised he was about to declare them man and wife and hadn't actually put the rings on yet. Blushes all round. As Gábor walked the couple back out along the aisle Andrea whispered to me.

"Did you know that the bride is pregnant?"

Outside everything got confusing. The traditional wedding pictures don't really happen here and instead the Dutch and the Hungarians hung about outside not talking to each other. Two traditional events did occur. The official cam-corder man spent more time surreptitiously filming Andrea and ignoring the bride and secondly we realised that we didn't know where the reception was so we had to watch other guests and hope that when they got in their car they were indeed going to the reception and not going to the DIY store instead. Fortunately the Lada family we chose did go to the reception.

We were all allocated to sit next to Father Gábor at the reception. Initially I was annoyed. No rude jokes then. I was pleasantly surprised. Gypsy dancing started the celebrations followed by both fathers making a speech. The Dutchman was full of platitudes and talked about all the links between Holland and Hungary.

"What links are they?" snorted Gábor in disbelief and then snorted harder when these links turned out to be friendship and love.

---

[55] try saying that one – say-kesh-fe-hear-varr

The aperitifs came round. I was delighted to see that Gábor followed his champagne with a Finlandia vodka. I took my usual Vilmoskörte. It is good to see a priest who likes a snifter, I thought.

First up was the traditional meat soup, Gábor wolfed his down, weddings are hard work obviously. He questioned Dries, the South African about life in South Africa and was delighted by the answers. They were the sort of questions you expect the Queen to ask. "Is the crime quite high there?" etc.

The food continued, schnitzel, pörkölt, so did the wine and the beer. The conversation turned to films and Andrea admitted to loving the romantic film 'Out of Africa.'

"What's the plot?" said Gábor.

"Well Meryl Streep has a marriage of convenience…"

"Hold on," said Gábor, "You mean she disrespects the act of marriage…"

"But she falls in love with Robert Redford."

"Who is not her husband…" said Gábor.

I could see that Gábor wasn't going to get this film. He finished off by pointing out something and referring to specific Catholic law that applied to Karen Blixen regardless of her Lutheran origins.

Next came the Dutch guests who sang, or shouted a few traditional songs. Gábor winced all the way through.

Afterwards he said, "I liked two things about that – just before it started and just after it finished."

Next came some jokes. This was Gábor's:

"Three men are in heaven playing golf, one is Jesus, one is Moses and the other man is not identified. Moses plays a shot and he hits it into the water. So Moses parts the water and plays his second shot and it goes into the hole. Jesus tees off and he too hits it into the water. Jesus walks on the water and plays his second shot straight into the hole. The third man plays his shot into the water, but as it hits the water a fish leaps from the liquid and swallows the ball. At the same time a bird appears and picks the fish up in his beak and flies off. The fish lets go of the ball above the green and the ball falls into the hole – a hole in one.

Jesus turns to the third man.

"You know Father," he says, "I really hate it when you do that."

This is a great joke but I think this one was even better.

Slobodan Milosevic is in hell and he is being shown around by Satan. Satan is showing him around the various areas and the kind of eternal damnation he can expect. In one room he sees Leonid Breshnev making mad passionate love to Princess Diana.

"Blimey," says Milosevic, "This looks pretty great for eternity. Can I have something like this?"

"Um," said Satan, "this is Princess Diana's punishment."

Once again we roared with laughter. I was curious as to why Diana was in hell and Gábor explained that a) Mother Theresa a true saint died in almost obscurity surrounded by the media frenzy around Diana and b) as a priest he has little sympathy with the way the Royal Marriage was lived.

There was a plate breaking incident which isn't traditional Hungarian. It got a little bit out of hand. I broke one, only one I swear.

"Tell me Ray," said Gábor later on, "what is your opinion of women? What is their role in the world?"

By this time I was extremely worse for wear. Another Vilmoskörte had been downed, as had too much beer and wine. I gave it my best shot.

"Um," I said, "I'm no expert. I just observe the world and make deductions from the data I collect but this is what I think," and told him.

Gábor gave me a strange look, which I now realise was a mixture of alcohol and respect. "You have just summed up two thousand years of philosophical thinking on the subject," he said. He was watching Andrea dance at the time.

I was encouraged by this and went on one of my anti television rants. After I'd finished Gábor said.

"Ray are you old fashioned?"

Meanwhile the bride and groom did something distasteful and went and consummated their marriage mid-reception. I didn't notice but Andrea reported the bride's dress was not done up properly when she returned.

The conversation turned to Communist stories, the realisation of the lies said, jeans, coca cola availability, the ease of which in the west we can get things off shelves. We do not realise what it is like not to be able to have them.

Suddenly it was 2 a.m. We had all danced the money dance with the bride in the red dress. Andrea had danced a lot, Dexter had drunk too much and discussed the world with his priest. It was a good night and time to go home. The problem was getting a slightly sozzled Gábor into the car. He was with the newly weds imploring them to read the Pope's new book, and, with the *elan* of a magician, he suddenly whipped a copy out of his briefcase. I guided him out of the door and plonked him on the front seat. The poor chap had Pentecost in five hours and it took one hour to get home.

Gábor spoke to Dries all the way home and I can't remember what he said as I was barely conscious. I do remember one classic as we zoomed into Budapest. Gábor was ranting about the lax socialist drugs laws two years ago (now you get two years for possession of one joint) and he slurred that all Communists were "brigands of Satan". Marvellous language.

Tuesday 22nd May

Back to school and a list of ways the Headmaster can drive you mad:

1)   Buy crappy plastic pencil sharpeners by the dozen that don't work.

2)   Having placed all the GCSE exam papers, sealed and annotated in a UPS plastic bag ready for transit I was greeted by him saying 'no, no' , removing them and trying to force them into an impossibly small envelope, for the simple reason that this is cheaper. He failed and was still trying to do it 20 minutes later. Even the secretary was scornful.

Tibor the one armed physicist sat with me at lunch today.

"I learnt a new Hungarian word today," he said as he ate his vegetable soup. "It is 'Solarium Brown.'"

He paused for effect as usual. "It is a reference to the skin colour of our gypsy population. Hungary is now politically correct. It is wrong to call a gypsy a gypsy, he is now a person with solarium brown skin."

Wednesday 23rd May

Dexter finally got pissed off over the lateness issue. Tony has been made Naima's scapegoat over lateness. Tony was late three times and got a telling off. Tony then sounded off about her and she overheard. Naima is still mad and keeps pestering me to talk about what she is doing wrong. I was busy preparing an exams timetable and tried to make re-assuring noises but she wouldn't let me.

"Ray," she said, "I am truly sorry but I will not let you work I must talk with you." She took my pencil out of my hand.

I looked at her. "What?" I said.

"What is to be done?" she said.

"Look," I said. "I have a pretty good idea of what a Headmaster should do and so do you. What is it?"

Silence.

"This is my definition," I said. " A person who is driven by a desire to provide the best education possible, a person who will discipline the children and discipline the staff as necessary when they fall below the high standards expected of his or her school. OUR Headmaster farms out these three tasks and does a thousand other irrelevant things like ordering stationary. He is never here, he is late and he is weak. The fact that you have the job as 'teacher discipliner' is ridiculous because the Headmaster should be doing it. Why does the Headmaster need to order books? He should give a damn about what I am doing in the classroom. I could be doing anything!"

Naima wasn't listening, or maybe she was. "But the governors and the Headmaster have entrusted me with this job and I said yes. "

"Yes, and I say you shouldn't be doing it."

"But he can't do it," said Naima, "he is not good at such things."

"So why is he the Headmaster?" I wailed. "He is late and always two minutes behind, he has no idea of priority," I said.

At this point the Headmaster came in. Naima said.

"Some of the staff think that you are always late and so they can be late," which wasn't exactly the context of my words but this caused the Headmaster to explain to me how busy he was and what was expected of the staff.

"LOOK!" as I felt I was surrounded by idiots, "I don't care less about your excuses." I was angry now. "The thing is lateness is endemic here. I guarantee that practically every period every day almost every class starts late. We are all late all the time because there is no bell. This morning Brittany has organised an important meeting, Ági and Jessica forget to come, you Headmaster walk in ten minutes late with a fax and start joking about it, then repeat the first of Brittany's announcements at the end, because you weren't here to hear them. So I am defending Tony because yes he was late but so are we all and no wonder he is mad because he knows the reality.

The Headmaster stared at me. "People are always late?" he said. "This is very serious. Naima you told me everyone was always on time!"

Naima looked subdued.

"Headmaster there is no bell so no-one knows when it is time," she began.

"We can't have a bell..."

"I know, but when do we go to class," I said. "Which clock is official? The staffroom clock is wrong..."

I didn't get any further because the Headmaster's attention span had gone and he was up on a chair adjusting the hands on the clock. When he had finished he said,

"This is the official clock."

"I don't care about the damn official clock," I yelled. "Everybody is always late. YOU," I yelled again, "have never got to class on time. You come in here late, start photocopying for ten minutes and then wander into class about twelve minutes from the end."

The Headmaster looked shocked. Naima was very quiet.

"In fact," I finished, " if you don't believe me come in here at 11.40 and see how many classes have actually started. I'll tell you how many – none."

The Headmaster of course didn't bother to come and see the laziness endemic in his staff. Jessica and Ági were not reprimanded for missing the meeting. Tony was still warned for his lateness even though I have been late three times and no-one has said a word.

Wednesday evening

Tonight was incredible. As the *L'equipe* newspaper reported about tonight "God is English." I am talking football of course. An English team played a German team to see who would be crowned champions of Europe. Being away from England it was difficult to sum up the mood in England but Sky news seemed to report that the whole country would be watching the match. I was watching it too and accompanying me were pals Fozzie (the man with the Trabant) and István. István has no TV but loves football and it has become a ritual for him to come round to my place to watch the Champions League games on my tv. He is of course a lucky charm in his perverse way. In every game he has come to see the English team have gone behind. Then, in his gloriously pessimistic[56] way, he tells the rest of the people in the room that 'well we might as well go home now it's all over' in Hungarian so as not to offend my English sensibilities. I always give him a look as if to say, this ain't over yet and the English team always do something miraculous. I did not want miracles tonight I wanted a simple easy victory. It was all getting too stressful.

Fozzie was an unknown quantity as far as football fanaticism is concerned. He was university educated you see and some such people look down on the game but he cracked open a Soproni Ászok beer and showed great enthusiasm.

"The Germans will get half a million Euro if they win tonight," he said.

The game started, the German team scored within six minutes, the English team looking confused. This sparked a conversation over lucky German teams of the last fifty years.

"Who was the best team in the 1954 World Cup?" said Fozzie. "Hungary of course. We beat those sausage-eating bastards 8-3 in the first round then we meet them in the final. Puskás is injured, it's raining and the bastard Germans win. Outrageous!"

"What about the penalty shoot-outs against England in 1990 and 1996?" I replied, one eye hopefully on the screen. "We outplay them for 120 minutes each time and then they get us on penalties!"

The English team was not playing well. István was starting to shake his head. Fozzie was screaming COME ON!! every time the ball went even close to the German goal, but there was no way these players were going to score.

"They have been eating pasta," said István cryptically.

"Sorry?" I said.

"In the 1986 World Cup Hungary played the Soviet Union and our coaches made a great play of how we would win because our team ate pasta the night before…we lost 6-0."

"That's it," I said, in a very jovial mood, I was convincing myself I didn't care about the result, "pasta."

Fozzie was still thinking about every racial German stereotype. The German team's huge shaven headed forward fouled an English team's player, but the referee, the world famous bald Italian referee with the bug eyes, waved play on.

"WHAT," he yelled. "What is this? Skinhead Nazi's together!"

The Hungarian's have little fondness for Germanic people.

István remembered another German atrocity in World Cups.

"Remember 1982 in Spain, the semi-final against France?"

We nodded in memory. The Germans had been outplayed for most of the game only to recover and win on penalties. This may sound honourable until you

---

[56] The Hungarians take pride in being the most pessimistic race in the world

remember the Schumacher incident. Batiston the French forward was clear through and certain to score. Schumacher, the German goalkeeper charged out from his goal and physically assaulted Batiston, knocking him unconscious, possibly fracturing his skull.

"Do you remember it?" yelled István. "The whole world was watching as the guy was carried off on a stretcher."

"You are forgetting the most outrageous thing of all," I said. "The referee didn't even give a free kick!! The man attacked him feet first and there isn't even a free kick!"

Batiston received a broken bone in the assault and one of France's best players was out of the game. Schumacher looked innocent and there the German recovery began.

"You know," said Fozzie, warming further to the story, "I think Schumacher killed Batiston on the pitch!"

We laughed.

"No seriously, I think Batiston died on the pitch, his head was completely knocked off and the referee says it was no foul."

"He didn't die," I said knowledgeably, "but it screwed Batiston up so much that he invited Schumacher to be his best man at his wedding."

"No, No," said Fozzie, "he died I swear."

"Well Schumacher claimed he dived whatever?" said István.

As I watched the English team give the ball away again, I decided that Fozzie must be right. "Yes," I said finally. "Batiston died and England is dying too."

The camera panned over some German fans singing and looking smug. "YOU ARE NOT GOING TO WIN AGAIN!" I bellowed. "WE IN EUROPE WILL NOT ALLOW IT!"

The comments from the Hungarians got far too racist at this point so I shall not record them.

Half time the English team need to make substitutes. István's girlfriend Zsusza had made us pancakes and we wolfed them down at half time: chocolate, jam, túró[57] Second half, no substitutes. It begins as the previous half began, English team attacking like a bee without a sting. However there are good signs for the rampantly optimistic. The Germans seem to be hanging on the for the one goal win. A German player receives the ball in the English area, then takes it all the way back to the German half.

---

[57] túro is basically milk curds, a bit like cottage cheese, but sweeter and considered a delicacy. I avoided it quite a lot of the time, like that other delicacy, tongue, but rarely did without my túrós táska (pastry with túro and raisins, and probably the number one chocolate bar in Hungary was *túrórud,*, which is chocolate bar filled with túro) on the way to the station every morning. Acquired taste though.

Substitutes at last! It has little effect. István purses his lips. I know what's coming.

"It's all over now," he said to Fozzie in Hungarian. I am losing my optimism too and sink into the sofa staring blankly at the screen.

Three things happen, the Germans hit the post twice, the English team's goalkeeper makes an incredible save, the Germans substitute their thirty-eight year old talisman in defence. Optimism creeps in. The Germans nearly scored three times and the English luck held. We only need one goal to get to extra time.

The English team play better. They get one on target, someone else makes the keeper make a save - a rarity for the English team tonight. Fozzie screams again. István wakes from his pessimism.

"Why didn't they play like this before?" he asks as the clock says two minutes to go.

"It's the goalkeeper's last game," I said. "He will come up for the last corner I guarantee. He's crazy."

Ninety minutes, the game is nearly over. The camera pans on German fans who have stopped their arrogant cheering and have resorted to stressed looks skyward, hands in prayer. I decided I would rather be me and hoping rather than them and praying. The fourth official says three minutes.

"Plenty of time," I say with my new found optimism.

"Corner", Fozzie yells, followed by "AAAAAAAAAAAGH" again, so do I. The goalkeeper does indeed run eighty yards to add his weight to the attack. The ball goes over – the keeper is there causing confusion, getting in the way, someone puts the ball in the box and the striker's on to it and IT'S IN. He looks to the referee to be sure it's O.K then charges away. The German players physically shrink and I don't know what happened next as the screams from three grown men in my living room deafen us all. I am out of my seat screaming out of the window to Budapest in general and immediately repair to the fridge. I return with beer and the team are still celebrating.

"Jesus Christ," I said as I sat down. "Now we've got to go through extra time."

"No they'll score again," said Fozzie.

We all laughed. What a fool.

Three minutes into time added on the English team have another corner.

"They'll score, I tell you," said Fozzie.

"COME ON!" I yell full of joy and knowing they won't.

The corner comes into the box the striker heads it on and the other striker sticks a leg out. The ball hits it and flies into the net. The German players all collapse on the floor.

"AAAAAAAAAAAAAAAAAAAAAAAAAAAAAAAAAAAAAAAEEEEEEEEEEE EEEEEEEEEEEEEAAAAAAAAAAAAAAAAAAAAAAAAAAAAGGGGGGGGGGGGGGGG GGGGGGGGGGHHHHHHHHHHHHHHHHHHHHHHHH," is the only sound I hear. It is the collective sound of three men incapable of believing what they have just seen.

In a daze I run to try and get on to my landing outside the flat but can't open the door for jumping up and down. So I just yell in the hall. I come back what seems like half an hour later to find the team still embracing each other.

I sit down again in a daze. I am hyperventilating. I am repeating the phrase "I don't believe it...I don't believe it."

The German's restart but immediately the referee blows the whistle. I am spent and sit there drenched in sweat still repeating the words. I say "I don't believe it" a few more times as Fozzie and István shake their heads and shout a lot. Tony calls.

"Fuck, that was a shitty game," he said, "and I don't believe the ending. It's a fairy tale." Tony likes football but will never understand it.

"I would take every damn loss to every German team ever for this moment right now," I said to him, recovering my speech. "A poor performance followed by large amounts of luck. We won the German way! I thought you would do your usual trick and switch off," I said.

Tony has a short attention span sometimes.

Andrea, who was in Miskolc, rang next. "They were bloody lucky," she said sternly. "I did it by the way. I was praying for it."

I returned with more beer for the boys.

"Time for a game," I said, as we watched the contrasting scenes on Hungarian television - ecstasy, despair, tears. "Let's bet on what German TV is showing now."

"Adverts!!" we all chorused.

I switched to RTL and there was an advert for *Bitburger* beer. We cheered.

"No beer for you Germans tonight," yelled Fozzie. "No half a million Euro!"

Then the RTL picture went black and white. "Look they can't even be bothered to colour the picture now can they," I yelled. "This is how we felt all those times before."

The Germans received their loser's medals. They didn't want them. Their talismanic leader almost threw his away. I spent the rest of the broadcast simply laughing at despondent Germans with mullet hairstyles, very bad form.

We had some more beer then settled down to the real work of the night. Fozzie works for MTV (not *that* MTV but Magyar television). He has just got the job and seems to work in the dubbing department, translating film scripts into English and my suspicion is that his superiors have given him a right stinker of a script to see what he is made of. The film he was charged with translating was "Number 17" a Hitchcock film made in 1932.

There are two problems with this film. The first is that in 1932 recording techniques were very primitive, making what some of the actors said somewhat indistinct. The second problem was that the film was British and the actors were speaking 1930s English with some frankly bizarre idioms and sayings. It was an impossible task, but Hungarian society is all about who you know and he knows an Englishman (me).

The worse problem was a character called Ben, who was a drunken cockney idiot and was played by a drunken Cockney idiot. He was completely indecipherable and it took an hour to work out the first ten minutes. He used words like 'guvnor', 'luvaduck', 'fag', and 'apples and pears'. He also dropped all his aitches except when he said 'hour' which he pronounced 'HHHour'. Poor Fozzie was completely confused when I explained what was actually said compared with what he thought had been said. Another example were the women who all pronounced their A's as a sort of E. So when a woman screams 'Dead! Dead!' Fozzie was justified in thinking she was saying 'dead'. But in fact she was saying 'Dad! Dad!' and a completely different slant was put on the mystery body on the landing. If Fozzie hadn't come to me nobody would have noticed. Some things we had to miss out, either the bad soundtrack or the voices defeated even me but we got the context, which brought another problem. There were references to Lloyd George, George Formby and a cigarette brand called Lord something which Ben, in a fit of class system sarcasm insisted he smoked one end while the eponymous Lord smoked the other.

The whole process took three hours and István gave up at 2 a.m. The film is pretty poor if you watch it frame by frame with some of the most wooden acting I have ever seen. However I did manage to spot the Hitchcock cameo – a first, and I have done MTV a service, and saved Fozzie's job.

Thursday 24th May

I wrote a snotty letter to the Headmaster as he, once again walked into the exam room and struck up a conversation with the invigilator. This time he walked in and said to Ági, "Do you know if Ray wants to do an experiment with the Balaton water? Where is he, I need to talk to him?"

Ray was next door teaching. The Year 11 students complained to me today saying he walks in and peers over their shoulders. He also walked in last week and started to ask me about the science course and each student's prospects whilst they did the exam. Now remember this exam is conducted in a room the size of your living room so it is very disturbing. So I wrote him a letter impolitely telling him he is banned from the exam room unless he has a very good reason to be there. "Casual chit chats," I wrote, "do not constitute a good reason." I also wrote, "it is a little embarrassing when we have told the kids they will get an instant detention if they disrupt an exam then find that the only persistent offender is the Headmaster himself."

Friday May 25th

The Headmaster apologised for disrupting the exams – sort of. He maintained his right as the Headmaster to wander in as he saw fit and explained that he had to see

Ági yesterday because he was out of school all day otherwise. Telephones don't seem to be an option here. Tony suggested I lock the door from the inside but I have tried it and the lock won't work.

Elsewhere Yifan a 16 year old girl asked me in secret to recommend a good school in London for next year. Tony has taken up the Chinese teaching mentioned previously. The Chinese wanted someone with an American accent and Tony needs the money more than me.

"It doesn't matter what accent your teacher has," said Tony to the students in their first lesson, "you'll all have a Chinese one anyway." Tony isn't a diplomat.

Saturday May 26th

With Andrea still in Miskolc it was up to me to amuse myself. Top of the list was a visit to Statue Park[58] –"gigantic memorials from the Communist dictatorship". This is the kind of place that Andrea has not the slightest desire to visit and the kind of place I have an OVERWHELMING desire to visit. What is this obsession with Communism? Is it because the Commies were the bad guys of my generation, the Indians, the Nazis, the Darth Vader? Is it because if there was one thing Communists could do well was make a good flag, make a great statue and have a great parade? I think it's the mirror image the society gives me. The 'what if a country tried a different way' factor, and the horror at the results. As I have said before I would have hated to live under a Communist regime so maybe my fascination with the near past is a little hypocritical. I don't think so. Maybe my interest is ghoulish but it is also a reality. It happened and I want to know about it.

Hungary did something no other former Communist country did: it kept most of its statues and placed them in a park a little distance out of Budapest. The journey on a yellow Volan[59] bus was pleasant and the weather was in the scorching. The bus was full but there were only a few tourists who alighted at the Statue park. In fact only three people had made the journe: me and two other Brits of the backpacking variety. I expect this was fairly typical. Why would a Hungarian go? A Hungarian either has no desire to be reminded or may believe the park is some kind of joke for the tourists. The latter isn't the reason this park exists. As the art historian Tibor Wehner said about the park…

"There is a joy in the absence of book-burning. The design aims to break down a minefield of objections, to achieve an accurate presentation of the statues free from any sense of barely conceived mockery - this is not a joke park, it is absolutely not that."

The architect, Ákos Eleőd, who designed it said, 'The park is a very delicate matter. I've been trying my utmost to treat this terribly serious theme with the proper

---

[58] From Budapest city centre on the 7 bus to Etele sq (terminus), and from there on Volán (distance) Bus (yellow) departing from stall number 2-3. (toward Diosd-Erd).
[59] Distance bus, i.e. it goes out of town

amount of seriousness. This park is about dictatorship. And at the same time, because it can be talked about, described, built, this park is about democracy. After all only democracy is able to give us the opportunity to let us think freely about dictatorship. Or about democracy come to that. Or about anything!"

On the other hand thinking isn't the highest priority of the free person in a democracy. It's the worker in the sweet factory analogy. They let you eat as many sweets as you like but after one day you've had all you need and ignore it. If the sweets were banned the workforce would be desperate to try more. Interpret the sweets as books. A free person never thinks about his freedom. So does our democracy mean people do think about dictatorship? I doubt it. And that is where the ideals fall down. Because backpackers go there and have their pictures taken casually on a statue of Lenin with a smug, dumb-ass look on their face.

The park is designed as a series of three concentric figures of eight straddling a straight path. This central path is straight as an arrow, "the one true path, one and indivisible" like Communism. The figures of eight are on their side, meaning not eight but infinity of course. Whichever path you take in the figures of eight you have no choice but to return to the true path in the centre. The central path of course suddenly ends. "You can progress no further. You have to turn back, It is a dead end." The entrance is a crude edifice, neo-classical in design, but made of brick. It is a façade, there is nothing behind it, the main gate is always shut, but if you are clever you can see the side entrance. So even the entry represents Communism. In the façade stands a ten metre high Lenin which stood near Heroes square until 1989. On the other side is a more modern Marx and Engels. Why Marx and Engels statues survived the statue purges always amused me. I suppose it's because they were philosophers and not murderers. Anyway I prefer the statue of them in Berlin. Inside there is the Soviet soldier from under the Liberation monument. A huge statue, 30 metres high, of a woman, the spirit of freedom stands on the Gellert hill on Buda holding a palm leaf out to the city. It is a symbol of Budapest but it was built by the Soviets who liberated Hungary in 1945. In 1989 the Hungarians removed the Red star, the statue of the Soviet soldier with the flag and the Commie stuff and left the woman. The soldier survived and now lives in the park. There was also another great statue of Lenin which stood outside the great iron works a Csepel. The story is that the statue was a gift from Krushchev and after ten years it was found to be so poorly made that it was corroded, full of holes and falling apart. The iron works hastily designed an exact replica and replaced the old one in the middle of the night without telling a soul. The famous Stalin statue is not there, it was destroyed in the 1956 revolution that was put down by the Soviets, and never replaced.

I had a great time and I resisted buying something in the gift shop. It seemed after all the insisting that this park was *not* a joke, that to sell a McLenins T-Shirt, or other ironic T-shirts wasn't what the designers wanted. I nearly bought a CD of Communist party songs too but again I respected my future wife's feelings on my flippancy.

In the afternoon I went round to Tony's. We were due to watch a football game – Ferencváros or Fradi as they are affectionately known, against the Székesfehérvár team Videoton. Fradi are the best supported side in Hungary and also have the most violent supporters, which caused Andrea to express concern.

"It's O.K," I said. Tony had done his research. "As long as we don't go into B sector we'll be O.K."

Andrea had only just forgiven me for a previous attempt to see Fradi. István invited me to go and see them play Újpest, one of the other big Budapest sides[60]. The two teams are like Rangers and Celtic but worse, because the hatred is so Nihilistic. There are always riots and fighting on the streets. The only reason we didn't go was because it was raining and we were lazy. Later on tv we watched the running battles on the streets round the stadium, the armed riot police charging the crowds faces covered with scarves, the water cannon, the CS gas and the mounted police and we laughed the kind of "Good grief we nearly died" nervous laugh you do on these occasions. Videoton were so irrelevant these days however that there would be no trouble today. However Tony insisted that we were fortified for our trip. He gave me some plum palinka and some beer before we left and then did his usual trick of taking me into the cheapest drunk joint to down a glass of wine of such awful quality it cost 10p for a whole glass. Then as I just adjusted my ears to the foul language in the bar Tony told me to drink up again.

We got to the stadium and made absolutely sure we didn't buy a ticket in B sector, drank some more foul but cheap wine and sat in our great £2 seats. Fradi are a goal down in a minute. B sector to our right are not impressed. Our section is a little more polite. Tony took tremendous pleasure in translating the appalling insults thrown at the players by the gentlemen surrounding us.

"**** you, **** your fathers, you **** old **** mother **** ****** ***** ****** *****" Most of the insults were beyond translation, English not being a particularly rude language. Still Fradi soon equalised and things settled a bit. In the second half Videoton had two attacks and scored both times, sending the fans into further swearing bouts. An old guy came and sat on the steps next to us. Tony and I had talked all through the game so it came as no surprise when he spoke to us in English.

"Where you fucking from?" he asked. He was drunk.

---

[60] Hungarian football has a glorious history and Hungary has made the World Cup *final* on more than one occasion. At the time of writing the Hungarian football system is in such disarray that hardly anybody goes to a live match at all, and Hungary had failed to qualify for a World or European Championship since 1986. Ferencváros were consistently good but Ujpest and Kispest Honved were much less successful than they had been. Modern Hungarian football was more likely to be dominated by the poorly supported and allegedly Jewish run MTK of Budapest, and various small town sides who found a local rich man and had success for one season before the money ran out and the players all moved away.

"Errr Amerikaiak vagyűnk,[61]" I said.

"And him?" said the man.

"Me too," said Tony in Hungarian. "California."

The man snorted. "*You* are American," he said pointing at me, "But you asshole," he said pointing at Tony, "no way. Your accent is all wrong."

We sniggered at this point. "I swear he's American," I said.

"I am!" said Tony.

"No way, I lived in California for ten years. I KNOW!"

Tony dismissed him with a wave of the hand and the old boy returned to his seat. The rest of the match was spent with him yelling all the swear words and homosexual references he had learned in his obviously brief time in the States at us.

"You see," I said to Tony, "I knew there was something strange about you. You're not a Yank at all are you. You've been lying all along. Here I am a proud American son and you are some pinko foreigner."

Fortunately the old man disappeared before he sent Sector B round to kill us. Fradi lost 3-1 and we went home with the 'fans' and got caught in some tribal chanting abusing Újpest again. Tony translated it with another chuckle . It was something like "**** Újpest, **** their fathers, **** their mothers, those gypsy ****s".

"And the great thing about this," said Tony beaming, "is that it rhymes beautifully in Hungarian!"

We escaped from the mob and repaired to the Mushroom, another appalling wino dive near Moszkva square. The wine was an exorbitant 20p a glass but wasn't watered down. Quentin Tarantino appeared to be in there unconscious, but it wasn't the place where I wanted spent an evening so we went to Marxim's[62], recently mentioned in the daily Telegraph because somebody didn't appreciate the idea of a theme spoof Communist bar. Somehow the Gulag pizza offended the palates. I can recommend the Sztalin[63] pizza though. The beer was good too. The place is deliberately scruffy, with tatty red flags and chicken wire hanging around. Ost Zone is better in East Berlin but this was cheap. It also is next to a real old factory that probably made irrelevant plastic pencil sharpeners by the million ten years ago. Tony and I had a great time and, as is the case on such occasions, I cannot recall any of the conversation, but I suspect you can probably guess!

Monday 28th May

Paper work paper work.

---

[61] "We're Americans"

[62] 2 Kis Rokus street, Buda

[63] This is not a typo, Russian names, being in Cyrillic are written the way they should be pronounced in Hungarian, as we do in English

Tuesday 29th May

This is rather pathetic but I am a little addicted to the game 'Free Cell' available on Windows. Brittany is likewise addicted to 'solitaire'. There has been a little creative game recently on what we change the name of each icon on the computer screen. I changed the solitaire box to 'Brittany's only addiction' and she changed the Free Cell one to 'Ray's only addiction except wine and women'. I retaliated by giving the Oxford dictionary definition of addiction in full in solitaire box. She returned with a simple, 'there is no addiction here. Nothing to see. Move along." Today I went to the computer only to find the free cell game called 'Poisson' and the solitaire called 'drug'.

"Is this you?" I asked to Brittany.

"What?" she said and looked at the screen in mystification. "It's not me Ray."

"Well who did it then and what drugs are they on?" I said.

"Well whoever it is," said Brittany, "they spelt poison wrong."

"Ahem," I said, "I think that's French for fish," and Brittany collapsed in embarrassed ignorance.

However as I am writing this I think that actually Brittany has hit the nail on the head. It is actually a poorly spelt poison and the anonymous person was referring to both games as narcotics or deadly chemicals. I am most disappointed as I now look like a pretentious fop and the titles aren't half as surreal as I thought they were.

The Headmaster explained to me today why I had no work permit.

"It is because the photocopy made of your teaching certificate was not an official one so they would not accept it.

"When was this?" I asked, "because we could have done it again," but the Headmaster wasn't going to explain this any further. I can accept this is *a* reason for not having one but it is not THE reason. I was pretty sure that there had been no great effort to get me a work permit.

Wednesday 30th May

I did my bit for the school today. I interviewed two parents in the absence of the Headmaster. Naima was delighted as she had found this Hungarian family and 'did not want them scared off'.

I was looking forward to having a go at persuading people to come to our school. I had three innovations already planned:- 1) I wore a tie – something our Headmaster seems to disapprove of 2) I planned to give the father a copy of the National Curriculum so that he could see what he could expect from an English school 3) I warned Jessica we would be coming down to visit them. The couple consisted of a very nice guy in his forties, the wife was younger and pretty, kids were crazy – boys aged four and six. I talked about the English system and outlined my philosophy of teaching, I answered a few questions and outlined our limitations as a school – but you turn them into bonuses. Then we went down to Jessica's room and the family could see the four children speaking American English and colouring 'I love the summer because…' posters. There was Jessica, beaming and friendly in the beautifully decorated room with kids who spoke English where they couldn't one year ago. YOU would have sent your children to our school!

"Unfortunately Jessica has to return to the States to get some work experience there," I said almost truthfully. "Her replacement will be a native speaker." I assured, although the Headmaster hasn't hired anyone yet and it is June.

"How much do I pay?" said the father.

"I don't know," I said. "You should contact the Headmaster at your convenience. He deals with the money."

So they'll have to meet the Headmaster after all.

June

Monday 4th June

The Headmaster spent his fifth day in a row away from the school. The reason is legitimate, the organisation poor. His mother's brother has died and his mother is also critically ill and he is spending much time there. Very justifiable, but he told nobody where he was and made no provisions for his absence. Who is responsible for what while he is gone?

I have completed my recent dalliance with Hungarian bureaucracy. It was slightly complicated and involved the marriage. In Hungary there is an official government office for marriages. You have to go to the registry office to fill in forms for your official papers. The church service is essentially irrelevant from an official point of view. Most Hungarian couples go to the registry office first to get the papers then go on to the church for the religious stuff. The reality is that the church has no interest whatsoever in the official stuff. From my point of view this means we have to book a date in a Budapest registry office some time before our church wedding. Before we can book the date we have to fill out the papers. One month before that I paid £70 to get the British Embassy to provide a document in Hungarian stating I am free to marry. I also translated my birth certificate. Then we took our documents to the office – open only three afternoons a week and only one person and a typewriter sits in the office. It is a first come first served job and the woman deals with one couple at a time, typing the forms for them, causing a huge queue to mount.

The first time we went we were told I needed to bring my residence permit until I pointed out I wasn't a resident nor had a work permit. Officially I work in England - thanks Headmaster! Next time we went with all our documents but the woman wouldn't allow Andrea to translate for me what was needed to be said in Hungarian so we would have to return again with a third party translator. The third time we took Andrea's boss, who simply had to ask me what my job was and was I free to marry. Then the woman asked us to check the documents. There were two mistakes on mine. One had got my mother's maiden name wrong but on inspection it was noted that the British Embassy had got it wrong. Potentially this could have meant we would have to start the whole process again but the woman was in a good mood. They also got my place of birth wrong but the official translation had too so I let it slide. We now must wait for thirty days to get permission to marry from some dodgy office. In the same office they wanted to know what Andrea would call herself after marriage and what the children would be known as. Blimey!

Brittany's flat was broken into at the weekend. The thief stole her lap-top, one hundred cds, $400 and, this is my favourite, a suitcase to take it all away in.

The Hungarian Girl Trap

Wednesday 6th June

The Headmaster has returned from Vienna where he has been buying up all the International School of Vienna's old books. I am hoping he doesn't think that these books are a substitute for new books.

Friday 7th June

Well term rather collapsed in on itself somewhat. After the exams had finished, the kids finished, as did the teachers, even though there was two days to go. Brittany insisted that school should finish early on both days but actually nothing happened at all on Friday except that teachers frantically wrote out reports for the deadline of Saturday. We were all beavering away in the staff room, egged on by Tony's contribution to the day – a tape he had recorded for me entitled 'The Best of Communism'. This tape contained all the classic Communist songs and it was a jolly rousing way to work I tell you. Some of the titles include, "We thank you Comrade Rákóczy", "Forward together with the party and the people", that foot-tapper known as "The KISZ welds us into unity" and of course the Soviet National anthem. As you can imagine it was all jolly funny but I was worried about how the Hungarians would take it. The young ones laughed and the older teachers went a little misty eyed as they heard the songs that reminded them of their youth. Only Éva, the rather fearsome secretary, had a real anti-reaction. She walked in, switched it off and walked out again.

It was time to go, Tony doesn't get paid. The Headmaster moans over procedure about report deadlines, then won't listen to explanations. Jessica's stroppy, Éva's mad. I walk out with Tony and say goodbye to no-one. Feel guilty but it's for the best.

I organised a little afternoon drinking session in a local café and Naima had the temerity to ask the Headmaster to buy us the first round of drinks. Amazingly he did. It was a hot, hot day, ninety degrees plus, so the only place to go was the air conditioned Rolling Rock Café.

"Right, Belgian beer all round then," said Tony on hearing the good news about the Headmaster's first round.

So we sat in the bar for about four hours in that leisurely way one can when you have been given three months wages in advance in $100 dollar bills. Tony was holding court in whatever the hell language you wanted. All the teachers came along, but by five o'clock only the hard-core of Tony, Brittany, her boyfriend Michael, Ági and I were left. Tony went (or staggered) back to his wife, Ági had to go and buy some meat (?) so it was left to Brittany, Michael and I to carry on the charge. Andrea was back in Miskolc.

"Let's go to Iguana," suggested Brittany, meaning the 'expensive' Mexican place near Parliament square[64]. "They sell great pitchers of margueritas."

So we did and we did indeed indulge in a jug or two of very lethal marguerita. The food was excellent and we were thrown out at 7.30 p.m. Michael had finally 'hit the wall' and had collapsed into his burrito. So Brittany carried him home. She was holding her drink remarkably well though I have no proof of this because a) I was hammered and b) I was hammered. I was alone, I had outdrank them all. Unfortunately when you have done that there is no-one left to drink with and I never drink alone so I fell home, realised how drunk I was and tried not to do anything functional at all, failed and was rather bemused to find I had a raging hangover at midnight.

Little snippets of conversation come back to me. The typical unsubtle Tony remark to Brittany about her being 'not the thinnest of chicks' as he referred her in comparison to the average Hungarian beanpole.

She took it well. "I'm glad I'm not sensitive or anything," she said.

Saturday 8th June

In the afternoon I went with Tony to watch another football game, this time it was at Vasas, a rather industrial area of Budapest. We took a few detours of local kocsmas[65] drinking wine at 36 forints a glass. This stuff is not 'wine', I have subsequently found out, but a lot of water, some wine and a lot of fermented sugar. The game was great: Vasas beat Ferencváros 2-1. The crowd were crazy, hanging on the fences and screaming but quite good-natured, urchin kids ran onto the pitch at the end of the game, the security guys making only half-hearted rugby tackles, I also liked the other 'hooligans'. Most are teenaged boys, who hero worship English hooligans but don't really get it. Half of the Vasas support seemed to be wearing gas masks, not because of some impending terrorist attack, but because it was some kind of uniform. Tony tried to buy beer (unavailable to the plebs) from a rich Ferencváros fan in the wired off executive section but he didn't want to know us. At the time Ferencváros were leading so after his shittiness I cursed them and was delighted Vasas came back to win.

Afterwards we went to Leroy's[66] for big steaks. Brittany and Michael joined us after dithering all day about what to do. They were too nervous to go on a bus to the statue park and ended up in a cinema accidentally watching a semi pornographic film. By the time Tony and I got to Leroy's we were a little drunk so the conversation

---

[64] 16 V. Zoltán street, Pest

[65] A Kocsma is the bottom end of the Hungarian bar system. Spit and sawdust, nor chairs, no politeness, a functional place to get wasted quickly and cheaply.

[66] 50/a Visegradi street, Pest

was riotous and funny, Tony leading the way. The main people to abuse were Budapest public transport ticket inspectors.

The ticket inspectors are fair game for abuse. They would climb on a tram and slip their red armband on at the last minute in order to catch fare dodgers. I found the whole thing a little bit distasteful, unfair and very unsporting. You sat there waiting to be accused of not having a ticket. Much as London Transport has its faults and that would probably make another book, at least it stops most people from trying to fare dodge before they do it, with the ticket barriers. Here the metros were unmanned. Anyone could walk in and theoretically take a train for free. They could only be caught by one of these spot checks and the gamblers in the city would always risk it. The controllers, when they descended, always found someone. There was a convention to these encounters, almost like a mini drama, with the actors overdoing their parts. The person without the ticket would spend ten minutes searching fruitlessly through their bag muttering about it being somewhere. This would be delayed as long as possible hoping that the controller would believe them and move on. However the controller, scenting money, simply stood there, the smug grin and rolled eyes becoming more obvious to the audience as every minute passed. Finally the victim would give up the charade, try and make a run for it, swear, curse, argue, weep, blame the Government for their poverty, plea for the return of good old Socialism, or hand over their identity card and pay the fine.

Andrea claimed the controllers were all arrogant ex-Communist pigs and hated them, as did most of the city. They worked on the simple principal that the rules were pasted on yellow boards at the entrance to each metro station or on every bus and tram, in Hungarian, English and German. Therefore if you were in breach of these rules you were guilty. They had heard every story in the world and would not budge once they had you. Andrea once had her pass taken away because she had placed it in a plastic sheath not issued by the Budapest Travel Company but one from her home town of Miskolc. These sheaths cost ten forints(3p), and were identical except for the colour, and were irrelevant to the pass. Some guy was just letting the power of the armband go to his head. I would lose count of the times that I saw hapless tourists in furious or tearful conversations with these smug-grinned, head shaking, small moustachioed fools. The tourist would explain that a) they didn't mean to, b) the ticket punching machine didn't work, c) that their ticket was valid and they were just lost in the metro station and were, in fact just trying to get out of the building, or, d) that there was nothing wrong with their ticket at all and the controller was just being a jobsworthy communist asshole. All these I had seen and every time I suspected that half the time the tourist was probably genuine. The fine for not having a valid ticket was 3000 forints (£7) so it hardly made a great deal of difference it was simply the atmosphere created by these fools. I suspected that many tourists left Budapest with a very negative opinion after an encounter with them. I also suspected that not all the tourist's fines were legitimate or found their way into the BKV's coffers. The Budapest Sun's letter's page was always full of incidents from tourists.

Tony just yelled at them, safe in the knowledge that he had a valid ticket and legally they couldn't physically touch you (so he was told by his buddies in his local bar). [67]

"I wouldn't buy a ticket at all, but since I've been married I've promised my wife I won't spend another night in jail," said Tony.

Sunday 9th June

Trip to Balaton.

I arrived at Budapest Déli station (it means South and has nothing to do with delicatessens) at 10 o'clock having realised, in Andrea's absence that I had neglected to pack any T-shirts. As I realised this half way to the station it was too late to go back. I hoped we were going to a place that sold them.

The kids and staff were all waiting when I got there. Chris, the 18 year old English boy was there smoking.

"I'm going independently," he said. "So I can do what I want."

"Does the headmaster approve," I asked pointlessly.

"He hasn't forbidden me," said Chris.

There was a good staff presence. Apart from me, Brittany and Michael, Jessica, Ági, the Headmaster, Naima, Gerry the owner, Peter a maths teacher and various others were all making the trip. Most however were just here for the Sunday.

The Headmaster had booked us on the cheapest, slowest train in the history of wheeled transport. We stopped everywhere, every house on the way seemed to have its own railway station. The train was typically East European, with exit doors that swung open all the time. This created potentially dangerous exits from lavatories if the train happened to be zooming round a corner at the time. Actually I was the only person brave enough to go into the toilet. It was a rusty bowl in the corner of a little room last cleaned in 1974.

Balaton is the biggest lake in Western Europe and Hungarians attach an almost religious significance to it. It is a great favourite with families in northern Europe who want a cheap, warm, safe vacation within a day's driving. The Germans even have their own name for it "Platensee", which annoys Andrea no end. This implies to her that the Teutons have it earmarked for invasion. It must be said that the

---

[67] An obvious reference at this point is the striking film "Kontroll" (2003) directed by Nimród Antal., starring talented actor Sándor Csányi as Bulcsú. It is set in the murky world of the Hungarian ticket inspector (although the film never specifically admits to being set in Budapest) The film tries too hard to be a realistic 'warts and all' look at their world, a cool serial killer flick and a Fight Club wannabe and fails because it isn't quite sure what it is it wants to be most. You do however come away with a very dark view of ticket inpectors. For the potential Budapest visitor it is probably worth watching to see how the Budapesti treat these inpectors – the film implies nobody buys a ticket!

Austro-German influence is huge here. Go into McDonalds and my poor Hungarian is answered back with German rather than English as it is in Budapest. They serve beer there too, not something seen in Budapest. There are strip clubs and 'zimmer frei' signs everywhere.

The hotel was reasonable although I found to my consternation that I was sleeping in the same room as Gerry and the Headmaster – not my first choice of room-mates. Some Chinese men arrive claiming to be the 'brothers' of some of our Chinese girls.

I went to bed at around 1 a.m. Gerry came with me saying he doesn't snore since he an operation to stop it. We stayed up drinking whisky (Gerry's) discussing educational theory. We go to 'sleep' at 2.30.

Monday 10th June

Last night was undoubtedly one of the worst nights I have ever spent in my life. Five minutes after I put the lights went out there was a loud snort from Gerry 'I don't snore any more' Ashcroft. Soon the snores had reached levels loud enough to damage human ears. And they weren't conventional snores. There were whoops, farts, whistles, sound effects from sci fi movies, chirrups, grunts, mutters and snorts, even the occasional pathetic 'oh god' was muttered after a particularly loud noise. It was impossible to sleep at all. Then the Headmaster comes in at 4 am having been talking by the fire with the maths teacher. Gerry wakes up briefly but the torrent continues. It is like being on the runway next to DC-10 jet about to take off. I lay there hopelessly. Even the sound of the kids running around all night was drowned out by the din. The final straw was my bed, far too short for me, and the mattress appeared to be made of some kind of itching powder. I moved my leg and dislodged a cup and saucer on the cupboard at the end of the bed. The cup rolled briefly round the saucer making a tiny noise. Gerry, still snoring like twenty sousaphones warming up, stopped snoring and, in his sleep muttered 'What the fuck was that?' before resuming his impression of a chainsaw.

I was in a particularly foul mood when I came down to breakfast. After my sleepless night, I opened my eyes to see the Headmaster naked in front of me and wanting to have a conversation about Bunsen burner tubing. Gerry then stopped snoring and went into the shower and broke it. I needed coffee but breakfast beverages consisted of only lukewarm lemon tea.

We took a coach to the town of Vesprém to see the zoo. It was pitiful and old and needs a huge modernisation. Gerry didn't come, he slept all day. We also saw the castle, but the Russian girls preferred the shopping centres. We came back to swim and me to continue my sleep deprived sulk. Ági saved my life. She dangled a key in front of me and said I could have a room to myself.

The Hungarian Girl Trap

Tuesday 11th June

I slept for five hours last night. The kids were still conducting their own sleep deprivation experiment, going for swims at three a.m and trying to force the other guests out of the hotel by staying up and talking until dawn. I was in a good mood. Gerry wasn't and I wondered if curses do work. He had had a sleepless night owing to the Chinese 'brothers' in the room opposite bellowing around all night.

"There was also some bastard who had an alarm clock that went off every five minutes," he reported. "It nearly drove me completely insane."

He told of various anecdotes about torture, sleep deprivation, Edgar Allen Poe's coffin, and insects in the ear. "But I tell you," he said, "none were worse than that fucking alarm clock!"

"Excuse me!" said Sasha, a Russian boy sitting next to him.

"Gerry gave him a hard stare. "Do you find the word 'alarm clock' offensive?" he said pompously.

The 'alarm clock' turned out to be the radiator in his room.

Wednesday 12th June

After various trips to local areas of interest: an ostrich farm, and some caves in Tapolca, it was nearly the end of the trip. As we sat on the strand outside the hotel, barbecue cooking, kids playing beach volleyball, staff getting tipsy on the surprisingly free-flowing wine, I cast my mind back to the last day of term and walking out with Tony. If I had any backbone I would not be here and I contemplated saying what I felt. Of course my resolve to stand shoulder to shoulder with my unpaid brother Tony was destroyed on the last day because I was paid for two months in advance, and now the positive vibes of Balaton were destroying my bad thoughts. I was enjoying myself, it was hard not to at Balaton.

As I sat there in the evening gloom the Headmaster did a little speech thanking all the leavers (all the foreign staff). When he came to my turn he was completely lost for words. "I don't know what to say'" he said, "I don't know how we will survive without you."

I stood up to receive the applause, the cards and the bottle of plum pálinka and wanted to tell them how it really was. Tell them that this school was the most shambolic, mis-managed disaster I have ever encountered, but in the end the Balaton atmosphere made me wish them a good future.

Thursday 13th June

I escaped today as Andrea and her family arrived in Balatonalmádi. They were a few hours late. The car had been shedding oil like the *Exxon Valdiz* all the way along the motorway. To make it here they had to buy a fresh bottle of oil every thirty kilometres.

We are staying at some distant relative's summer house, who, judging by the state of it, comes here once every ten years. There are two proper rooms, one toilet room and one shower room with no door, just a curtain. The kitchen is an annex next to the structure and only accessible by going outside and round. The dining area is simply the space between the kitchen and the main house, covered by a corrugated plastic roof. Vines grow haphazardly over it. Of course it is perfect for the job it has to do, which is provide a place to sleep as you live an outdoor life. What's more interesting to me is the décor, which is frozen in 1970s time. There is a scale model of the Soviet warship "Swerdlow" on one wall, various cheap prints of Mont Matre and the Eiffel Tower, a drinks cabinet made out of an old television set and containing one bottle of *metaxa*. There is also a wild boar skin on another wall and two rather pathetic weasels on either side. Monstrous metallic green beetles fly around causing me to exclaim loudly. Apparently they are St. John beetles but look like something from a science fiction book.

The weather is at its regular summer temperature of at least 35°C. I am wiser now and have only worn shorts and sandals for two weeks now. We are eating only yellow peppers, tomatoes, peaches and water melon. Each tasted of heaven. None of that chemical crap from the supermarkets here.

Friday 14th June

We got the Wartburg fixed and pottered around trying to change some English pounds into forints. The first place we try won't exchange pounds.

"Where can we change pounds?" asked Andrea.

"I don't know anywhere," says the girl and returns to her magazine.

I walk into the shop next door and change pounds without any problems at all.

Saturday 15th June

Balaton is truly enormous. The now firing-on-all-cylinder Wartburg takes us to Tihany today. Tihany is a little knob of land sticking out from the north side of Balaton. On its highest hill stands an abbey of classic Hungarian design: burnt orange walls, onion dome spires. The views from here really do make the lake look like a sea but without the fishing boats and the tang of salty air.

One of the other strange things about Balaton is the 'Sense and Sensibility' seasonal movements. All of Budapest society is currently around Balaton. So you can visit all your pals. Last night we went to see one of Andrea's work colleagues at the American firm. She looks like a blond boy, in the way only an East European woman can. She appeared to be married to Lagzi Lajcsi, a large singer, popular on television[68]. We cooked goulash[69] in a pot over an open fire as the sun went down and the lake turned from bright blue to milky white and finally black with the twinkly lights of Siofok the only thing left to see. Láci tried to initiate conversation but his accent was so harsh and my Hungarian so poor that we had the worst 'conversation' of the last 5000 years.

Sunday 16th June

Why don't Hungarians take siestas? It's hot enough. Andrea's sister has turned up with her new boyfriend, who, I am told, bears an uncanny resemblance to a recent Prime Minister. He also speaks English in the way that many young Hungarian men do – as a low growl. We went to Balatonfüred, the next big town along. It's full of Dutch, Germans, Austrians and Slovaks and parking spaces are gold dust. It was early evening and Balaton was going that silvery milk colour again and the temperature was still baking hot. Balaton is a wine region of some note, the ordered rows of vines cover the hills all around and creates such a beautiful scene. They hold the wine festival here along the shore. There must have been fifty different vineyards selling wine from wooden huts interspersed with sausage stands and lángos stalls[70]. The place was buzzing with life. I even heard that rare thing English accents from a bunch of telephone engineers based in Zalaegerszeg. A glass of wine cost 100ft and most were excellent. The winemakers all seemed to be related, tight-knit and all with the same eyes: darting, proud, yet protective of the life's work. Afterwards we ate at a lakeside restaurant and were brought back down to earth by the awful live keyboard based musak that Hungarians seem to think should accompany fine dining.

Monday 17th June

Siófok is one of the coolest towns on Earth. This is one hell of a statement, but to me today it was like Miami depicted in a Will Smith video. It is St. Tropez. It is NOT Ibiza, which is great because the British will never come. We caught the ferry from Balatonfüred and crossed Balaton in fifty minutes (I told you it was big). Siofok was waking up from another party night, but what a place. Imagine the opening credits from some California based teen drama series! American cars cruise the streets, all the guys seem to work out, the girls are ridiculous. All the Germans and Dutch seem

---

[68] Real name Lajos Galambos, just google the name to see what he looks like
[69] Or *gulyás* as it is spelt here. Goulash is really a soup, not the paprika pork stew we associate the word here. Pork, pakrika and vegetables, preferably cooked outside on the open fire, where of course, like in all cultures, the man suddenly takes over the cooking in some prehistoric throwback when they never show any interest in the cooking inside
[70] A savoury doughnut with garlic sauce, sour cream and cheese. Magnificent

to come here to meet their wives. Every other place is a bar, everyone is wearing swimming costumes.

In the evening we visited Zsuzsa and Erik, the Hungaro Dutch couple we saw married in May. Predictably they have a summer house just up from us and it has the kind of view over vineyards and the lake that makes you want to pick up a paintbrush. Erik met Zsuzsa in a Balaton night club four years ago and, to my relief, knowing the Dutch people's ability with languages, he had not one word of Hungarian. We sat under a pear tree, which had the annoying habit of dropping ripe pears onto your head every so often, and talked wine, football and our little Balaton secret. Later we ate in the open, but this time the food was an acquired taste I guess. You light a fire and then get a big lump of bacon fat, an onion and heat it over the fire. As the fat melts you take it off the fire and drip it onto some bread. Add more onion and that's your supper. The beer flowed and I was delighted to see that Erik was similarly bamboozled. Of course it is just a feeble excuse to sit around a fire at night and talk and sing and realise that all is well with the world. Sometimes I think the British have lost the simplicity of tales told around a fire.

Saturday 22nd June

This last week has been spent in mild panic as I needed to get baptised and Gàbor insisted (quite rightly) that I had a Roman Catholic as my Godfather. Well none of Andrea's immediate family, who were the obvious candidates were neither Catholic, nor in Budapest, so we ended up going to Tony, whose Sicilian background was perfect. He was quite useful and we spent the preceding few days wandering round Budapest going into churches so I could familiarise myself with what Catholics do in church. Of course these visits were interspersed with visits to local bars as well.

The ceremony took place in Gábor's church, a modern building somewhere on Váci út[71]. The congregation consisted of almost exclusively of people over the age of sixty. I wondered whether they got religion as their lives neared an end, or whether they had always been religious. The cynic in me suspected the former. Either way they were very interested in us.

The baptism and confirmation went by without much of a hitch. The problems started in the communion straight after. Tony, Andrea and I had gone up first and afterwards Tony guided me through what was going on by whispering to me.

Afterwards in Gábor's office Gábor was furious with Tony.

"How dare you talk through the sacred Communion service," he screeched.

"I'm sorry, but in the States everybody talks through the Communion, it's sociable and friendly."

"That, my friend, says more about America than you think," said Gábor.

---

[71] This is not Váci Utca, but a long road out of the city starting at Nyugati station. The blue metro line goes right up it

Tony then made things worse by referring to the Pope's picture on the wall of Gábor's office as 'The Polish guy', but by now Gábor had regained some control. He turned to Andrea and said,

"I assume that you will be responsible for most of Ray's education into Catholicism."

Epilogue

Saturday 27th July

WEDDING DAY

2.55 p.m

I'm making my first confession to Gábor five minutes before the ceremony is about to start. We are alone in the backroom of the church is Miskolc. Unfortunately I haven't had a chance to do anything bad in thought, word or deed since the baptism, mainly because Andrea and I have been single-handedly arranging the wedding. In Hungary there is no "bride's father pays for it all and organises it all" tradition. So the cakes have to be ordered from a woman in a village 20km away, the wedding cake from a pal who owns a cake shop around the corner. I could go on. The reception site, a restaurant as close to the castle as Andrea could get, came to us not long ago in tears because they would have to charge us more than they quoted because their quoted price was less than the price quoted in mafia protected businesses nearby. Usual stuff.

So I make a few platitudinous confessions and even Gábor is unimpressed, as if he was anticipating lots of bad behaviour, and tells me to say a derisory amount of 'hail Marys'. Gábor clearly sees me as one of his great achievements, as he tells me that he has decided to make the service a full service, with communion, which will come in at ninety minutes. I protest that the English will be lost but I can see he doesn't care.

The irony for me is that, in the eyes of the law, we're already married. As I have mentioned before you have to have a civil service first of all. Most couples do it just before arriving at church, but because of my technical residence being Budapest, we had to do it there, last week. So the family got in the Wartburg and came to Budapest, I invited Tony, I said one word, "Igen", which was ridiculous because I was supposed to say "yes" and have it formally translated by the official translator. After twenty minutes we were through and sitting in Andrea's father's favourite restaurant, the Golden Fish[72].

Later

Apparently I spent most of the service looking as if I was about to faint. There are various approaches one can make to writing about one's wedding: the picture postcard, romantic way, but, in the modern world, where everybody camcorders everything, what's the point? Borrow the video! The bride wore white, I was in

---

[72] No idea where it is, it is not a tourist place though. It's in the suburbs

morning suit, people cried. The things that stood out for me were the out of the ordinary things: Andrea arriving at the ceremony in a Mitsubishi Colt. The whole congregation, out of practice, attempting to genuflect properly through the service that seemed to last forever – even though there was hardly a regular church goer in the whole congregation. This was highlighted finally when there were absolutely no takers for communion apart from my wife and I, and the lack of singing in the joining-in bits.

I was more concerned to ensure that I didn't screw up, having been coached by Gábor when to stand and sit via surreptitious nods, or "when I say 'áld meg'". I don't think I did, but I was horribly aware of the English people in the congregation. When we had seen Gábor officiate before he has kept the service short and sweet, and did the whole service bilingually (this is his unique selling point, the reason he gets the foreign trade), but here, because he wanted the service to be special, there was a hell of a lot more Hungarian and a hell of a lot less English. He still did most of his cute turns of phrase; 'brothers and sisters' always struck me a particularly cute way of addressing a congregation.

I remember Tony breaking wind and the hard wooden pews amplified the sound far louder than he expected. His wife was furious, but apparently he got away with it by doing that trick where one turns around furiously looking for the culprit.

I remember my best man getting flustered at one crucial point. There is a kind of Hungarian ritual of ring exchange, which to the untrained eye, looks like a game of 'one potato two potato' played under a sacred cloth. At some stage during this it seemed to me that the best man was married to Gábor.

I remember thinking that many of the English guests would be disappointed by there not being a formal, 'you can now kiss the bride' section. This being the whole point of the service to the English. The only kiss was a chaste peck after what seemed like an hour's worth of Hungarian and many would have missed it as they drifted into their own thoughts.

I remember the rush by the congregation outside to have a cigarette after ninety minutes of high Catholicism. I remember my English friend Al was legless already because the waiters at the reception restaurant played a joke on him and told him they needed someone to try all their pálinkas to decide which was the one to use at the wedding. There were six different ones. They thought it was very funny. It was cruel really, Al had only just recovered frommy stag night held traditionally only forty-eight hours ago. Control freak that I am I held it in the 'Old Man's' Blues bar and everyone had a great time.

I remember being delighted that someone had finally managed to paint of over the graffito 'Satan lives' which had been spray painted on the church's white walls with a determined hand at least six months ago.

Outside the church we stood proudly, bridesmaids hovering. The congregation formed a spontaneous queue to congratulate us (this is the way to learn a language – forced repetition. After this I shall never forget that 'gratulálok' means 'I congratulate you'). Everybody kisses you. It takes forever, but there is warmth there, tears in the eyes of the older members of the family, for whom their final wishes is to see the family continue.

Suddenly Andrea's mother's boyfriend László leaps out of nowhere and congratulates us. He is dressed in shorts. He couldn't come to the wedding, but couldn't resist a quick visit.

"Strawberry Fields forever," he grinned.

"Magical mystery tour," I replied.

"I don't want to spoil the party," he said, about to go. "Let it be,"

"But it's 'a day in the life!'" I said.

He stopped, thought for a while, and then said, "Everybody's got something to hide except me and my monkey." Then he was gone.

Reception

Having walked through the village to curious looks and causing the Diósgyőr dog population to go apoplectic we are at the reception. Hungarian receptions are much less formal than British ones and we have had to weld in some British formality to the events. There is an initial two hour chat over drinks. The bar is free of course, the British are astonished. I start to relax a bit and get chatting. Everyone was there.

Dinner lasted all night, meat soup, followed by the meat from the meat soup (which caused hysterics in the English contingent – chicken feet in a bowl). Next was a meat course, then cakes galore. Later stuffed cabbages were served at 1 a.m and I think food was pretty much available all night.

Andrea and I did the circulations. I gave a speech in Hungarian, which got huge cheers (hopefully for the right reasons). Then I gave my traditional groom's speech, which I had translated not word for word but in a more reported fashion, which worked because you got the guffaws from the English followed by a pleasing ripple from the Hungarians and great cackle from Andrea's bohemian father.

The Doctor, looking smarter than usual, but no less drunk, was sitting next to a furious looking woman, arms folded across her chest so tightly she looked like she was in a straitjacket.

"This is my wife," said the Doctor. "she used to be my nurse."

"I see," I said.

"No you don't," said the Doctor. "The English language is too simple. In Hungarian I must address all my nurses in the formal manner. If I don't it means I want to fuck them. It's a kind of come-on."

"And let me guess," I said.

"Yes, I got formal," he said.

"I love her," he said, "but she doesn't like me drinking. I took her to America and she hated it too, well until I took her Niagara falls, then she didn't want to come home." He recalled that Americans didn't understand why he didn't want to move there.

"I can have a Mercedes here too and my friends are here. I live well."

"How long have you been married?" I asked.

"Two months," he admitted. "well she was pregnant. I had to look after her."

At this point I should have put my head in my hands and walked away to find some food, but instead I decided that the Doctor's wife needed my wisdom. So I proceeded to talk to her in Hungarian, and as I can't remember what I said I am now quite frightened.

Next I see Tony, still in denial about the farting incident. He wasn't denying he did it, just not seeing anything wrong with it. I was delighted to hear that his wife is pregnant, Tony, very keen to inform me of his special method to guarantee conception, which was a private thing between godfather and godson. He seemed quite happy. He was settled in his Budapest life. He had already moved on to the next international school. A new one appears every year.

There's Zsuzsa and István putting on a brave face, even though they have broken up. Zsuszsa is off to Australia with a Frenchman (of course!). István can now concentrate on making films and kicking against Hungarian society whilst being fiercely proud of being Hungarian: quite an oxymoron. I never see Zsuzsa again, but István becomes part of the Budapest art scene. I see him whenever I am in Budapest and listen to his latest script ideas, which usually involve violently beautiful films with naked girls sporadically placed in them.

There's Andrea's boss Angela, shivering in the cold, wearing the best man's spare combat trousers. She's following us to England to run British Gas or something.

There's Brittany and her boyfriend Michael. They have delayed their return to the States until Monday and I am glad they did. Brittany is going to Houston to begin teacher training and she is going to be great. I just know it.

Jessica couldn't make it. She went to Albania to help in a Christian refugee camp. She sent me her diaries. She enjoyed herself, but didn't enjoy herself if you know what I mean. She married soon after. Christians do it really quickly.

Larry wasn't there either. I never saw him again. I spot his name on the credits of the occasional article in the Budapest Sun, or lecturing in circus skills to various Jewish groups, or advertising his now pan Europe basketball talent agency. He won't have changed. I never even find out if he went back to Churchill.

I never hear from Naima either, but the Headmaster's name stopped appearing on the Churchill adverts in the paper not long after. Gerry was still involved too. I wish the school well.

There's Andrea's father, in full dinner jacket, proud and happy, eyes red with tears, speech prepared in English and Hungarian. Andrea fears it 'will start from Adam' and last a long time. It didn't.

There's Andrea's cousin Gábor. Apart from Easter I last saw him unconscious at New Year's after a heavy night on the spirits. Then he had given out Nihilistic vibes. I remember writing to friends about how Hungarians had no belief in a bright future, nothing to look forward to, based entirely on the drunken, hopeless state Gábor was in that night. I was wrong, he was just partying with friends. Travel writers always make this mistake of defining a country by fleeting observations. It's why I don't read travel books. Gábor now has a job, he's become desperately interested in Hungarian history and is the only person I know in Hungary whose clothes aren't covered in slogans in bad English. He wears patriotic t-shirts, decorated in old maps with the old boundaries bearing the legend 'the lion shall rise again'.

The traditional dancers surprise me by speaking perfect English and explaining to the Brits the origins of all the dances. The dance of the red dress and the show passes without a hitch, as I have seen enough of them to know what to do. We got to bed at five after paying for the reception in cash as the last taxi pulled away.

And the next day we came home and started a new life in England…

The Hungarian Girl Trap

Lightning Source UK Ltd.
Milton Keynes UK
UKHW011858161221
395765UK00001B/71